Sylvia Plath

Sylvia Plath © Rollie McKenna

Sylvia Plath

The Wound and the Cure of Words

STEVEN GOULD AXELROD

The Johns Hopkins University Press   Baltimore & London

© 1990 The Johns Hopkins University Press
All rights reserved. Published 1990
Printed in the United States of America

Johns Hopkins Paperbacks edition, 1992

The Johns Hopkins University Press, 701 West 40th Street,
Baltimore, Maryland 21211-2190
The Johns Hopkins Press Ltd., London

∞

The paper used in this book meets the minimum requirements of the
American National Standard for Information Sciences—Permanence of
Paper for Printed Library Materials, ANSI Z39.48-1984.

Library of Congress Cataloging-in-Publication Data

Axelrod, Steven Gould, 1944-
Sylvia Plath : the wound and the cure of words / Steven Gould Axelrod.
    p.   cm.
Includes bibliographical references (p.   ).
ISBN 0-8018-3995-5 (alk. paper) ISBN 0-8018-4374-x (pbk.)
1. Plath, Sylvia—Criticism and interpretation.   I. Title.
    PS3566.L27Z517   1990
    811.54—dc20   89-43481

This book is for Rise, Jeremiah, David, and Melissa,
for my father, Dr. Bernard Axelrod,
and for the blessed "memory on the wall,"
my mother, Martha Gould Axelrod

CONTENTS

A biography of the imagination, this book meditates on Sylvia Plath's struggle for voice. It combines the rhetoric of psychoanalysis with the rhetoric of literary criticism, assuming with Freud that the self may be read as a text and with Robert Lowell that a text may become "by a wild extended figure of speech, something living . . . a person" ("After Enjoying" 112). Since a text is the work of a desiring body but also of a network of social and linguistic relations, I have studied the interactions among Plath's personal experiences, her cultural conditions, and the institution of literature. I have attempted to explain by complicating rather than by simplifying. I have added my own discourse to Plath's, causing what Roland Barthes called a "second language" to float above the first (*Criticism* 80).

The introductory chapter suggests the outlines of Plath's textual project. It examines the uncertain boundaries separating her inscribed texts from her psychic semiosis, while revealing the political and linguistic voids that surrounded and penetrated both. Succeeding chapters study the deeper strata of Plath's discourse; the plot flows through the systems of her family relations.

Chapter 2 explores the way that Plath's biological father and her male literary precursors interfered with her creativity even as they helped to shape it. The chapter concentrates on four exemplary texts in which the "I" first submits to and then rebels against the father: "Snakecharmer," "The Colossus," "Daddy," and "Words."

Chapter 3 studies Plath's ambiguous, charged relations with her mother and with the literary women who assumed a maternal role in her creative development. The chapter reads *The Bell Jar* in the context of Virginia Woolf and examines "Mussel

Hunter at Rock Harbor," "Metaphors," "Elm," and "Lady Lazarus" in the context of Emily Dickinson. The concluding section considers Plath's most powerful evocation of female generativity, "Three Women."

The last chapter ponders Plath's doubling relationship to her husband (the poet Ted Hughes) and her redirection of that doubling impulse to her texts. The chapter focuses on poems of the mirror and the shadow, in which the self's creative double remains hidden; on texts like "In Plaster" and "Daddy," in which the double splits off from the self in malign form; on poems like "Stings," in which the creative double transforms the self; and finally on poems like "Edge," in which the double dies. The book concludes by constructing a link between Plath's discontinuous narrative of the double and her own fate.

ACKNOWLEDGMENTS

I particularly thank six readers of this book in manuscript: Carole Fabricant and John M. Ganim for their acuity; John T. Irwin and Linda W. Wagner-Martin for their generosity; and Rise B. Axelrod and Alice Wexler, who together saved the ·project by providing line-by-line critiques just at the moment when I was most bewildered.

For stimulating ideas and encouragement, I am grateful to Jeremiah Axelrod, Helen Deese, Kimberly Devlin, Paul Douglass, George Haggerty, Ralph Hanna, Richard D. Lehan, Jay Martin, Jean-Pierre Mileur, Marshall Van Deusen, and Claudia Yukman. Nan Dorsey provided me with sympathetic understanding of the father-daughter relation in Plath's texts; some of the insights in chapter 2 are ours together. Aurelia Schober Plath kindly answered my queries.

I have had good guides in the writing, most of whom should be readily apparent: Freud, Robert Lowell, Roland Barthes, Harold Bloom, Sandra M. Gilbert, Susan Gubar, John T. Irwin, Margaret Homans. In addition, I am indebted to a host of Plath critics, above all A. Alvarez, Pamela J. Annas, Christopher Bollas, Mary Lynn Broe, Lynda K. Bundtzen, Judith Kroll, Marjorie Perloff, Jon Rosenblatt, Murray M. Schwartz, Margaret Dickie Uroff, Susan R. Van Dyne, and Linda W. Wagner-Martin.

My project may have begun nine years ago when a student, whose name I have forgotten, asked if I had noticed the allusion to *King Lear* in the last lines of Plath's "Words." My immediate answer was "no"; my considered responses are the second chapter's concluding section and this book in general. When I was in the middle of the project, I introduced a Plath class with the words, "Welcome to my obsession." To my good fortune, many students have consented to share that obsession and have shared their insights with me as well. I especially want to thank Neda Baric, Syd Butler Bartman, Diana Garber, Mary Hunter, Steve Giuliani, Sydney Johnson, Erik Kruger, Kathryn O'Rourke, Stan Orr, Bethany Schroeder, Eva Shinnerl, and David Thomas.

Over the years I have spent many hours in libraries, and like Camus's Sisyphus, I was happy. I much appreciate the care and effectiveness of Ruth Mortimer and the staff of the Neilson Library at Smith College and of Saundra Taylor and the staff of the Lilly Library at Indiana University. I am additionally indebted to the staffs of the following libraries: the British Library; the Library of the University of California, Berkeley; and the Tomas Rivera Library of the University of California, Riverside.

I thank Melinda Rosenthal and Ann Mosher for their excellent bibliographical assistance, Clara Dean for her efficient typing, and Eric Halpern, Carol Zimmerman, and Alice M. Bennett for helping me to get the book into final form. I also acknowledge support from the Research Committee of the University of California, Riverside.

Thanks are due to the editors of *American Poetry Review* and *Contemporary Literature* for allowing me to reprint portions of this book that first appeared in their journals. Because scholars now find it difficult to obtain permission from Plath's executors to quote, I have quoted nothing not in the category of fair use.

Finally, I am grateful to Sylvia Plath for being herself. It is, finally, enough.

Axes
After whose stroke the wood rings,
And the echoes!
—Sylvia Plath, "Words"

CHAPTER ONE

"Great Works May Speak from Me"

Possessed of speech, possessed by it, the word having chosen the grossness and infirmity of man's condition for its own compelling life, the human person has broken free from the great silence of matter. . . . But this breaking free, the human voice harvesting echo where there was silence before, is both miracle and outrage.
—George Steiner, *Language and Silence*

Notion of a book (of a text) in which is braided, woven, in the most personal way, the relation of every kind of bliss: those of "life" and those of the text, in which reading and the risks of real life are subject to the same anamnesis.
—Roland Barthes, *The Pleasure of the Text*

SYLVIA Plath's struggle to find her "voice in writing" (*LH* 241) became the central desire of her life and texts. At happy, "healthy" times, her "joy" whirled "in tongues of words" (*LH* 234), and she sensed that "great works" might "speak" from her (*J* 194). At unhappy times, she felt like a "vacuum" who could be filled only with "other people and their words" (*J* 86), if she could be filled at all. Plath felt "dependent on the process of writing" (*LH* 211) because she thought that writing alone could create her identity out of the void, could give her "a name, a meaning" (*J* 196). In addition to exemplifying the intensely personal nature of the poetic enterprise as defined by Robert Lowell, her career reveals the "charged relation" that often subsists between a woman author and her texts (Jacobus 17). As she wrote in one of her final poems, her "blood jet" was "poetry," and there was no stopping it (*CP* 270).

Uncertain of boundaries and burdened by pain, Plath hoped that poetic language could heal her "bloody private wounds" (*J* 188). Her ambivalence toward her father, mother,

3

and husband; her desire for status and belonging within a system of human relations; her wish for coherence; her horror at historical catastrophe; her sense of contingency, marginality, and loss — all of these were transformed into her battle for textual power. In this drama, rooted in her fear of non-being, she moved with great effort from muteness to textual "voice" (*LH* 231, 248, 336; *J* 185, 297) — or to what Wordsworth called "Shadows / And Images of voice" ("On the Power of Sound"). Textual "voice," for Plath, was less a means to communicate than a power exercised for its own sake. She called in order to be calling, to dramatize her calling, to establish an identity of words.

Prefiguring the speculations of Roland Barthes, Harold Bloom, Walter Ong, and Donald Wesling, Plath thought of "voice" as a category in which her body could pass through language, generating a verbal form that constituted another self. Moreover, "voice" evoked for her an intertextual space in which her web of obsessions might define itself in relation to the institution of literature. Seeking to reinvent her subjectivity by revising the words of the precursors, she both wished and feared that her "voice" might prove "Woolfish" (*J* 186) or that it might resemble Lowell's (*J* 222). Thus, instead of mimetically duplicating her empirical speech, Plath's textual voice superseded that speech, revealing patterns hidden and unspoken within it. The psychological sequence may have been: to be dead is to be without speech; in my everyday life I seem to lack freedom of speech; therefore my texts, which afford me access to speech, will permit me to enter into existence. The dread, expressed in *The Bell Jar,* of finding oneself as "blank and stopped as a dead baby" (*BJ* 282) implies a double fear: of dying ("stopped") and of being unable to write ("blank"). Freud remarked that in the psychic life made manifest in dreams and literature, "dumbness is to be understood as representing death" ("Three Caskets" 250). Split between a mark and a void, Plath indicated that whereas inscribed utterance was an "expression of life" (*J* 81), to be "dumb" was to be a "death's head" (*BJ* 22).

LANGUAGE

PLATH's compulsive orality appears throughout her discourse in the linked figures of *mouthing* and *eating*. These metaphors suggest that her need to voice poems was connected to disturbances in her earliest experience of parental nurturance. The style of that experience may have conditioned her enduring sense of hunger, suffocation, and deprivation as well as her need to keep proving oral prowess, envisioned not as the source of discrete products but as a continuous, life-sustaining process.

Her memory of childhood in "Ocean 1212-W" (*JP* 20–26) provides some clues to the nature of her adult absorption in writing. In this memoir, written when she was separated from her husband and composing the poems of *Ariel*, Plath recalls (or constructs) the chilling separation from her mother that occurred when her younger brother was born: "I who for two and a half years had been the center of a tender universe felt the axis wrench and a polar chill immobilize my bones. I would be a bystander, a museum mammoth" (*JP* 23). The moment becomes, at least in recollection, a negative epiphany: "As from a star I saw, coldly and soberly, the *separateness* of everything. I felt the wall of my skin. I am I. That stone is a stone. My beautiful fusion with the things of this world was over." She labels the moment "the awful birthday of otherness."

Although this recollection of her mother's "desertion" may well be a screen memory for an even earlier disturbance in maternal care, we note that Plath places the event just at the time when her mother stopped feeding her. At two years old, the little girl had grown old enough to feed herself, especially since her mother now needed to nurse a new baby. Thus, at least in memory, food and love were withdrawn together. Not by accident, food imagery predominates in Plath's recounting of this primal event. She recalls her grandmother's refusing to speak to her while kneading bread (*JP* 23); she remembers wandering past "ice-cream and hotdog stalls" prematurely boarded up; and she associates herself with the "hollowed orange and grapefruit halves" and the empty shells shaped like "ice-cream cones" that the sea has swallowed and regurgitated. The tide, formerly "motherly" (*JP* 20), has now "sucked back into itself," leaving the little girl, like the other detritus, a "reject" (*JP* 23). The child mimics in her own behavior what she believes has happened to her: whereas in the past she had "sometimes nursed starfish alive in jam jars of seawater and watched them grow back lost arms," on this day she "flung the starfish against a stone. Let it perish" (*JP* 23).

In order to understand this eloquent essay, we should recognize the correspondence between the child as a "bystander" or "reject"—deserted by her mother who had once "nursed" her "alive," newly imprisoned in a "wall" of skin, trudging in the direction of a "forbidding prison" (*JP* 23)—and Plath's habitual conception of the artist as the "rebel," the "odd" (*JP* 55). Plath's memoir suggests that just as she once watched starfish grow new arms, so she herself developed a new and pleasurable capacity that compensated for the lost feelings of warmth and union. In addition to placing this epiphany at the time when her mother stopped feeding her, Plath places it at the moment of her entrance into the symbolic order of language. Words themselves fragmented the two-year-old's "beautiful fusion" with the world, precipitating her "awful birthday of otherness." Yet words, which caused this split, could also repair it. As Emily Dickinson wrote, "To fill a Gap / Insert the Thing that caused it" (poem 546).

It is also significant that Plath locates her epiphany at the seashore. Harold Bloom has suggested that precursor texts symbolically constitute a "sea of poetry, of poems already written" and that therefore "poets tend to incarnate by the side of ocean," since incarnation necessarily results from poetic influence (*Map* 12–17). Northrop Frye, on the other hand, has asserted that "the narrative myth of dissolution is so often a flood myth" (20). To these associations we might add Roland Barthes's conflation of text with the mother's body (*Pleasure* 37) and Whitman's intricate interweaving of ocean, mother, death, and poetic utterance in "Out of the Cradle Endlessly Rocking." Plath, who called the ocean her "poetic heritage" (*LH*

345), seems to have incorporated all elements of this complex into her oceanic drama of the daughter's death and her rebirth as poet, of the mother's death and her rebirth as text. In Plath's "memory" or "vision" (*JP* 20), the sea tosses up a "monkey of wood" to the young girl, which she interprets as a "sign of election": "The sea, perceiving my need, had conferred a blessing. My baby brother took his place in the house that day, but so did my marvelous and (who knew?) even priceless baboon" (*JP* 24). An earlier passage indicates the precise nature of this election. There Plath recalls her mother's reading her (feeding her) Matthew Arnold's "The Forsaken Merman," a poem in which sea beasts "feed in the ooze." Plath felt that "a spark flew off Arnold and shook me, like a chill. I wanted to cry; I felt very odd. I had fallen into a new way of being happy" (*JP* 21).

Thus commenced Plath's lifelong feast of words. The "spark" and "chill" of poetry replaced the "polar chill" of separation that had immobilized her; a new way of being happy in the throat replaced the old way; poems became "like water or bread" to her (Interview 172). Plath's memoir expresses her wish to feel that *Ariel* had compensated her for her mother's initial withdrawal, her father's subsequent death, and her husband's ultimate abandonment. Her displacement of eating to the vocalization of literary language explains the dichotomy often remarked in her life between her need to maintain a large and well-kept kitchen, decorated with hanging globes of garlic and gleaming pans, and her "ravenous" desire to be a poet (*JP* 208) — a duality present in her discourse as a juxtaposition of "poems" and "potatoes" (*CP* 106). The displacement also clarifies her otherwise extravagant association of writing with living. A sort of transitional object mediating between inner and outer reality (see Winnicott 1–25), Plath's writing psychically sustained her, just as her mother's nurturing had done during her first years of life. Both satisfied her voracious need for love.

As a final hypothesis, we may posit that Plath as a young girl was made to feel that her demands for food and love were excessive. Perhaps she felt guilty about expressing her needs, believing she must steal what was not "rightfully" hers. Parental deprivation may have induced her lifelong sense not simply of rebellion and oddness but even of criminality. A Dickensian orphan, always wanting "more," she knew that she deserved her "forbidding prison" (*JP* 23) and her punishing "jailer" (*CP* 226). On this score, compare Esther Greenwood's compulsive stealing of food (*BJ* 31–32) to her appropriation of her mother's "secreted" writing paper (*BJ* 142), and compare both to Plath's own stealing of writing pads (*J* 204–5). Plath seems to have conceived of both writing and living as thefts from the powerful and the dead. Her existence struck her as marginal and doubtful, like that of a concentration camp victim; she felt herself menaced by effacement and erasure at every moment; she needed to purloin her signifier if she was to live.

"Too big to go backward" (*CP* 133), at least overtly, Plath chose to "mouth" poems (*J* 33) that would confirm a self. Surveying the canon that resulted, Margaret Homans criticizes Plath for dissolving the distinction between empirical and textual "I" in a "poetics of literal truth" (*Women Writers* 223). Although Homans raises an important issue here, her key term seriously misrepresents Plath's aim in writing. If Plath blurred the division between self and text, she did not do so in an effort to reproduce the "literal truth." She conceived of her project as inherently figurative, as her vocabulary of "allegory," "metaphor," "simile," "muse," and "white flying myth" attests (*CP* 293, 116; *J* 28, 194; *JP* 26). Understanding with Stevens that "it is a world of words, to the end of it" (Stevens 345), she knew that veristic "cries of the heart" would not suffice (Interview 169), that creativity depended on "culture" and "libraries" (*LH* 471). Besides, she conceived of the self as itself a shifting world of words. Her "I" could never anchor or master her utterance, since it was as indeterminate as the other. If her psychic text, like her inscribed text, was but a structure of tropes, a language of desire, then she would simply test the boundary separating different figurative systems. She would treat the frontier between them not as a dividing line but as explorable territory—a "potential space" of creative, if also transgressive, play (see Winnicott 41–56, 106–10; Kristeva 280–91).

Plath libidinized her texts by permitting energy and identity to flow back and forth between self and writing as well as between self and represented "I." She affirmed the organicity of her texts just as she granted the fictional aspect of her real life. Whereas Lacan envisioned the self as "not a poet, but a poem . . . that is being written" (*Four Concepts* viii), Plath conceptualized the text as a poet, "born all-of-a-piece" and capable of traveling "among strangers, around the world" (*JP* 65). Although she would probably have endorsed Bloom's formula that "a poem is always a person, always the father of one's Second Birth" (*Map* 19), she would have denied, in her healthy periods, the antithesis that he constructs between the "person-in-a-poet" and the "poet-in-a-poet" (*Map* 19). She was very much aware of the erotic and linguistic interplay between her "desire to be many lives" and her "writing" (*J* 16), between "world-making" and "word-making" (*J* 193).

Understanding figuration as a link between breathing and making, Plath termed "the world . . . a blank page" (*J* 317), while seeking to compose "a paper image . . . like a live skin" (*CP* 164). On the one hand, her texts portray the human subject as inherently linguistic: one speaker describes herself as a "letter in this slot" (*CP* 248), another feels composed of "panic in capital letters" (*JP* 152), another wishes to "walk into *Phèdre*" and leave her "mark" (*JP* 175), another has a scar on her face that "marked" her like a "scarlet letter" (*JP* 264), and yet others feel "papery" or "erased" (*CP* 235, 233). On the other hand, the texts often depict words as animate, whether "looking for a listener" (*CP* 203), "travelling . . . like horses" (*CP* 270), or taking control of a poem away from the poet (*JP* 62–63). In Plath's view, only a fool like Buddy Willard would call a poem a "piece of dust" (*BJ* 65). She conceived of "metaphors" as stages of a pregnancy (*CP* 116), "words" as fertile spawn (*CP* 202–3), and "poems" as children (*CP* 142). Although it may seem paradoxical that a dualist like Plath should enact exchanges between subject and object, that aim may explain her association of writing with health: composition was the one act in which she could diminish the otherness that oppressed her.

If Plath enthusiastically traced connections between body

and text, she exhibited some ambivalence about her identity relations with her represented "I." At times she insisted that the "I" was a virtual stranger: a woman in a maternity ward, a partly Jewish young woman, or a "good, plain, very resourceful woman" (*CP* 176, 293, 294). She distanced the written "I" from her personal beliefs and from the poem's ideology. As Michel Foucault's division of the "author-function" into a plurality of egos (*Language* 125–31) suggests, Plath's various subjective positions—as psychological being, as author, and as textual "I"—always manifest difference. Yet Plath also loved to muse about her resemblance to her represented double. At such moments she meditated on the nature of fictiveness itself.

Her depiction of Esther Greenwood's writing process in *The Bell Jar* provides a ready example. Scribbling on a "virgin sheet" of paper, the virginal Esther wants to invent a character

Plath, in *Mademoiselle* magazine, August 1953
        "Come on, give us a smile."
        I sat on the pink velvet loveseat in Jay Cee's office, holding a paper rose and facing the magazine photographer. . . . I didn't want my picture taken because I was going to cry.—*The Bell Jar*.

Source: Courtesy Mademoiselle. Copyright ©1953 (renewed 1981) by the Conde Nast Publications Inc.

"who would be myself, only in disguise" (*BJ* 142). Esther has chosen "Elaine" as her heroine's name because it has the same number of letters as her own. We note that both names have the same number as "Sylvia," and that Esther's surname, "Greenwood," duplicates one of Plath's maternal family names, Greenwood, in addition to anglicizing "Sylvia." Beneath the "disguise" of Plath's pseudonym "Victoria Lucas," then, "Sylvia," "Esther," and "Elaine" lie concealed as interchangeable variants. "Victoria Lucas" partially reveals as well as conceals, since the last two letters of the first name duplicate those of "Sylvia" (just as the first letter of "Elaine" duplicates that of "Esther"), and the last name, "Lucas," has the same number of letters as "Plath." Moreover, Esther at several points adopts the persona of "Elly" (*BJ* 13, 25, 156), a shortened version of "Elaine." Esther's choice of this persona suggests that her literary invention functions as an alter ego, as what Jay Martin would call her "fictive personality." Since "Elly" comes from Chicago, she may also represent Esther's fantasy identification with one or two "unconventional, mixed-up" boys she knows who attend the University of Chicago (*BJ* 157)—just as Plath identified herself with her unconventional Chicago pen pal, Eddie Cohen, who also attended the University of Chicago for a time and who belonged to a "group of neurotics" with "suicidal tendencies" (Cohen letter, January 24, 1951, Indiana ms.).

The four sentences of her novel that Esther manages to compose mimic her own situation and sensations as she writes, and they echo or prefigure the prose style of *The Bell Jar* as well (*BJ* 142-43). As Esther writes, she dirties her virgin sheet of paper (142), an image that connects her composition to her earlier self-description as a "dirty, scrawled-over letter" (*BJ* 23). Just as the letters that inscribe her invented character are really herself "in disguise," so she herself is but a "letter" (in both senses of the word). This reciprocal relation of self and letter recalls Dickinson's "letter to the world," Poe's "purloined letter" that is bearer and barer of hidden identities, Hawthorne's allegory of a woman whose subjectivity condenses to a single scarlet letter ("Hester" and "Esther," incidentally, being cognates), Melville's tale of a scrivener whose work in the "dead letter office" absorbs his future, and, in Esther's own phrase, the "alphabet soup of letters" that constitutes Joyce's autobiographical fiction (*BJ* 147). Whether she wishes to dictate "thrilling letters" or to think of herself as a "scrawled-over letter" (*BJ* 89, 23), Esther is a woman of letters, an Aristotelian being of the word, her identity bound up with language. Organized as a grammar, her psyche expresses itself as text and as the desire to compose text. Her suicidal descent begins when she fails to gain admittance to a writing course (*BJ* 135), and as she breaks down, so does her linguistic capacity. Words are "dimly familiar but twisted all awry, like faces in a funhouse mirror" (*BJ* 147). Letters grow "barbs and rams' horns," separate from each other, and "jiggle up and down" (*BJ* 147)—just as they do for the protagonist of "The Wishing Box" (*JP* 205) and as they did on occasion for Plath herself. Eventually Esther can neither read nor write (*BJ* 160). At the nadir, her consciousness is wiped out "like chalk on a blackboard" (*BJ* 256). She recovers by discarding the rigid dualities that have ordered her language of the self ("dirty" versus "virgin," for example), exchanging that coercive rhetoric for a less structured one that includes numerous "question marks" (*BJ* 290).

Plath's sense of writing as being "essential" to her life (Interview 172) reflects the aesthetic assumptions of her postromantic precursors. In her late essay "Context" she wrote: "The poets I delight in are possessed by their poems as by the rhythms of their own breathing" (*JP* 65). As examples, she mentioned Robert Lowell, Theodore Roethke, Elizabeth Bishop, and Stevie Smith. Of these, Lowell had the strongest personal impact. He was her professor at Boston University at a time when she was trying to "change" her "ways of writing" (*J* 294). Under his guidance, she composed many of the poems she collected in her first book, *The Colossus*. She later said that Lowell's "breakthrough into very serious, very personal, emotional experience" facilitated her own development (Interview 168–69), though at other times she stressed his rhetorical powers (*J* 294; *JP* 205). Whether essentially personal or rhetorical, Lowell's texts elaborate a trope of creative labor. *Life Studies*, for example, focuses on its author's development from a rebellious young boy to a poet of self (11–46, 59–90). Believing that "the artist finds new life in his art and almost sheds his other life" ("Talk" 43), Lowell claimed that he *was* his "words" (*History* 203). Studying with him validated Plath's wish to conflate "my writing, my desire to be many lives" (*J* 16), since he himself conflated "one life, one writing" (*For the Union Dead* 68).

Thus, as a result of emotional need, creative desire, and poetic influence, Plath devoted her life to inscribing an enduring immanence, another self of writing. In studying the interactions between her positions as person, author, text, and represented "I," we witness her quest to achieve satisfaction and authority in the symbolic order of language. For if words (as a form of separation and loss) wounded her, words (as a form of connection and fulfillment) also promised to cure that wound.

SILENCE

In a discourse so obsessed with voicing, we should expect to find that silence also plays a crucial role, and it does. Plath's writing reveals two distinct types: a political silencing that originates in human relationships, and a more ambiguous linguistic fading that inheres in words themselves.

Since she was a "political person" (Interview 169), Plath generally understood silence in its former aspect, as a "dead silence" in the head (*JP* 209), as what Tillie Olsen calls the "unnatural thwarting of what struggles to come into being, but cannot" (xi). More particularly, she discovered that in a patriarchal culture, figurative language, like analytical language, putatively belongs to men. Standing outside language, Plath frequently felt that she "could hardly speak" (*CP* 223), that the verbal act was proscribed to her. Yet she also believed that she could not "live" without inscribing her utterance (*LH* 313; Interview 172). When Hélène Cixous describes a woman's difficulty in voicing, she evokes a crucial aspect of Plath's situation:

Every woman has known the torment of getting up to speak. Her heart racing, at times entirely lost for words, ground and language slipping away—that's how daring a feat, how great a transgression it is for a woman to speak—even just open her mouth—in public. A double distress, for even if she transgresses, her words fall almost always upon the deaf male ear, which hears in language only that which speaks in the masculine.

It is by writing, from and toward women, and by taking up the challenge of speech which has been governed by the phallus, that women will confirm women in a place other than that which is reserved in and by the symbolic, that is, in a place other than silence. (251)

In just this spirit did Plath rebel against masculine law that associates women with dumbness or with degraded language, and against her own self-doubts and inhibitions as well.

Plath related her struggle against silence to the larger struggles of oppressed peoples everywhere (see *JP* 64; Interview 170). Silence in this sense signifies the destruction of powerless or dissident individuals by "governments, parliaments, societies, / The faceless faces of important men" (*CP* 179). Although her texts do occasionally welcome silence, when anger overwhelms language or when words seem exhausted, those instances are either ironic or despairing. More typically, she strives to defeat the ever-threatening moment when the "tongue" is "stuck" in the jaw (*CP* 223), "swollen and stuck out" (*JP* 156), or made "of stone" (*JP* 261); when the self "has no voice" (*CP* 263) or "no tongue" (*CP* 266); when the "breath" vanishes (*CP* 244–46) or the mouth is gagged, veiled, or vaporized (*CP* 193, 243, 209); when one can speak only with a "hollow voice" or a "zombie voice" (*BJ* 140) or can type only the words of a male other and never one's own (*JP* 16, 84; *BJ* 89); when one stews in the sour air of the bell jar (*BJ* 222). For Plath, muteness signified exclusion from the "uttering tongues" (Whitman 34) and "voices" (Eliot 48) of history. It meant social nonbeing.

The irony of Plath's career is that despite all her efforts, silence won a major victory over her in the end. Her premature death led to the loss and destruction of a significant portion of the texts she had already written. If we are to fathom the social and biographical significance of her relation to silence, we need to consider the fate of her manuscripts. The story reveals what was truly at stake in her struggle to speak, while suggesting how tenuous her grasp on language finally was.

After her death Plath's husband and executor, Ted Hughes, destroyed one of her unpublished manuscripts and lost another. In his foreword to the published *Journals*, he explains that the manuscripts were additional journals that "continued the record from late '59 to within three days of her death. The last of these contained entries for several months, and I destroyed it because I did not want her children to have to read it (in those days I regarded forgetfulness as an essential part of survival). The other disappeared" (*J* xiii). Although Frances McCullough, coeditor with Hughes of the *Journals*, plausibly claims that the journal is Plath's "most important work" next to her poems (*J* ix), its climactic three years, constituting a third or more of the entire text, are now gone. Those were the years when Plath found new and more capable modes of literary expression. Particularly in her last six months, when she had separated from Hughes, she wrote "terrific stuff," as if domesticity had "choked" her (*LH* 466). Having located her gift "in time to make something of it" (*LH* 480), she exclaimed, "I am a genius of a writer; I have it in me" (*LH* 468). Out of that period came most of the poems her reputation rests on today. At the same time, she continued to work on another major text, her journal. We can reasonably surmise that, qualitatively, the later journal entries were to the earlier ones as the poems of *Ariel* are to Plath's earlier poems. Hughes himself has confessed: "Looking over this curtailed journal, we cannot help wondering whether the lost entries for her last three years were not the more important section of it" ("Her Journals" 153).

Even the preserved sections of the journal have been edited in a way that often distorts Plath's voice. Marjorie Perloff bluntly terms the editing of Plath's work a "scandal" ("Extremist Poetry" 585; see also McCullough, Letter; Perloff, "Two Ariels"; Tabor, 43–44). The text of *Journals*, based on a typed version provided by Hughes, contains numerous marked and unmarked omissions. McCullough explains in her "Editor's

Note" that "there are quite a few nasty bits missing — Plath had a very sharp tongue and tended to use it on nearly everybody" (*J* ix). Yet many of the deletions occur when Plath seems poised to use her "sharp tongue" on one person in particular, her executor-to-be: "Grumpy with Ted, who sometimes strikes my finicky nerves [omission]" (*J* 212); "No criticism or nagging. [Omission.] He is a genius. I his wife" (*J* 259). Other omissions occur for no apparent reason. Although scholars may read a few of the suppressed passages in the Smith College library, they may not quote from them. And most of the deleted material, which apparently bulks twice as large as the published material, has been sealed away from all eyes.

If the omissions may someday be restored, the destroyed portions can never be. Of the twenty-seven disappointing pages of notes that have been printed as the *Journals'* conclusion, McCullough remarks: "Because only work notes survive from this last section of the journal, it almost gives the impression that Plath died long before she actually did end her life" (*J* 357). This impression, however, is wholly false, a reflection of the executor's disposition of the manuscripts rather than of the writer's mind and art. The poetry, fiction, and correspondence from Plath's last three years demonstrate that, for all her torment, she had never been more alive. Her journal, in the state she left it, undoubtedly exposed that vibrancy. A blank page, testifying to all that Plath wrote and that Hughes destroyed and lost, would have made a more meaningful conclusion than the notes that have been printed, which clearly were not journal entries at all but drafts destined for the wastebasket. The essential ending of Plath's surviving journal occurs in December 1959, when she and her husband returned to England from the United States. The rest is "blackness and silence" (*CP* 173).

In addition to the destroyed and lost portions of the journal, a novel also "disappeared" in about 1970. Hughes reports that this manuscript, which Plath planned to title *Double Exposure* (or *Double Take*), contained only 130 pages (*JP* 1), though she herself implied at times that it was nearly finished (*LH* 467, 473, 490). Since her suicide closely followed the ebbing of her literary inspiration, it seems possible that she had essentially completed the draft. As soon as she finished *The Bell Jar* in spring 1962, she immediately began work on a sequel that would depict Esther Greenwood's successful marriage and the birth of her daughter. This novel, dedicated to Hughes, was not the one that "disappeared" in 1970. Plath burned this manuscript herself after discovering Hughes's infidelity in July 1962, a discovery evoked in "Words heard, by accident, over the phone" and "The Fearful" (*CP* 202–3, 256). She then began writing a new novel, which she termed in her letters her "second" and which Aurelia Plath amends in *Letters Home* to "third." This is the novel that vanished after her death. Although its exact contents remain a mystery, its title, *Double Exposure*, suggests that it explored, as Plath wrote in another context, the way time "blooms, decays, and double-exposes itself" (*JP* 61) — and particularly the way time can reveal a marriage to be a sham. In October 1962, writing to her mother about the marital degradation she had endured, Plath remarked: "I shall never forget and shall commemorate in my next novel" (*LH* 471). In November she told her patron Olive Higgins Prouty that the novel concerned a husband who was a deserter (Smith ms.). Judith Kroll, who has seen an outline of the plot, reports that its principal characters were a "heroine," a "rival," a "husband," and the "rival's husband" (66). Linda Wagner-Martin states that the novel revealed "the gradual corruption of a naive American girl . . . by a powerful and inherently dishonest man" (236).

If we judge by the general quality of Plath's writing in her last six months, and by her particular enthusiasm for the novel as she worked on it, *Double Exposure* appears to have been another important book, perhaps surpassing *The Bell Jar*. Writing to her mother, who she knew would resent any private revelations, Plath termed both novels "potboilers" (*LH* 490), casually promising to publish them anonymously. But her intention to dedicate the new book to Olive Higgins Prouty (*LH* 491) suggests that she would not in fact have published it under a pseudonym. She valued her "terrific second novel" (*LH* 473) too highly to omit her name from the cover. In her last months she described herself interchangeably as a "novelist" and a "poet," speaking of her new novel in the same breath that she used to describe the poems of *Ariel*.

The accidental loss, if that is what it was, of the novel attests
to the extent of Plath's bad luck, but the intentional destruction
of the journal goes beyond luck to malice. Hughes claims he
destroyed the journal's conclusion because he did "not want
her children to have to read it" (*J* xiii). Without knowing precisely what the entries contained, we can still suspect Hughes
of disingenuousness on this point, because he had reasons of
his own for not wanting those pages ever to see print. In her
last year, and especially in her last six months, Plath must have
focused her journal entries on Hughes himself—his character,
his behavior. Since Plath had a "sharp tongue" in her journal,
her portrait of her husband must have been devastating. After
the "shock" of Hughes's infidelity (*LH* 465), after a period of
"agonized" life with a man who no longer loved her (*LH* 460),
after the "final blows" of his desertion and temporary disap-
pearance (*LH* 462), and after the "humiliation and begging
money from deaf ears" (*LH* 463), Plath felt she had been
through "the most incredible hell" (*LH* 467). Her way of recovering herself was through the "potential space" of writing: "I
love and live for letters" (*LH* 471). She centered her existence
on her creative productions—her poems, her new novel, and
her journal. The journal, like *Double Exposure* and "The Jailer,"
must have suggested her feelings about the man she was divorc-
ing. Yet Hughes decided that "her description of neighbors and
friends and daily happenings is mostly too personal, her criticisms frequently unjust" (*JP* 8). And he found himself in a position to prevent those unjust criticisms from ever seeing light.

What he really did with the last years of the journal and
when he did it remain unclear. We have seen his statement in
the *Journals*, published in 1982, about "those days" when he
sought "forgetfulness," presumably a time in the distant past.
But just four years earlier, in his 1978 introduction to *Johnny
Panic and the Bible of Dreams*, he wrote: "How much of it"—
apparently the journal in its entirety—"ought to be published
is not easy to decide" (*JP* 7–8). He then proceeded to publish
three excerpts from the years he subsequently claimed were
destroyed or lost. A question also exists concerning the num-

ber of manuscripts that vanished. In one account Hughes speaks of a novel that "disappeared somewhere around 1970" (*JP* 1). In another he speaks of a journal notebook that "disappeared" at some unspecified time (*J* xiii). Were these two mysterious losses separate, or were they one and the same? In his public statements, Hughes has been curiously ambiguous in explaining the fate of Plath's manuscripts. In a revised version of the *Journals* foreword, for instance, he comments that the journal that disappeared "may, presumably, still turn up" ("Her Journals" 152). It is just barely possible that Plath's words have not been destroyed or lost at all, but have been hidden away.

In his critical comments about Plath, Hughes constantly returns to the theme that "all her writings appear like notes and jottings directing attention towards that central problem — herself" (*JP* 8). But his careful editing of her manuscripts; his elimination of "The Jailer," "The Rabbit Catcher," and "Purdah" from *Ariel*; his efforts to exert control over the work of Plath scholars; his sister Olwyn's collaboration on a hostile biography (Anne Stevenson's *Bitter Fame*) and his own attempt to gut an evenhanded one (Linda Wagner-Martin's *Sylvia Plath*); his apparent destruction of manuscripts; and even his loss of manuscripts — all of these may be designed to make his assertion seem truer than it is. For it is possible that the writings he has suppressed or misplaced have directed attention toward other central problems — for example, the problem of Hughes himself. Adrienne Rich has written that male culture "has every stake in opposing women actively laying claim to our own lives" (*On Lies* 14). The posthumous stilling of Plath's voice provides striking evidence for Rich's charge and further suggests the validity of Plath's fear that external forces jeopardized the inscription of her utterance.

Yet why did Plath leave herself open to this sort of silencing? Why did she leave her texts in the possession of a man whom she evoked in her poetry as a "vampire" and an "enemy" (*CP* 224, 244)? One answer might be that she wished to continue to be his victim even after death, that she wished her work to share in her suicide. We uneasily note some eerie parallels: her

actions of burning her novel and then gassing her body six
months later, her willingness to allow her husband to dominate
her in life and to mutilate her memory and texts after death.
But such an explanation belies what Rich called Plath's "struggle for survival" (*On Lies* 121) and what Plath herself called her
"fight for air and freedom" (*LH* 465). An alternative answer,
initially suggested by A. Alvarez in *The Savage God* (33–38), is
that Plath did not expect to die at all and thus did not concern
herself with the disposition of her manuscripts. She planned
the suicide attempt at a time when she was expecting a visitor,
leaving the telephone number of her doctor prominently displayed: she did not expect to have literary remains. Nevertheless, she certainly knew there was a chance she would die. In
her interior conflict between self-abnegation and self-assertion,
perhaps the former had won a devastating victory over the art
as well as the life. Or was Plath simply enacting the fate of
women's words in a patriarchal culture? Was she representing
herself in yet another way as a being who "could hardly speak"
(*CP* 223)? In making her inscription vulnerable to dismemberment by male hands, was she lodging her final protest, delivering her final proof, writing her final text, the most bitter and
unanswerable yet?

DISTINCT from the political silence enforced by the other is the
silence that plays dialectically with utterance in the dualism of
language. This inherent silence — often manifested as fragmen-
tation or contradiction — unmakes what utterance makes, dissolving rather than defining the subjectivity of the author.
Thomas Giannotti has remarked that "the language of silence
would seem to be embedded in the post-romantic consciousness as a phenomenological condition" (34). With the decline
of metaphysics, a belief that absence is encoded in every sign
leads to a valorizing of silence against any linguistic self-
assurance. Modernist and postmodernist writers discover in
the play of silence and language a consolation for the loss of
certitude.

Plath, however, who was in search of her "name" (*J* 196), did
not easily accommodate the intrusion of silence into her dis-

course. Although she would have sympathized with the speaker of Beckett's *The Unnamable* when he declares, "I'm in words, made of words," she would have recoiled when he adds, "I'm something else quite different, a quite different thing, a word-less thing in an empty place" (139). Whereas Beckett destabilized discourse, Plath sought to discover the words that could construct a meaningful self-presence. Whereas he exploited the holes in language, she, who felt herself falling vertiginously down those holes, tried to grasp the crumbling ledges as though they were secure handholds. Nevertheless, the unwelcome sense that language provided no ground for settling identity and no sky for transcending it haunted her discourse. The represented "I" of the poems often reveals herself to be a "cut-paper shadow" (*CP* 161), inhabiting a world of papery "holes" (*CP* 226), looking out on "nothing but a great space" (*CP* 169). Plath knew that literary language provided her with "a place to stand on, but no rocks, / No floor" (*CP* 79).

In the last weeks of her life, she brought her relation to language to a crisis. In "Words" (*CP* 270), for example, axes divide echoes from their origin, sending them "off from the center like horses." In one sense utterance and self have become opposites, but in another they have identically returned to nonbeing. The decentered words are "dry and riderless" (writerless), while the wordless "life" lies motionless underwater. In "Contusion" (*CP* 271), imagery of absence similarly predominates: the sea pivots on a "hollow," the mirror is "sheeted." In one of Plath's final two poems, "Balloons" (*CP* 271–72), the eponymous "soul animals" figure language itself (as do the echoes, horses, sea, and mirror of the preceding poems). A little boy, thinking he glimpses a "pink world he might eat" on the other side of a balloon, bites it and discovers its emptiness. "Edge" (*CP* 272–73), Plath's other final poem, concludes on an even deeper note of disenchantment. As the indifferent moon stares at a dead woman, its "blacks crackle and drag"—the sound of silence registering not as language at all but as noise, as radio static.

Thus, whether figuring political violence or linguistic vacancy, silence threatened Plath's project of textual self-creation. Although she sought to defy the authority of the other by speaking, the other retained power over her discourse. Although she meant to refute the void by making her mark, her mark inevitably wandered from her intention, returning in a guise as strange as it was familiar. Yet at the same time, silence inhered in her project, motivating and shaping it. Plath's writing explores the ironic relations between utterance and silence, and it also tests the relations between utterance and matter. It unsettles the role that fictive discourse plays in a human life by inventing "a language lined with flesh" (Barthes, *Pleasure* 66), by troping along the border of body and text. An uncertain, flickering image of voice arises, speaking words that at once reveal and conceal, betray and redeem.

CHAPTER TWO

"Jealous Gods"

If you want to be a top-notcher, you have to break with everyone.
You have to show up your own father.
—F. Scott Fitzgerald, *Letters*

I rose—because He sank—
I thought it would be opposite—
—Emily Dickinson, Poem 616

WHEREAS George Steiner states that "speech is the core of man's mutinous relations to the gods" (37), Harold Bloom suggests that speech is the core of man's mutinous relations to the fathers (*Map* 80). Bloom figures poetic history as an "agon" that recuperates the Freudian pattern of human history in general: the ephebe (the son) contests the precursor (the father) for poetic immortality (the mother). Freud himself proposed that writing may assume "the significance of copulation," since it entails "making a liquid flow out of a tube on to a piece of white paper" (*Inhibitions* 16). But what happens when the writer is a daughter? How does the female poet receive instruction and achieve authority? Sandra M. Gilbert, Susan Gubar, Margaret Homans, Barbara Mossberg, and Cheryl Walker have all, in different ways, answered those questions by positing an agon not among women writers, but between the woman writer and patriarchal culture. They suggest that speech is the core of woman's mutinous relations to man.

Mossberg suggests that Emily Dickinson, the mother of American poetry, was caught between her pose as a dutiful daughter and the anger and power she experienced as a poet (198). Gilbert and Gubar argue, more generally, that whereas nineteenth-century women writers secretly undermined patriarchal myths and metaphors (*Madwoman* 73–74), their twentieth-

23

century descendants have publicly fought for verbal territory
(*No Man's Land* 1:3–4). Walker similarly describes American
women poets as progressing from acquiescence or subversion
to open warfare against male domination (17, 148). Taking a
more rhetoricized approach, Homans catalogs the ways women
have established themselves as writers despite being constructed by male ideology as objects lacking figurative capacity
(*Bearing* 5, 29–33). These studies illuminate a crucial aspect of
Plath's situation. She martyred herself to patriarchal tradition
and rebelled against it; revered men's texts and defaced them;
was inhibited by self-doubt and plotted to invent a language of
her own. She often portrayed herself as either a servant or a
thief.

The latter self-concept provides a clue that helps us loosen the
knot in which her poetic identity lies hidden. Jacques Lacan
taught that relations between the living and the dead inevitably
involve elements of theft and sacrifice, while T. S. Eliot observed
that strong poets steal from their predecessors, and Alicia
Ostriker has shown that women writers steal language from the
men who possess it. Thus it is no accident that Plath liked to
write on stolen paper (*J* 203–5), nor that she imagined herself a
plagiarist (*BJ* 143; *JP* 207), a trespasser (*JP* 162–63), and a thief
of poetry (*CP* 103). Plath was a person who felt "cheated" (*J* 269,
299) and who needed to cheat in return to gain her ends.

Having been bereaved of her father when she was eight—the
verb "to bereave" deriving from the same root as "to rob"—she
stole back everything that was hers: love, status, and the figurative language by which she lived and died. Every letter she
wrote was in effect purloined, from her dead father and from
the male institutions that perpetuated him. She sought to as-
suage her father's death by alternately taking from him and
holding vigil for him. She yearned "to pay" him "back" in two
senses (*BJ* 196). Thus it is proper for us to begin our inquiry
here, examining the paternal presence so pervasive in her
psychic and written texts and so demanding of her self-
sacrifice or rebellion. There are even deeper deeps than these,
but these are waters that Plath herself knew well, inhabited by
an "old man" who was for her a "myth of origins" (*CP* 92).

A PATRIARCHAL EDUCATION

SYLVIA PLATH's father, Otto Plath, undoubtedly helped initiate her wish to write by providing an example of a life devoted to, even consumed by, writing (Wagner-Martin 20–28). On the other hand, his intimidating authority, together with his withdrawn and demanding personality, made it difficult for her to have faith in her own creativity. When Otto Plath died after refusing treatment for his diabetes, his young daughter felt "lost and betrayed" (*JP* 312). Just as she had initially stolen his love, an act she feared had killed him (*CP* 117; *J* 279), so she now needed to steal her existence back from him, who had sought her death as well as his own. Why else had he abandoned her so young, leaving her but a "ghost of an infamous suicide" (*CP* 117)? Why else did he seem to entice her to follow suit, as she eventually did?

Beyond being both endowed and impoverished by her father, she was in competition with him for the power of his sign, a relation metonymically suggested by her comment, "I know nothing of bees. My father knew it all" (*J* 318). He wrote about bees in *Bumblebees and Their Ways*, just as she would write about them in innumerable stories and poems. She conceived of him as a "faulty" but authentic artist (*J* 316), just the kind she herself would become. It was crucial to her that he had generated language, whereas her mother only transcribed it. He had dedicated his book to his "teacher and friend" William Morton Wheeler and had merely acknowledged the "service" of his wife "in editing the manuscript and in proofreading" (*Bumblebees* xi), possibly motivating Esther Greenwood's remark in *The Bell Jar*, "the trouble was, I hated the idea of serving men in any way" (*BJ* 89). Like Esther, Plath wanted to dictate her "own thrilling letters" rather than transcribe words dictated by men (*BJ* 89), wanted to be an "arrow" rather than "the place an arrow shoots off from" (*CP* 239; *BJ* 83). Thus her conflicted feelings about her father went into her construction of her writing identity, conditioning the kind of poetry and fiction she would write and the sort of relationship she would have with male precursors.

In her psychic text and in her literary texts, Plath attempted
to make contact with her beloved yet distrusted father through
her grief. Since he had given her life, his connection to her
from the other side of the grave confirmed her existence in life.
Further, as her writing double, he could help her to inscribe
her literary immanence. When she wrote, she repetitively
figured herself in relation to him — as his daughter, his enemy,
or both. Yet to make too complete a contact was to risk loss of
self, since the object of her mourning might become a vampire
feeding on her (*CP* 224; cf. Freud, "Mourning" 249–51). In actuality and in her writing, therefore, she alternately wished to
"kill" him (*CP* 222) and "howled" her loss (*BJ* 199). She needed
to be disloyal and loyal at once — Goneril and Regan as well as
Cordelia. That she maintained her balance for as long as she
did on her fragile tightrope testifies to her enormous skill and
desire.

As we have seen in the introductory chapter, Plath conceived of art as a compensation for loss. Of all her losses, the
most obvious one (though not the first) was the death of her
ambivalently loved father. In her adult life, she attempted to
restore that loss by preserving her father in her creative life as
a "buried male muse" (*J* 223). But the loss was repeated when
she was deserted by her ambivalently loved husband, whom
she had fancied was her father "risen" from his grave "to be my
mate" (*J* 223). The latter bereavement hurled her first into a
creative frenzy and then, when that mania faded, into extinction. In a sense her writing career amounted to an extended
exercise in mourning. But because her grief went underground
and never seemed to end, it verged on what Freud termed
"melancholia": "In mourning it is the world which has become
poor and empty; in melancholia it is the ego itself" ("Mourning" 246). According to Freud, the melancholic does not gradually withdraw libido from the lost object, as the normally
grieving person does, but rather identifies the ego with the
abandoned object. Thus "the shadow of the object" falls "upon
the ego" (249) — conceivably in the guise of a double or a buried muse. Just as the wish "to recover" the lost object (*CP* 222)
causes the melancholic to incorporate it into the self, so resent-

ment causes the melancholic to reproach the lost object or even to want "to kill" it (*CP* 222) once it is there. Freud concludes that sufferers usually "succeed, by the circuitous path of self-punishment, in taking revenge on the original object. . . . It is this sadism alone that solves the riddle of the tendency to suicide which makes melancholia so interesting—and so dangerous" (251–52).

When Plath read Freud's essay in late 1958, she called it "an almost exact description of my feelings and reasons for suicide" (*J* 280). Astonishingly, she then applied its insights only to her feelings about her *mother*. We can understand this strange reaction by turning from Freud to John Bowlby. Whereas Freud thought that ambivalence turns normal mourning into pathological mourning, Bowlby has more recently found that ambivalence frequently appears in normal mourning as well. He suggests that mourning is always a difficult and partially unsuccessful process. Pathological mourning merely involves "exaggeration or distortions" resulting from "defensive processes" that have interfered with and diverted the normal course (31). As Plath's application of Freud's insights to her mother rather than to her father implies, Plath's defensive processes were powerful indeed. In the period preceding her first suicide attempt, she denied the significance, or even the actuality, of her father's death: "What do I know of sorrow? No one I love has ever died" (*J* 19). Similarly, when her husband left her, she caromed dangerously between devastation and denial. Her efforts to repress her feelings of grief at that time may have distorted them to the point that suicide, again, seemed the only answer.

When capable of self-analysis, however, Plath understood that her complex relationship to her father was an organizing theme of her psychic life, and she recognized that his death was a point of her vulnerability. Every loss, every grief reminded her of that one: "Crying and crying with this terrible pain; it hurts, Father, it hurts, oh, Father I have never known; a father, even, they took from me" (*J* 123). This grief powered her creative activity: "I rail and rage against the taking of my father. . . . My villanelle was to my father; and the best one. I lust for the knowing of him" (*J* 128). She thought that although "the

bottom fell out" of her emotional life when her father died, she
could "restore" herself by writing "stories, poems, and the
novel" (*J* 162). Her father's death left a "hole" in her that words
alone seemed able to fill (*LH* 289).

Yet we might venture that it was not her father that she ultimately depended on so much as his loss, since it was precisely
the loss that provided her with the only worldview and the only
artistic identity she possessed. Her mature writing reflected "a
heaven / Starless and fatherless" (*CP* 262), and it entailed a
sloughing off of "dead hands, dead stringencies" (*CP* 239).
Without her father's death, she would be nothing — not words
in a hole, but merely a hole in her father's dominion of signs.
Her nostalgia for origins — for a lost paradise in which paternal
order prevailed, words were at one with things, and desire was
at one with satisfaction — thus played against her sense of self-
preservation, her need to maintain herself in a fatherless state.
Her nostalgia also conflicted with her fury at an authoritarian
father who loved her best when she was absent (Wagner-
Martin 27) and who seemed to have abandoned her just when
she needed him most.

Thus, as much as she wished to idealize her father as "intel-
ligent, loving, liberal" (*LH* 162), as a "buried male muse" (*J*
223), or as "a giant of a man" (*JP* 306), she also needed to
deflate his memory, to keep him small, impotent, and distanced. Her unresolvable ambivalence appears in her journal
comment, "He was an ogre. But I miss him" (*J* 268). Alice
Denway's professor-father in "Among the Bumblebees" suggests the dimensions paternity assumed in Plath's imagination.
A sort of sea deity, Alice's father resembled "a king, high on a
throne" (*JP* 308). His daughter "worshiped [him] because he
was so powerful, and everybody did what he commanded
because he knew best and never gave mistaken judgment" (*JP*
306). But he also possessed a malevolent nature. Alice would
observe him correcting student papers with "vicious little red
marks . . . the color of the blood that oozed out in a thin line
the day she cut her finger with the bread knife" (*JP* 309). Thus
he served a double function: to inspire writing and to censor it.
When Alice's father "would get cross and raise his voice like

thunder," he made her shiver, just as he made his students tremble with fright (*JP* 311, 308). No wonder Plath wrote her honors thesis about a character, Ivan Karamazov, who asked, "Who does not desire his father's death?" No wonder she wished to dig her father up only "to prove that he existed, that he was really dead" (*J* 299). But at the same time, she must have shared Alice's lingering destitution at his death: "In all the rest of her life there would be no one to walk with her, like him, proud and arrogant among the bumblebees" (*JP* 312).

Bowlby observes that "what is impressive about mourning is not only the number and variety of response systems that are engaged but the way in which they tend to conflict with one another" (31). Undoubtedly Plath's psychic text was more complicated than most. As a child of eight, she must have at once denied that her father would die and been terrified of it. Since he was already part of herself, his death would be a devastating loss. At the same time, she must have felt she had caused his death, since children presume themselves magically powerful (Piaget 123–251, 389–94). Believing on another level that he had "deserted" her (*J* 280), she would have experienced anger at that loss, guilt at the anger, and a sense that she deserved to be punished. Moreover, we must add to that emotional complex the longing for him; the sense that she would never be complete without him; the competition with him; and the fear of him, as her childish fantasies gave him gargantuan proportions. In all these ways, as Freud put it, "an object-loss was transformed into an ego-loss" ("Mourning" 249). Plath asked not simply Melville's question, "Where is the foundling's father hidden?" but Where will he reappear? and In what form? She must have dreaded his revenge against her, since she might have kept him alive had she only known how and since her angry thoughts perhaps killed him in the first place.

Plath apparently could not acknowledge and work through these feelings in her contacts with others. Noting this failure, Alice Miller asserts that "the reason for her despair was not her suffering but the impossibility of communicating her suffering to another person" (255). Nevertheless, Plath found that she could express her suffering in poems and stories. Although

artistic expression could not make up for her inability to communicate such feelings in the context of her life in the world,
it did provide catharsis and at least temporary relief.

As we have seen, Plath describes or imagines her discovery
of poetry's power in "Ocean 1212-W" (*JP* 20–26). She recalls her
mother's reciting lines from Arnold's "The Forsaken Merman"
about the merman's caverns:

> Where the sea-beasts rang'd all round
> Feed in the ooze of their pasture-ground;
> Where the sea-snakes coil and twine
> Dry their mail and bask in the brine.   (*JP* 21)

She further recalls her reaction to hearing this poem: "I saw
the goose-flesh on my skin. I did not know what made it. I was
not cold. Had a ghost passed over? No, it was the poetry. A
spark flew off Arnold and shook me, like a chill. I wanted to
cry; I felt very odd. I had fallen into a new way of being happy"
(*JP* 21). If we bring to mind the recurrent images in Plath's
poems of the primeval father who is variously dead, ghostlike,
archaic, risen, bestial, or godlike, her reaction seems momentous. Her discovery of poetry reflects not only on her relation to
her mother, as we saw in chapter 1, but also on her relation to
paternity. She had identified her muse, the male force who
engendered her creativity even as he annulled it. The ghostly
chill that moves her to tears yet tells her of a "new way of being
happy" suggests that the solution to her dilemma lies in taming
the sea god who ruled the "still, stagnant, putridly and potently
rich sea" of her "subconscious" (*J* 73).

To hear Arnold was to hear re-created, in the potential space
of literary language, feelings from her own depths that were
connected to her father; and in hearing them she learned how
she might withstand and even use that terrible presence. In
combination with the Arnoldian discovery, Plath's habit of cir-
cling words in her father's thesaurus (Wagner-Martin 166)
assumes special significance. It indicates her creative determi-
nation to use language to control her unconscious world—to
"dike" the flood (*J* 99, 188). "Ocean 1212-W" recollects or constructs the moment when the young girl recognizes her voca-

tion and passion, her destiny as an artist. At the same time, it suggests that her vocation, passion, and destiny all derive together from a complex of motives: first, her use of poetry as a way to be "happy" by venting and transforming the unconscious, that is to say, her excruciating feelings about her identity in relation to her father; second, her profound need to write *for* her father, whom she still wished to please; third, a wish to *be* her father, with whom she identified; fourth, a parallel and terrifying wish to be *with* him; and finally, a conviction, arising from her feeling of guilt, that she does not (or should not) exist. Relentless and pervasive, Plath's emotional system combines generative and destructive power. At the same time that her Arnold story implies a paradigm of artistic activity — out of the "ooze" of the unconscious the "sea-beasts" of the imagination feed, out of the "caverns" of the psyche the "sea-snakes" of poetry coil and twine — it suggests the psychological forces that precipitated and haunted that activity as well.

One of Esther Greenwood's metaphors in *The Bell Jar* crystallizes Plath's creative situation. Esther says that she recognized a sudden uncertainty about her writing ambitions "the way you recognize some nondescript person that's been hanging around your door for ages and then suddenly comes up and introduces himself as your real father and looks exactly like you, so you know he really is your father, and the person you thought all your life was your father is a sham" (*BJ* 39). We note here the assumption that the father is the double of the female self (he "looks exactly like you"); the belief that one's inability to judge the father's character connects to the inability to know oneself; and again the association of a writing career with the image of the father. The metaphor indicates that Plath's father was both basic to her imagination and inimical to it, a "buried male muse" and a "panther" on the stairs, stalking her discourse (*J* 223; *CP* 22).

Plath's unresolved feelings about her father eventually transferred to her husband ("Ted . . . is a substitute for my father" [*J* 280]); to men in general ("I hated men because they didn't stay around and love me like a father" [*J* 268]); and to the patriarchal literary tradition ("Why do I freeze in fear my mind

and writing: say, look: no head, what can you expect of a girl
with no head? . . . Fear of losing male totem: what roots?" [*J*
273]). Paternal power froze her voice, scorned her as if she had
no head, and neglected her as if she did not exist. She felt that
no matter how hard she struggled, she could neither measure
up nor escape. Her ambivalent grief for her father had set the
stage for an ambivalent awareness that femininity itself, as
socially constructed, was imprisoning. Therefore she wrote in
male metaphors, which she increasingly sought to undermine
or to explode. Whereas in early poems like "Snakecharmer"
and "The Colossus" she tried to neutralize the father's ghost, in
"Daddy" she confronted the ghost directly, and in "Words" she
appropriated the ghost's authority. She tried first to propitiate
the "paternal source of godhead" (*J* 223) and then to defeat him.

PLATH's sense of herself in relation to male literary power,
though founded on her experience of her father, became form-
alized when she attended high school and college. Before then,
she lived with books of all kinds. Aurelia Plath recalls reciting
"poetry to my babies from the day they were born. . . . Nursery rhymes, all of A. A. Milne, Stevenson's poems for children,
The Wind in the Willows, and a lovely anthology, *Under the Silver
Umbrella*" (Letter, August 14, 1983). Family favorites included
Horton Hatches an Egg, Alice in Wonderland, The Yearling, and *The
Hobbit*. As soon as Sylvia learned to read, she and her mother
read together, a practice that Aurelia Plath remembers continuing until her daughter left for England in 1955, just before her
twenty-third birthday. Aurelia Plath recalls that "we made no
distinction in our reading as to whether something was written
by a man or a woman" (Letter). Thus, in addition to classics
written by men, they read poetry by Elizabeth Barrett Browning, Amy Lowell, and Edna St. Vincent Millay, and such prose
works as Alcott's *Little Women*, Charlotte Brontë's *Jane Eyre*,
Emily Brontë's *Wuthering Heights*, Buck's *The Good Earth*,
Cather's *Death Comes to the Archbishop* and *My Ántonia*, Colette's
Memoirs, Dinesen's *Seven Gothic Tales*, Edgeworth's *Castle Rackrent*,
Eliot's *Adam Bede, The Mill on the Floss*, and *Romola*, Wharton's
Ethan Frome, and novels by Dorothy Canfield Fisher, Zona

Gale, and Ellen Glasgow (Letter). While this recalled list may be inexact, it demonstrates that Aurelia Plath modeled reading for her daughter, just as Otto Plath modeled writing, and that she exposed her daughter to a wide variety of texts by women.

At Wellesley High School, however, Sylvia Plath encountered a very different literary canon, which delegitimated the one she had learned from her mother. The school's virtually all-male curriculum implied that whereas an amateur reader might read works composed by women, a professional read books by men. Since Plath's love of literature and her personal literary ambitions developed together, her high-school education must have deeply affected her identity as a writer. Her favorite class at Wellesley High was an English course taught by Wilbury Crockett. She found that studying literature stimulated her with ideas for new poems and joked that she mustn't let Shakespeare get too far ahead of her (Indiana ms.). Although she clearly wanted to compete with Shakespeare, she complained that the "fellows" thought that "no serious thought has ever troubled my little head." This dilemma undoubtedly reflected her family structure. As she remarked to her pen pal Eddie Cohen, her father had written a book on bumblebees and many scientific articles, whereas she herself was "more subjective than objective, and take after my mother." The schema seems to have been that to be male was to be objective and to write books, whereas to be female was to be subjective and to appear to have no serious thought. Although it originated in the family, this schema was reinforced by her school. In Crockett's class, Plath wrote papers on T. S. Eliot, Nathaniel Hawthorne, Sinclair Lewis, Shakespeare, and Tolstoy. In a paper on the immortality of literature, she chose a male as an example of "the creator's spirit": Charles Dickens. Except for a single paper on Virginia Woolf's *Mrs. Dalloway*, none of Plath's high-school papers, class notes, or letters focuses on a text by a woman (Indiana mss.). Like others of her generation, she was taught that language, whether scientific or figurative, belonged to men.

At Smith College, which Plath attended on a scholarship, the situation did not differ greatly, even though the students

there were all young women. She studied with Mary Ellen
Chase and Elizabeth Drew, but even they generally assigned
books written by men. Plath wrote essays on W. H. Auden,
Jacques Barzun, Chekhov, Dostoevsky, F. Scott Fitzgerald,
Erich Fromm, Hardy, Mann, Milton, Nietzsche, John Crowe
Ransom, Saroyan, Synge, Dylan Thomas, Robert Penn Warren, and Yeats (Indiana mss.). She also compiled a notebook
on Joyce's fiction and wrote an honors thesis, "The Magic Mirror," on Dostoevsky's *The Double* and *The Brothers Karamazov*
(Indiana mss.). In her years at Smith she wrote only three
short essays on texts by women — two on Edith Sitwell and one
on Amy Lowell. In a course in modern American fiction
taught by Robert Gorham Davis, she read Dos Passos, Faulkner, Fitzgerald, Hemingway, and Lewis. In a course in modern
poetry taught by Elizabeth Drew, she read heavily in Auden,
Eliot, and Yeats and more lightly in Hart Crane, Joyce, Marianne Moore, Ransom, Stevens, and Thomas. Drew did not
teach Pound and Williams, whom she thought minor, nor any
female poet except Moore. Plath's only major-author course
was in Shakespeare.

Named the outstanding English student in her class at
Smith, Plath was one of only four students to graduate summa
cum laude. Adlai Stevenson, the nation's most eloquent propo-
nent of liberalism, and Plath's political idol, gave the commencement address that year. More explicitly than any of her
professors, he assigned Plath her place in a patriarchal culture.
Stevenson argued away the frustration Smith graduates were
likely to feel when they contrasted their college life, in which
they "wrote poetry," with their domestic life to come, in which
they would write only "the laundry list":

Women "never had it so good" as you. In short, far from the vocation of marriage and motherhood leading you away from the great
issues of our day, it brings you back to their very center and places
upon you an infinitely deeper and more intimate responsibility
than that borne by the majority of those who hit the headlines and
make the news. . . .

This assignment for you, as wives and mothers, you can do in
the living room with a baby in your lap or in the kitchen with a

can opener in your hand. If you're clever, maybe you can even practice your saving arts on that unsuspecting man while he's watching television. I think there is much you can do about our crisis in the humble role of housewife. I could wish you no better vocation than that. (Quoted in Friedan 60–61)

At Cambridge University, where Plath earned a master's degree as a Fulbright scholar, she once again found a challenging woman professor to guide her, Dorothea Krook. Krook recalls feeling that "the things I said, we said, her authors said, mattered to her in an intimate way" (50). Yet every essay she wrote at Cambridge concerned a male European author: Aeschylus, Augustine, Bentham, Blake, Chekhov, Coleridge, Corneille, Henryson, Hobbes, Hooker, Hume, Ibsen, Langland, Locke, Mill, Racine, Strindberg, Synge, Tourneur, Webster, Yeats, the Cambridge Platonists, and above all Plato (two essays), Lawrence (two essays), and Chaucer (six essays). Krook sensed in Plath a "strong suppressed resentment" at Cambridge (55), one source of which may have been its restricted definition of authorship. Nevertheless, while still at the university Plath married Ted Hughes, who also encouraged her to read only texts written by men: Shakespeare primarily, but also Blake, Chaucer, Donne, Hopkins, and Thomas (*J* 246; *LH* 235). Soon after marrying Hughes, Plath wrote to her mother, "He literally knows Shakespeare by heart and is shocked that I have read only 13 plays. . . . I could never get to be such a good person without his help" (*LH* 267).

When Plath came to teach literature herself, at Smith College in 1957–58, she composed teaching notes that are witty, engaged, and informative—and almost entirely about texts written by men (Indiana mss.). In a course in nineteenth-century American fiction, she taught three authors: Hawthorne, Melville, and James. For a course in modern poetry, she made plans to include Hopkins, Yeats, Eliot, Thomas, Auden, Ransom, Cummings, and "if possible" a bit of Moore, Stevens, Bishop, and Wilbur. In the surviving notes, she discussed a total of seventeen male authors (those just mentioned, plus Poe, Strindberg, Webster, Joyce, and Dostoevsky), while mentioning only two female authors (Moore and Bishop).

Whereas in her early life she and her mother read many
women writers, and whereas in her later life she discovered
innumerable other women writers on her own, her formal education had taught her to admire canonized authors who were
normatively white and male.

Plath's personal library reflects this orientation. Her various
anthologies were edited by men (Conrad Aiken, William Rose
Benet, Donald Hall, Louis Unterecker, Oscar Williams, and
others) and included mostly male poets, virtually none of
whom belonged to the ethnic groups with which she tended to
identify herself, such as Jews, African Americans, and Asians.
Indeed, her library prepares us to understand Plath's identification with minority cultures. In the anthologies and on the book-
shelves, women also constituted a small and endangered
minority. Although she bought some books by women, she by
no means made a collection of their work. Of the books she
stored at her mother's house, 123 were written or edited by
men, 17 were by women, and 2 were joint efforts of a man and
a woman (Indiana volumes). Of the books she kept with her in
England, 119 were by men and 16 were by women — fully half of
them by one author, Virginia Woolf (Smith volumes). All told,
she owned 243 books by men and 34 by women. In *American
Poetry Now*, an anthology of new poetry she edited in 1961, she
included thirteen male poets (Robert Creeley, Edgar Bowers,
Anthony Hecht, Daniel Hoffman, W. S. Merwin, Lucas
Myers, Howard Nemerov, Hyam Plutzik, Louis Simpson,
George Starbuck, W. D. Snodgrass, William Stafford, and
Richard Wilbur) and only four female poets (Barbara Guest,
Denise Levertov, Adrienne Rich, and Anne Sexton). The proportion of women to men was higher than in most poetry col-
lections of the time, but not radically so. In her letters and
journals, too, Plath wrote more frequently about male writers
than female ones. The poets she mentioned most often were, in
order, Eliot, Yeats, Shakespeare, Auden, Moore, Lowell,
Spender, Rich, and Thomas; the novelists she mentioned most
often were Woolf, Lawrence, Joyce, and James (see Axelrod,
"Literary Relations").

If Plath's education, library, and much of her correspondence reflect a patriarchal conception of culture, her poetry and fiction exhibit a more independent view. She increasingly recognized that to become a serious writer, she would need to unlearn one of the main lessons of the classroom and of her library. Those sources of authority seemed to sanction her to write only the language of popular literature, as found in the texts of Val Gendron, Phyllis McGinley, Olive Higgins Prouty, Mary Ellen Chase, and the contributors to the *Ladies' Home Journal*. Yet that was hardly a language that could "purify the dialect of the tribe," in the Mallarméan-Eliotesque phrase Plath had been taught to admire. The paradox of her education was that she had been instructed to value the language of high culture but to doubt her own capacity to employ it. Little wonder, then, that when she was not worshiping men and attempting to play their games, she tended to regard them as "heartless," "jealous," and obsessed with conserving their power (*LH* 106; *CP* 179; *J* 273). Little wonder that as she exercised her gift, she moved from self-subordination to a stance of revolt.

THE DEVELOPMENT of Plath's literary identity interlaced with her conflicted relations with the male writers of the canon, whom she regarded as highly powerful, like her biological father. She figured them as "kings" and "gods" (*J* 181), while portraying God himself as "the Supreme Stylizer" (*LH* 314). Each male precursor was, like Alice Denway's father, a "giant" (*JP* 306), or like Elizabeth Minton's brother, "a colossus astride the roaring sea" (*JP* 304). At times she viewed them as protecting geniuses or spiritual company. In the last months of her life, for example, she felt that Yeats was blessing her (*LH* 477–80; Roche 86). More often, however, she thought of them as threats, as "big, conquering boys" (*J* 99). Just as Esther Greenwood claimed that "women-haters were like gods; invulnerable and chock full of power," so Plath envisioned the poetic gods as women-haters who "descended" and then "disappeared": "You could never catch one" (*BJ* 127).

Thus Plath regarded her male forerunners with a confused mixture of admiration, awe, fear, and resentment. She felt torn between Alice Denway's worshiping attitude and Elizabeth

Minton's defiant one, between sacrificing herself to the poetic gods and attempting to curtail their authority. Although she eagerly read male writers and modeled her writing on theirs, she worried that she was "not worth the really good boys" (*J* 108). She often found that they seemed to obstruct rather than foster her aspirations. For example, she confessed that Auden's exquisite lyrics struck her as "conservative obliterating snow" (*J* 73). Thus, on the one hand she believed that she needed to read "what influences my writing" (*J* 129), but on the other hand she found that "too much blind worship of modern poets" (*J* 32), indeed too much reading of any sort (*LH* 342), made her feel "stifled, weak, pallid, mealymouthed and utterly absurd" (*J* 32). Although (or because) she wished to "become Shakespeare" (*J* 139), she felt that Shakespeare and the other male poets of the canon paralyzed her creativity (*J* 129). In *The Bell Jar*, Esther Greenwood envies a friend who "had managed never to read a word of Shakespeare" (*BJ* 148), whereas in real life Plath was troubled that she had read only thirteen of his plays. She alternately posed reading and not reading the classics, and reading and not reading the moderns, as her creative salvation.

Plath explored her sense that the patriarchal tradition excluded and threatened her in "The Wishing Box" (*JP* 204–10). In that early story, a man's fluent fantasies put to shame his wife's more "fragmentary" and "glowering" imaginings (*JP* 205–6). The self-preoccupied Harold has dreams that resemble "nothing if not meticulous works of art" (*JP* 205): multicolored visions of white leopards and purple deserts (*JP* 205); Hughesian fantasies about a "fox" or a "pike" (*JP* 207); imagined meetings with William Blake, William Carlos Williams, Robinson Jeffers, Robert Frost, and a poet who must be Robert Lowell (*JP* 204–5). His wife Agnes resents being "perpetually exiled" from these dreams and from the male alliances that seem to generate them. Ashamed of her own "tedious" dreams and nightmares, she feels she has been "ousted" from the "benevolent painted dream worlds" inhabited by her husband and his friends, the male poets (*JP* 206). After abandoning a desperate plan to plagiarize dreams out of Freud, she finally admits, "I don't dream anything. Not anymore" (*JP* 207). Growing up in a patriarchal culture epitomized by Harold, Agnes has lost her creative potential. "Choked" and "smothered" by the knowledge that the imagination speaks in a code "unintelligible" to her (*JP* 209), she commits suicide, her features set in a "secret smile of triumph, as if, in some far country unattainable to mortal men, she were, at last, waltzing with the dark, red-caped prince of her early dreams" (*JP* 210). "The Wishing Box" undoubtedly figures Plath's marital disillusionment; when she wrote it, she herself, like her protagonist, was newly married to an "imaginative" but "didactic" husband (*J* 145, 246). But it also expresses what Gilbert and Gubar call the female "anxiety of authorship," an anxiety "built from complex and often only barely conscious fears of that authority which seems to the female artist to be by definition inappropriate to her sex" (*Madwoman* 51).

Over the next several years, Plath's anxiety grew. Because her poetic fathers undermined her sense of her own competence, she began to dread them. She advised herself not to "copy" (*J* 199); she fretted that she was living and teaching "on rereadings, on notes of other people" (*J* 203); she felt ashamed of her inability to be "original" (*J* 203); she experienced a shock of recognition when she viewed the early paintings of De Chirico, filled with "long shadows cast by unseen figures — human or stone it is impossible to tell" (*J* 211); she fantasized that the "kings" and "gods" turned into a "white-bearded grandfather drowning in the sea surge" (*J* 181).

In the last years of her life, Plath attempted to rescue herself from this incapacitating anxiety by openly rebelling against male poetic authority. Although she never ceased to admire the poetic gods, she increasingly sought to put on their knowledge through resistance rather than through acquiescence to their power. In August 1958, about two years after the creative despair of "The Wishing Box," she foresaw her acquisition of a revolutionary stance in a novel plot she dreamed but never wrote. At this time she was just emerging from an extended period of anger at her poet-husband, in which "the strangling noose of worry, of hysteria, paralysis" prevented her from writ-

ing (*J* 253); and she was unconsciously priming herself to enter
her major phase as an artist. Brooding about her marital conflicts, she confided to her journal: "Dreamed last night I was
beginning my novel . . . : a girl's search for her dead father —
for an outside authority which must be developed, instead,
from the inside" (*J* 258). This dream novel, about abandoning
the quest for paternal authority, resulted in a catharsis. Hours
later, she appended this note to her entry: "Still tired, but curiously elated, as if absolved from suffocation — projects bubble.
. . . Or is this a lull in a merry-go-round of panic blackouts?"
(*J* 258). The panic attacks recurred, forcing her to return to
her psychiatrist, Dr. Ruth Beuscher, for further analysis, but
the writer's block lifted, and Plath began fitfully to compose the
majority of the poems published in *The Colossus.* Thus a dream
rescued her from her horror of dreamlessness. On an unconscious level, she assimilated the lesson of her dream novel
about resisting the "outside authority" of males and developing
her own authority "from the inside." Sensing that male muses
and god-creators were "jealous gods" who would "degrade" her
(*CP* 179; *J* 292), she began to look to women "for a parallel" (*JP*
61); she began to defy the tradition that Esther Greenwood
would satirize as "those smug men writing tight little couplets
and being so dead keen on reason" (*BJ* 148). In that sentence
Esther seems to have Dryden, Pope, and Swift specifically in
mind, but the context implicates the whole Bloomian-Batean
"burden of the past," and more particularly the male discursive hegemony that has inhibited women from speaking.

Let us now trace Plath's extended struggle with the patri-
archs through four key texts: "Snakecharmer," written in late
1957, in the floodtide of her apprenticeship to paternal power;
"The Colossus," written in October 1959, during her transition
to a more mature poetic voice; "Daddy," written in October
1962, when her voice of rebellion was speaking most powerfully; and "Words," written in February 1963, when the final
tone of her voice was heard.

SACRIFICE

BECAUSE the father insatiably "ransacks the land," as Plath notes in an early poem, his need "compels a total sacrifice" (*CP* 22-23). Yet identifying with him brings doom, not relief. "Snakecharmer" (*CP* 79), composed during her first semester of teaching at Smith, exposes with particular clarity the counterpoint between her wish to escape the father and her equally deep wish to incorporate him. Quite obviously, the poem functions as an allegory of writing. The snake charmer pipes into existence a "snaky sphere" from "the snake-rooted bottom / Of his mind" (st. 1, 4). Plath specifically genders him as a male, in contrast to Henri Rousseau's precursory painting "La Charmeuse de Serpents." As Margaret Dickie Uroff rightly says (105), Plath's snake charmer is a god of origins, but a more destructive one than Uroff allows, for the power that ennobles him also makes him arrogant and dangerous: he "rules the writhings" that make manifest his "snakehood and his might" (st. 6). While his invocation, "let there be snakes!" (st. 7), indicates a Godlike power, his resemblance to Lucifer in the image of a snake ambiguates the text, preventing it from being something so simple as a tribute to the creative artist at work. Resting in part on Plath's characteristic, ambivalent equation of God with Satan, the poem suggests her precarious position as a writer. As she struggles to create, she must shape her utterance around the snake charmer's songs, around the father in both his good and his bad guises.

On a simple level of interpretation, "Snakecharmer" allegorizes the relationship of art to psyche. The snake charmer/artist begins by piping green water—the stuff of creativity, the imaginative soup of the unconscious—until it wavers and undulates. Eventually the "green river / Shapes its images around his songs" (st. 2-3). At this moment of imaginative triumph, however, he "tires of music," piping the "cloth of snakes" back "to a melting of green waters" (st. 8-9). The maker's rage for order sated, he falls asleep, letting his writhings/writings cease, his snake texts vanish, his keener sounds become silent. In "The Idea of Order at Key West," Stevens emphasizes the

text's ability to perform such functions as "arranging," "deepen-
ing," and "enchanting" the otherwise "meaningless" physical
world. But contrary to what Arnold's "Forsaken Merman" had
seemed to promise her, Plath's allegory reveals that the text has
no such power. It remains "pliant," "flickering," and subject to
instant evanishment (st. 3, 6, 9), leaving nothing in its wake,
no "order," no "dimly-starred words," simply silence and stu-
por, a restoration of chaos and old night.

"Snakecharmer" valorizes not texts per se but rather the
power of text making. It does not pit the "fixing" capability of
song against the "fluttering" quality of the world, nor the
"poem as icon" against nothingness, as does Stevens's "The
Rock." Rather, it poses the vitality of the creative act — marked
by "swayings and coilings," Ovidian fusions of "tree and
human" (st. 4, 5) — against the waste sad time stretching before
and after. Plath allows temporality to enter her script, believing that the poetic process rather than the finished product
proves the "maker is alive" (Lowell, *History* 194). Her artistic
consolation was thus transitory, more analogous to lovemaking
than to the birth of a child: instead of Hillis Miller's "linguistic
moment," the creative moment. And yet that moment cannot
withstand the blankness that surrounds and penetrates it.
Even at the height of his powers, the piper pipes "no rocks, /
No floor," only a "wave" of flickering tongues (st. 3). The poet's
frustration appears in both the snake charmer's deception (his
cloth of snakes becomes a "melting" of water) and his eerie
indifference (he is consumed by "yawns," like a Baudelairean
figure of ennui) (st. 9, 7). Creativity was no Stevensian "cure of
the ground," but merely free play between identity formation
and annihilation.

On a deeper level, implicating Plath herself as an "interpretable being" (Barthes, *Grain* 192), "Snakecharmer" provides a
paradigm of her poetic process. Not counting Rousseau's painting, the poem includes two separate texts, the first belonging to
the creative-destructive power of the father, the second to the
female poet who evokes him. Even as Plath wished to utilize
her sense of the father's power over her, he exercised that power
all the same. Even as she sought to live in her art, she found

her creativity overtaken by the suffocating sense that it was not wholly her own. Her poetry was flawed by the snake charmer at its center, controlling, misleading, depriving, refusing to care. Unable to free her "deep self" or "deep voice" from the grip of a father who perpetually returned to life (*J* 165, 297, 325), Plath feared that, like the young woman of "Electra on Azalea Path," she must forever remain her father's ghost (*CP* 117). As much as art was for Plath an assertion of power, a "way of being happy" (*JP* 21), it was also a ritual of preservation, a charm against the final consumption, enacted on black lines of text that endeavored to evoke, and then to withstand, the white abyss they bordered.

As she describes a cosmos in which male "gods" begin one world, "man" another, and the male "snakecharmer" the third (st. 1), Plath establishes herself as the paradoxical inhabitant of a patriarchal universe that apparently excludes her. In fact she is describing the complicated conditions of her imaginative existence, which must always incorporate her perception of a paternal presence with whom she constantly exchanges positions along the line of aesthetic and emotional authority: daughter as poet, father as "sea-god muse" (*J* 244); father as poet, daughter as amanuensis; and later, father as tyrant, daughter as assassin. Presented with a creative cosmology that forbids females from entering, she realizes that she is cut off from the very creativity she posits as her life's salvation. Thus her internalization of her father was both the source of her creativity and the power that inhibited its free expression. The poet's resentful recognition of the father figure's ability to ward off her desire, to deny her competence, and to prevent her legitimation as an artist manifests itself in her largely negative depiction of both the snake charmer and the "snake-bodies" he summons forth (st. 5). His habitual "moon-eye" (st. 1) implies sterility as well as cruelty, deception, obliviousness, and deathliness. His "snake-rooted" mind (st. 4) is aggressively phallic, menacing, poisonous, and again deceptive. He is the despotic ruler of a world that writhes and writes at his command: brute power with an ophidian face. Both self and other, he is the Rappaccini-like father/god/lover/poisoner who checks all cre-

ativity. But at the same time, because Plath is imprisoned by
her longing for him and her rage to free herself from him, he
forces her to be creative, to make into words her inexpressible
emotional prison — or at least to try.

"Snakecharmer" implies that even at moments of comparative peace, Plath could not trust the surface of her mind, for
what was submerged might arise at any time, indifferent, inexorable, irresistible, out of control. Anger and despair lie barely
submerged in the poem, just as a "world of snakes" exists just
below the calm surface of the snake charmer's green river.
Through that deadly counterpoint, the poem enacts with precision the snake charmer's role and the poet's identification
with him. Since the piper has created women, Plath's feelings
about herself, as artist and woman, depend on the shifting
topography of his snaky sphere. But he is her creation, too;
and so she is accountable as he mesmerizes her. If he is the
charmer, she is the snake, evil and guilty; if he is the snake,
then she is the charmer, hoping to write well enough to keep
him, and to keep him away. The poem reveals the impasse of
a woman whose early terrifying and internalized experience
with her father, reinforced by an education that emphasized
male power, was threatening her creativity and threatening
her. Her poetry of this period repeats two interwoven questions. First, How can she come to figurative life when her culture tells her she cannot? And beneath that question a more
deadly one: How dare she come alive if her father is dead?
Each new poem was an attempt to re-create the world, and each
new poem could only disguise or relieve the past, never resolve
it. Only "death," she feared, could make her "real" (*CP* 25); only
death could return her to the father; only her father could make
her real, even as he interfered with her living reality.

IN FALL 1959, about a year after her dream novel about learning to resist paternal authority and only months after completing both her second period of analysis with Dr. Beuscher and
Lowell's poetry-writing course at Boston University, Plath
spent ten weeks with her husband at Yaddo artists' colony
before returning permanently to England. Her visit to Yaddo

represented, Hughes later said, "an end and a new beginning" for her ("Notes" 191). Initially depressed and plagued by nightmares, spending her days strolling through autumnal landscapes dotted with corroding statues, she complained to her journal: "When will I break into a new line of poetry? Feel trite. . . . I dream too much, work too little" (*J* 321). Then suddenly, on October 19, she reported that she had just written two poems that pleased her. One was an unnamed poem to her unborn child (she was three months pregnant with her first child at the time); the other was on "the old father-worship subject. But different. Weirder" (*J* 323). The latter poem was "The Colossus." "Old" yet "different," this poem represented both a culmination of her poetic career up to that time and a departure. It inspired the idea of a new book of poetry, distinct from the others she had planned and discarded over the years: "The main thing is to get rid of the idea [that] what I write now is for the old book. That soggy book. So I have three poems for the new, temporarily called *The Colossus and Other Poems*" (*J* 323). In the days that followed, Plath wrote some of her strongest poems yet: "The Manor Garden," "Blue Moles," "Poem for a Birthday," "The Burnt-Out Spa," and "Mushrooms." All were published in *The Colossus* (which ended up including the best of her earlier work as well).

Many Plath critics have noted the autobiographical implications of "The Colossus" (*CP* 129–30). Eileen Aird, taking Hughes's hint about "a group of poems that she wrote at this time about her father" ("Notes" 190), presents the poem as being about "the father-daughter relationship" (29); Suzanne Juhasz says that the poem explores "very private, very personal experience, her relationship with her dead father" (*Naked* 94); Calvin Bedient agrees that the poem concerns Plath's "family romance" (10–11); and Murray Schwartz and Christopher Bollas, in a psychological analysis, assert that in the poem "Plath tries symbolically to reconstitute her father" (185). Details from Plath's personal life support this line of reasoning. The poem mentions the "thirty years" the speaker has worked to restore the statue, while Plath at the time was turning twenty-seven; the speaker is in perpetual "mourning," just as Plath herself was; the statue is a "colossus," and Plath, as we have seen, remembered her father as "huge" (*LH* 289); and finally, the word "colossus" echoes the name of the patriarch of her Oija board, "kolossus," who enunciated her father's spirit (*J* 245; *LH* 346; Wagner-Martin 119). So it makes sense to read "The Colossus" as another in a series of texts treating what Plath termed her "Electra complex" (*J* 318), a series she had enlarged only a few months before in "Electra on Azalea Path."

Yet in what way is "The Colossus" "different" from and "weirder" than its predecessors? In this poem, even more than in "Snakecharmer," Plath projected her conflicted feelings about her father onto the scene of writing. Conceiving of her text as a "substitute" for self (*J* 312), she transformed family romance into textual romance, sexual politics into textual politics. Moreover, beyond simply acknowledging or suppressing her anxiety that she was "unable to invent, to create" a text of her own (*J* 222), she began to work through such feelings. However hesitantly, subversively, and humorously, she attempted to combat her fear of creative incompetence.

Even if we accept John Reichert's contention that some poems ask to be read as affirmative utterance rather than invented speaker's monologue, we still cannot read "The Colossus" in terms of Homans's "poetics of literal truth," since Plath did not, after all, live on a desert island. Like so many of her major texts, the poem is an allegory. Although Judith Kroll has recognized its allegorical quality (84), she portrays the poem, to my mind misleadingly, as a retelling of the "dying god and mourning goddess myths" that Plath found in Graves and Frazer. Plath never actually cared much about *The White Goddess* except when she was feigning an interest in topics of interest to her husband. More to our purpose, Lynda K. Bundtzen says that the poem illuminates "woman's psyche as it is shaped by a patriarchal culture" (186); Mary Lynn Broe describes the poem as an image of Plath's "unreconstructed" art (*Protean Poetic* 72); and Margaret Dickie Uroff calls it a study of Plath's "creative exhaustion" (90). Given the poem's strikingly literary ambience, I propose that it specifically allegorizes poetic relations. In the weeks preceding its composition, Plath was reading a wide variety of contemporary writers, most of them women: Elizabeth Bishop, Mavis Gallant, Katherine Anne Porter, Ezra Pound, Jean Stafford, May Swenson, and Eudora Welty. "The Colossus" reflects this literary orientation in its emphasis on "lips," "mouthpiece," "throat," "tongue," "ear," and speech (st. 1-2, 5-6); in its allusion to Apollo, the god of poetry, who was represented as the colossus of Rhodes; and in its intertextual relationship to *The Oresteia* (st. 4). (Lowell, incidentally, began to translate Aeschylus's trilogy in the early 1960s, and if he spoke about the trilogy in his class, Plath may have associated it with him.) I believe that Plath transformed her conflict with her father's memory into a larger argument with cultural memory, with the literary tradition's "colossal" list of books (*J* 72), with the canonical writers she thought of as "god-eyed" (*J* 78), and with the male "superiors" who neglected, misunderstood, and overshadowed her (*J* 306).

"The Colossus" conjures the creative self-doubts that filled Plath's journal during her first weeks at Yaddo. "Desperate" at being "verbally repressed" (*J* 316), she lashed out at the "accusing, never-satisfied gods" who surrounded her "like a crown of thorns" (*J* 314), and at the literary colossi who seemed to hold her back—such as John Cheever and Robert Penn Warren, members of the board at Yaddo (*J* 315). Although she regarded artistic creation as "a gift from the gods" (*J* 318), she bitterly thought that her own "menacing" gods had denied her their gift (*J* 321). She felt "barren," "unable to write," "already dead," and caught "between the hope and promise of my work . . . and the hopeless gap between that promise and the real world of other people's poems and stories and novels" (*J* 321–22). Beneath those angry emotions, undoubtedly, lay her unexpressed guilt over her father's death and over her own high aspirations. Finally, after consoling herself that once she began "all would be well" (*J* 321), she wrote "The Colossus." In this poem she restored herself to textual life and acquired poetic identity by allegorizing her feelings of belatedness, powerlessness, and guilt.

In Plath's allegory, the "colossus" suggests a monumental image of patriarchal poetry. Plath habitually considered poems

already written as "mummified" (*J* 320), whereas poems in process were alive; and she visualized the male masters as "big"
and godlike (*J* 99, 181, 240), whereas she herself was small. The
poem's "I" represents herself in relation to the colossus as a
figure of incapable imagination. She wishes merely to rebuild
the "historical" patriarch, to "dredge the silt" from his throat
(st. 2). Like Plath, who felt that "too much blind worship" of
other poets weakened her (*J* 32), the speaker sacrifices her own
creative potential to her task of devotion. The "great stone god-
block" (*J* 328) stands in her way, since she restores his text
rather than composing her own. Overvenerating the petrified
remains of what has already been created, the belated female
assumes a subordinate role similar to the one Plath's patriarchal education had reserved for her — though her effort to voice
her text also suggests a hidden will to mastery equivalent to the
one Plath herself harbored (a point to which I shall return).

Because the colossus of patriarchal poetry repels his devotee's
archaeological efforts, she fails even in her menial labor: "I
shall never get you put together entirely" (st. 1). But why
should she bother to restore his "barnyard" brays, grunts, and
cackles? Why should she not practice her own singing instead,
or make something radically new out of the pieces of the
colossus — a statue of Sappho perhaps? She bothers, first of all,
because the colossus (perhaps alluding to Eliot's "Little Gid-
ding") presents himself as a spokesman of the dead or of the
gods (st. 2). He is the father of all speech, the male "totem" of
"creative power" (*J* 273), as immense as she is small and incon-
sequential. He is a great "cornucopia" (st. 5), who alone can satisfy the "ravenous" appetite for imaginative utterance (*JP* 208)
that typifies all of Plath's personae. Furthermore, without the
colossus Plath's "I" would be deprived of anything to speak of
or anyone to speak to. He is her only topic of discourse and,
since she addresses him as "you," the only other participant in
her circuit of communication.

Yet the colossus is a disabling father, taking away what he
almost offers. After thirty years, his devotee is "none the wiser"
(st. 2). Although she regards him with scalding irony, by the
end of the poem her complaints and ironies disappear. She

seems resigned to her fate, no longer even listening for "the scrape of a keel" (st. 6) that might rescue her from his "island of words" (*J* 321). From this perspective, "The Colossus" appears to be a conservative, deterministic poem in which a potentially Emersonian self-assertor is reduced to building the sepulchers of the fathers. Wedded to ruin and remembrance, the female ephebe finds herself without the materials, and finally without the desire, for independent creation. No Ezra Pound resuscitating traditional forms, no "artist-prince" constructing his own "poem or monument" (as in Bishop's "The Monument"), she is merely an antiquarian and idolator. Clearing the grave mounds of the precursor's eyes, she makes herself, in a sense far different from that imputed to the colossus, a "mouthpiece of the dead" (st. 2–3). Perhaps, in her melancholy, she feels that she has died with him; or perhaps, in an attack of creative frustration similar to that experienced by her author, she feels that her imagination is "dead" (*J* 322). Thus, like Agnes in "The Wishing Box," the speaker of "The Colossus" appears to subordinate herself completely to the speech of the archetypal male who both models voice and extinguishes her own. The poem implies that if the colossus of poetry is inherently male, a woman can choose to devote herself to it as a copier and a restorer (like Hawthorne's Hilda), or she can have no existence in art at all. In "The Colossus," Plath imagines accepting the terms of that choice; evokes the depression that such a choice would certainly bring to a woman who once dreamed of being a "Kid Colossus" or "small god" herself (*J* 56, 131); and translates that depression into a doom that makes the choice seem not a choice at all but a necessity.

Plath emphasized her poem's melancholic awareness of the power of the past by making a monument its central feature. She thereby placed the text in the shadow of prior canonical texts about monuments, ranging from Yeats's "The Statues," Pound's Malatesta Cantos, Crane's *The Bridge*, and Stevens's "The Owl's Clover" to Lowell's "The Quaker Graveyard in Nantucket," "Christmas Eve under Hooker's Statue," "Between the Porch and the Altar," "Inauguration Day: January 1953," and "For the Union Dead." (Although this last poem was not

published until 1960, Plath may have known about it, since
Lowell began work on it in spring 1959, when she was still
attending his class.) In *The Final Sculpture*, Michael North argues
that such poems generally treat sculpture as a metaphor for
the uncertain status of poetry in the twentieth century. Both
arts are "public" yet with "a subject matter almost entirely of
isolated, musing individuals" (43). The monuments embody
the poets' divided aims in their own discourse—their wish to
speak to their culture and at the same time their alienation
from that culture. Lowell called one of his poetic sequences a
"figure" cut from "marble" (prefatory note to *History*), a metaphor that helps us understand Plath's poem, in which a monument similarly symbolizes her poetic process.

Nevertheless, Plath's use of a monument in "The Colossus"
points up an alternative code in the poem that undermines the
one we have thus far been examining. Despite the poem's depiction of subservience to the patriarch, Plath herself swerves so
sharply from Yeats, Lowell, and her other male precursors as
to belie her tone of domination and defeat. Rather than the
male poet's ambiguous relation to his public, the monument in
"The Colossus" symbolizes his powerful grip on the creative
potential of his female ephebe. Since the male poet prevents
the female poet's emergence as a speaking subject, she must
resort, as Gilbert and Gubar, Homans, and Walker indicate, to
strategies of subversion. Thus while "The Colossus," like
"Snakecharmer," inscribes female defeat, it also encodes the
survival of female difference and the victory of her voice. This
code of insubordination manifests itself variously: in the
speaker's amusing and scornful portrayal of the colossus's brut-
ish speech ("it's worse than a barnyard") and dilapidated estate
(acres of "weedy" brow that must be scrubbed with "pails of
Lysol") (st. 1, 3); in the very fact that *she* is representing *him*,
reversing the standard genderization of the subject/object relation; and in the disfiguring metalepsis that the text performs
on Yeats's and Lowell's statuary poems. While seeming to portray the female ephebe as a weak reader, the poem proves her
to be a strong misreader. It thus poises her tenuously between
silence and voice, between sacrificing herself to the dead patri-

arch and sacrificing him to her speech, between allowing him to steal her creative spark and stealing his instead. The poem demonstrates its author's creativity while lamenting the incapacity of its invented speaker, the author's textual double.

In "The Colossus," Plath learned to portray her putative imaginative failure in language so complex and revisionary that it paradoxically redeemed her voice and momentarily relieved her anxiety. She approached her poetic strength by exploring the margins of her weakness—her sense that her father's memory, patriarchal culture, and her own creative inadequacy all conspired against her. Employing a self-subverting poetics of self-doubt, she declared the chapel hopelessly bare and thereby discovered the grail.

REVOLT

THE COVERT protest of "The Colossus" eventually transformed itself into the overt rebellion of "Daddy" (CP 222–24). Although this poem too has traditionally been read as "personal" (Aird 78) or "confessional" (M. L. Rosenthal 82), Margaret Homans has more recently suggested that it concerns a woman's dislocated relations to speech (Women Writers 220–21). Plath herself introduced it on the BBC as the opposite of confession, as a constructed fiction: "Here is a poem spoken by a girl with an Electra complex. Her father died while she thought he was God. Her case is complicated by the fact that her father was also a Nazi and her mother very possibly part Jewish. In the daughter the two strains marry and paralyze each other—she has to act out the awful little allegory once over before she is free of it" (CP 293). We might interpret this preface as an accurate retelling of the poem; or we might regard it as a case of an author's estrangement from her text, on the order of Coleridge's preface to "Kubla Khan" in which he claims to be unable to finish the poem, having forgotten what it was about. However we interpret Plath's preface, we must agree that "Daddy" is dramatic and allegorical, since its details depart freely from the facts of her biography. In this poem she again figures her unresolved conflicts with paternal authority as a textual issue. Significantly, her father was a published writer, and his successor, her husband, was also a writer. Her preface asserts that the poem concerns a young woman's paralyzing self-division, which she can defeat only through allegorical representation. Recalling that paralysis was one of Plath's main tropes for literary incapacity, we begin to see that the poem evokes the female poet's anxiety of authorship and specifically Plath's strategy of delivering herself from that anxiety by making it the topic of her discourse. Viewed from this perspective, "Daddy" enacts the woman poet's struggle with "daddy-poetry." It represents her effort to eject the "buried male muse" from her invention process and the "jealous gods" from her audience (*J* 223; *CP* 179).

Plath wrote "Daddy" several months after Hughes left her, on the day she learned that he had agreed to a divorce (October 12, 1962). George Brown and Tirril Harris have shown that early loss makes one especially vulnerable to subsequent loss (Bowlby 250–59), and Plath seems to have defended against depression by almost literally throwing herself into her poetry. She followed "Daddy" with a host of poems that she considered her greatest achievement to date: "Medusa," "The Jailer," "Lady Lazarus," "Ariel," the bee sequence, and others. The letters she wrote to her mother and brother on the day of "Daddy," and then again four days later, brim with a sense of artistic self-discovery: "Writing like mad. . . . Terrific stuff, as if domesticity had choked me" (*LH* 466). Composing at the "still blue, almost eternal hour before the baby's cry, before the glassy music of the milkman, settling his bottles" (quoted in Alvarez, *Savage God* 21), she experienced an "enormous" surge in creative energy (*LH* 467). Yet she also expressed feelings of misery: "The half year ahead seems like a lifetime, and the half behind an endless hell" (*LH* 468). She was again contemplating things German: a trip to the Austrian Alps, a renewed effort to learn the language. If "German" was Randall Jarrell's "favorite country," it was not hers, yet it returned to her discourse like clock work at times of psychic distress. Clearly Plath was attempting to find and to evoke in her art what she could not find or communicate in her life. She wished to com-

pensate for her fragmenting social existence by investing herself in her texts: "Hope, when free, to write myself out of this
hole" (*LH* 466). Desperately eager to sacrifice her "flesh,"
which was "wasted," to her "mind and spirit," which were
"fine" (*LH* 470), she wrote "Daddy" to demonstrate the existence of her voice, which had been silent or subservient for so
long. She wrote it to prove her "genius" (*LH* 468).

Plath projected her struggle for textual identity onto the
figure of a partly Jewish young woman who learns to express
her anger at the patriarch and at his language of male mastery,
which is as foreign to her as German, as "obscene" as murder
(st. 6), and as meaningless as "gobbledygoo" (st. 9). The
patriarch's death "off beautiful Nauset" (st. 3) recalls Plath's
journal entry in which she associated the "green seaweeded
water" at "Nauset Light" with "the deadness of a being . . .
who no longer creates" (*J* 164). Daddy's deadness — suggesting
Plath's unwillingness to let her father, her education, her
library, or her husband inhibit her any longer — inspires the
poem's speaker to her moment of illumination. At a basic level,
"Daddy" concerns its own violent, transgressive birth as a text,
its origin in a culture that regards it as illegitimate — a judgment the speaker hurls back on the patriarch himself when she
labels *him* a bastard (st. 16). Plath's unaccommodating worldview, which was validated by much in her childhood and adult
experience, led her to understand literary tradition not as an
expanding universe of beneficial influence (as depicted in
Eliot's "Tradition and the Individual Talent") but as a closed
universe in which every addition required a corresponding
subtraction — a Spencerian agon in which only the fittest survived. If Plath's speaker was to be born as a poet, a patriarch
must die.

As in "The Colossus," the father here appears as a force or
an object rather than as a person. Initially he takes the form of
an immense "black shoe," capable of stamping on his victim
(st. 1). Immediately thereafter he becomes a marble "statue"
(st. 2), cousin to the monolith of the earlier poem. He then
transforms into Nazi Germany (st. 6–7, 9–10), the archetypal
totalitarian state. When the protagonist mentions Daddy's

"boot in the face" (st. 10), she may be alluding to Orwell's comment in *1984*, "If you want a picture of the future, imagine a
boot stomping on a human face — forever" (3.3). Eventually
the father declines in stature from God (st. 2) to a devil (st. 11)
to a dying vampire (st. 15). Perhaps he shrinks under the force
of his victim's denunciation, which de-creates him as a power as
it creates him as figure. But whatever his size, he never assumes
human dimensions, aspirations, and relations — except when
posing as a teacher in a photograph (st. 11). Like the colossus,
he remains figurative and symbolic, not individual.

Nevertheless, the male figure of "Daddy" does differ significantly from that of "The Colossus." In the earlier poem, which
emphasizes his lips, mouth, throat, tongue, and voice, the colossus allegorically represents the power of speech, however fragmented and resistant to the protagonist's ministrations. In the
later poem Daddy remains silent, apart from the gobbledygoo
attributed to him once (st. 9). He uses his mouth primarily for
biting and for drinking blood. The poem emphasizes his feet
and, implicitly, his phallus. He is a "black shoe" (st. 1), a statue
with "one gray toe" (st. 2), a "boot" (st. 10). The speaker, estranged from him by fear, could never tell where he put his
"foot," his "root" (st. 5). Furthermore, she is herself silenced by
his shoe: "I never could talk to you" (st. 5). Daddy is no "male
muse" (*J* 223), not even one in ruins, but frankly a male censor.
His boot in the face of "every woman" is presumably lodged in
her mouth (st. 10). He stands for all the elements in the literary
situation and in the female ephebe's internalization of it, that
prevent her from producing any words at all, even copied or
subservient ones. Appropriately, Daddy can be killed only by
being stamped on: he lives and dies by force, not language. If
"The Colossus" tells a tale of the patriarch's speech, his grunts
and brays, "Daddy" tells a tale of the daughter's effort to speak.

Thus we are led to another important difference between the
two poems. The "I" of "The Colossus" acquires her identity
only through serving her "father," whereas the "I" of "Daddy"
actuates her gift only through opposition to him. The latter
poem precisely inscribes the plot of Plath's dream novel of 1958:
"a girl's search for her dead father — for an outside authority

which must be developed, instead, from the inside" (*J* 258). As
the child of a Nazi, the girl could "hardly speak" (st. 6), but as
a Jew she begins "to talk" and to acquire an identity (st. 7). In
Plath's allegory, the outsider Jew corresponds to "the rebel, the
artist, the odd" (*JP* 55), and particularly to the woman artist.
Otto Rank's *Beyond Psychology*, which had a lasting influence on
her, explicitly compares women to Jews, since "woman . . . has
suffered from the very beginning a fate similar to that of the
Jew, namely, suppression, slavery, confinement, and subsequent persecution" (287–88). Rank, whose discourse I would
consider tainted by anti-Semitism, argues that Jews speak a
language of pessimistic "self-hatred" that differs essentially
from the language of the majority cultures in which they find
themselves (191, 281–84). He analogously, though more sympa-
thetically, argues that woman speaks in a language different
from man's, and that as a result of man's denial of woman's
world, "woman's 'native tongue' has hitherto been unknown or
at least unheard" (248). Although Rank's essentializing of
woman's "nature" lapses into the sexist clichés of his time
("intuitive," "irrational" [249]), his idea of linguistic difference
based on gender and his analogy between Jewish and female
speech seem to have embedded themselves in the substructure
of "Daddy" (and in many of Plath's other texts as well). For
Plath, as later for Adrienne Rich, the Holocaust and the
patriarchy's silencing of women were linked outcomes of the
masculinist interpretation of the world. Political insurrection
and female self-assertion also interlaced symbolically. In
"Daddy," Plath's speaker finds her voice and motive by identifying herself as antithetical to her Fascist father. Rather than
getting the colossus "glued" and properly jointed, she wishes to
stick herself "together with glue" (st. 13), an act that seems to
require her father's dismemberment. Previously devoted to the
patriarch – both in "The Colossus" and in memories evoked in
"Daddy" of trying to "get back" to him (st. 12) – she now seeks
only to escape from him and to see him destroyed.

Plath has unleashed the anger, normal in mourning as well
as in revolt, that she suppressed in the earlier poem. But she
has done so at a cost. Let us consider her childlike speaking

voice. The language of "Daddy," beginning with its title, is
often regressive. The "I" articulates herself by moving backward in time, using the language of nursery rhymes and fairy
tales (the little old woman who lived in a shoe, the black man
of the forest). Such language accords with a child's conception
of the world, not an adult's. Plath's assault on the language of
"daddy-poetry" has turned inward, on the language of her own
poem, which teeters precariously on the edge of a preverbal
abyss — represented by the eerie, keening "oo" sound with
which a majority of the verses end. And then let us consider
the play on "through" at the poem's conclusion. Although that
last line allows for multiple readings, one interpretation is that
the "I" has unconsciously carried out her father's wish: her discourse, by transforming itself into cathartic oversimplifica-
tions, has undone itself.

Yet the poem does contain its verbal violence by means more
productive than silence. In a letter to her brother, Plath referred to "Daddy" as "gruesome" (*LH* 472), while on almost the
same day she described it to A. Alvarez as a piece of "light
verse" (Alvarez, *Beyond* 56). She later read it on the BBC in a
highly ironic tone of voice. The poem's unique spell derives
from its rhetorical complexity: its variegated and perhaps
bizarre fusion of the horrendous and the comic. As Uroff has
remarked, it both shares and remains detached from the
fixation of its protagonist (159). The protagonist herself seems
detached from her own fixation. She is "split in the most complex fashion," as Plath wrote of Ivan Karamazov in her Smith
College honors thesis. Plath's speaker uses potentially self-
mocking melodramatic terms to describe both her opponent
("so black no sky could squeak through" [st. 10]) and herself
("poor and white" [st. 1]). While this aboriginal speaker quite
literally expresses black-and-white thinking, her civilized
double possesses a sensibility sophisticated enough to subject
such thinking to irony. Thus the poem expresses feelings that
it simultaneously parodies — it may be parodying the very idea
of feeling. The tension between erudition and simplicity in the
speaker's voice appears in her pairings that juxtapose adult
with childlike diction: "breathe or Achoo," "your Luftewaffe,

your gobbledygoo" (st. 1, 9). She can expound such adult topics as Taroc packs, Viennese beer, and Tyrolean snowfall; can specify death camps by name; and can employ an adult vocabulary of "recover," "ancestress," "Aryan," "*Meinkampf*," "obscene," and "bastard." Yet she also has recourse to a more primitive lexicon that includes "chuffing," "your fat black heart," and "my pretty red heart." She proves herself capable of careful intellectual discriminations ("so I never could tell" [st. 5]), conventionalized description ("beautiful Nauset" [st. 3]), and moral analogy ("if I've killed one man, I've killed two" [st. 15]), while also exhibiting regressive fantasies (vampires), repetitions ("wars, wars, wars" [st. 4]), and inarticulateness ("panzer-man, panzer-man, O You—" [st. 9]). She oscillates between calm reflection ("You stand at the blackboard, daddy, / In the picture I have of you" [st. 11]) and mad incoherence ("Ich, ich, ich, ich" [st. 6]). Her sophisticated language puts her wild language in an ironic perspective, removing the discourse from the control of the archaic self who understands experience only in extreme terms.

The ironies in "Daddy" proliferate in unexpected ways, however. When the speaker proclaims categorically that "every woman adores a Fascist" (st. 10), she is subjecting her victimization to irony by suggesting that sufferers choose, or at least accommodate themselves to, their suffering. But she is also subjecting her authority to irony, since her claim about "every woman" is transparently false. It simply parodies patriarchal commonplaces, such as those advanced by Helene Deutsch concerning "feminine masochism" (192–99, 245–85). The adult, sophisticated self seems to be speaking here: Who else would have the confidence to make a sociological generalization? Yet the content of the assertion, if taken straightforwardly, returns us to the regressive self who is dominated by extravagant emotions she cannot begin to understand. Plath's mother wished that Plath would write about "decent, courageous people" (*LH* 477), and she herself heard an inner voice demanding that she be a perfect "paragon" in her language and feeling (*J* 176). But in the speaker of "Daddy," she inscribed the opposite of such a paragon: a divided self whose veneer of civilization is breached and infected by unhealthy instincts.

Plath's irony cuts both ways. At the same time that the speaker's sophisticated voice undercuts her childish voice, reducing its melodrama to comedy, the childish or maddened voice undercuts the pretensions of the sophisticated voice, revealing the extremity of suffering masked by its ironies. While demonstrating the inadequacy of thinking and feeling in opposites, the poem implies that such a mode can locate truths denied more complex cognitive and affective systems. The very moderation of the normal adult intelligence, its tolerance of ambiguity, its defenses against the primal energies of the id, results in falsification. Reflecting Schiller's idea that the creative artist experiences a "momentary and passing madness" (quoted by Freud in a passage of *The Interpretation of Dreams* [193] that Plath underscored), "Daddy" gives voice to that madness. Yet the poem's sophisticated awareness, its comic vision, probably wins out in the end, since the poem concludes by curtailing the power of its extreme discourse (as I shall argue in chapter 4). Furthermore, Plath distanced herself from the poem's aboriginal voice by introducing her text as "a poem spoken by a girl with an Electra complex"—that is, as a study of the *girl's* pathology rather than her father's—and as an allegory that will "free" her from that pathology. She also distanced herself by reading the poem in a tone that emphasized its irony. And finally, she distanced herself by laying the poem's wild voice permanently to rest after October. The aboriginal vision was indeed purged. "Daddy" represents not Dickinson's madness that is divinest sense, but rather an entry into a style of discourse and a mastery of it. The poem realizes the trope of suffering by means of an inherent irony that both questions and validates the trope in the same gestures, and that finally allows the speaker to conclude the discourse and to remove herself from the trope with a sense of completion rather than wrenching, since the irony was present from the very beginning.

Plath's poetic revolt in "Daddy" liberated her pent-up creativity, but the momentary success sustained her little more than self-sacrifice had done. "Daddy" became another stage in her development, an unrepeatable experiment, a vocal opening that closed itself at once. The poem is not only an elegy for the

power of "daddy-poetry" but for the powers of speech Plath discovered in composing it.

When we consider "Daddy" generically, a further range of
implications presents itself. Although we could profitably consider the poem as the dramatic monologue Plath called it in
her BBC broadcast, let us regard it instead as the kind of poem
most readers have taken it to be: a domestic poem. I have chosen this term, rather than M. L. Rosenthal's better-known
"confessional poem" or the more neutral "autobiographical
poem," because "confessional poem" implies a confession rather
than a making (though Steven Hoffman and Lawrence Kramer
have recently indicated the mode's conventions) and because
"autobiographical poem" is too general for our purpose. I shall
define the domestic poem as one that represents and comments on a protagonist's relationship to one or more family
members, usually a parent, child, or spouse. To focus our discussion even further, I shall emphasize poetry that specifically
concerns a father.

Poems about parents, about the parent-child relationship,
and about the aging and death of a parent hardly existed in
English before 1800. But in the nineteenth century, with its
increasing interest in human development, family poems
began to appear with some regularity. We can divide such
poems into two types: the relatively straightforward eulogy or
elegy, typified by Matthew Arnold's "Rugby Chapel" (1857),
John Greenleaf Whittier's "Snow-Bound" (1866), e. e. cummings' "my father moved through dooms of love" (1940), and
May Sarton's "A Celebration for George Sarton" (1978); and
the more complex (and for our purpose more relevant) poem
of development, which emphasizes the child's maturation and
separation from the parent as well as ambiguities in the
parent's character and in the child's feelings.

A key early poem in this latter mode is Whitman's "There
Was a Child Went Forth" (1855), which recalls all that "became
part of that child" in order to ascertain his adult identity. The
poem's most intense passage focuses on the child's relations
with his parents. In a characteristic Whitmanian movement,
the passage begins with positive or innocuous details, intro-

duces disturbing matter, and then represses such matter in a
renewed flow of bland idealization:

> They gave him afterward every day, they became part of
>   him.
> The mother at home quietly placing the dishes on the
>   supper-table,
> The mother with mild words, clean her cap and gown, a
>   wholesome odor falling off her person and clothes as
>   she walks by,
> The father, strong, self-sufficient, manly, mean, anger'd,
>   unjust,
> The blow, the quick loud word, the tight bargain, the
>   crafty lure,
> The family usages, the language, the company, the furni-
>   ture, the yearning and swelling heart,
> Affection that will not be gainsay'd.   (*Leaves* 365)

This passage and the one immediately preceding it are reser-
voirs of material resembling personal memory, placed in an
otherwise impersonal and abstract context of "shadows, aureola
and mist, the light falling on roofs" and so on. The outbreak of
charged reverie—particularly the sudden representation of the
father as "mean, anger'd, unjust"—seems to be the emotional
center of the poem. That apparent uncovering of repressed
Oedipal material lays a foundation for many domestic poems
to come, obviously including "Daddy." The ambiguity of feeling toward the father and the allegorical suggestiveness of the
father-child relation when the child happens to be a developing
poet, are interrelated features that endure in the poems that
succeed Whitman's. The poem laments that the "strong, self-
sufficient" father does not need the child—an attitude quite
"unjust" indeed from the child's point of view, consigning the
child to a lonely, bitter struggle for his own strength and self-
sufficiency. And yet, as the poem also makes clear, such self-
sufficiency is a harmful self-deception. The child's parents
"became part of him." In allegorical terms, the precursors'
"usages" and "language" help to determine the young poet's
own utterance. Whitman assuaged his anxiety at this threat to
his autonomy by attributing an angry and manipulative self-
sufficiency to the father figure while retaining a more open and

humane strength for himself. Yet the anxiety that gave the poem birth and that impelled him to distinguish so sharply between "father" and "child" governs the entire poem, even its most apparently innocuous passages.

We encounter a similar pattern of ambivalence and internalization in the poems that follow Whitman's. Whether the paternal figure in Emily Dickinson's poetry appears in human or divine form, he is frequently presented as neglectful, secretive, and rejecting (poems 49, 112, 127, 141, 191, 215, 445, 1021, and 1258). Dickinson thought her father was "too busy" to "notice" what she did (letter 261). As a result, she often directed her anger, as Barbara Mossberg has observed, "toward a father — the masculine world — who [did] not notice, and [would] not notice, in what ways she [was] powerful, just like him" (71). Yet in a fundamental way, Dickinson's poetic development depended on her father: "If she could communicate with him, she would not need to write the poem" (Mossberg 81). Although Dickinson's textual "I" resides in her "father's house" (poem 824), she often articulates herself, like Plath's "I" in "Daddy," by protesting his behavior toward her: "Burglar! Banker — Father! / I am poor once more!" (poem 49).

Whitman's inheritor Hart Crane portrays another impoverishing, all-powerful father in the "Van Winkle" section of *The Bridge* (1929): "Is it the whip stripped from the lilac tree / One day in spring my father took to me . . . ?" The same poem's "Indiana" section represents the parent-child relation somewhat differently. In this section the father is long dead — a repressed anxiety that, one might postulate, is certain to return — and the poet-voyager-son is about to replicate the father's journey. The son's quest, however, discredits the father's, since it is implicitly for poetry, spiritual gold, whereas the father's quest was for material gold. We begin to see a family resemblance among the poetic fathers represented by Whitman, Dickinson, and Crane. They are domineering, withholding, and greedy — men of the "tight bargain, the crafty lure," burglars and bankers, seekers after "gilded" promises of personal fortune.

As a variant example of this tradition, we might include

Eliot's *The Waste Land* (1922), written several years after the
death of his father and including a voice that muses "upon the
king my brother's wreck / And on the king my father's death
before him" (3.19–20); Williams's diptych about parents,
"Adam" and "Eve" (1936); and Lowell's "In Memory of Arthur
Winslow" (1946), in which he mourns the grandfather's passing
while condemning the "craft" that netted him a million dollars
in gold. As fictional examples, we might adduce Fitzgerald's
Tender Is the Night ("Goodbye my father. Goodbye all my fathers"—
a line Plath underscored in her copy), Hemingway's *For Whom the
Bell Tolls*, Joyce's *Finnegans Wake*, Lawrence's *Sons and Lovers*, and
Woolf's *To the Lighthouse*.

All the texts mentioned thus far may be considered precursors of "Daddy." In the 1950s the "domestic poem" proper
appeared on the scene, with its own conventions and expectations, and with its own complex cultural and literary reasons
for being. Perhaps the precursive poems made the genre's eventual flowering inevitable, while its precise timing depended on
a reaction against modernism's aesthetic of impersonality.
Theodore Roethke wrote several early poems that initiated the
genre: "My Papa's Waltz" (1948), "The Lost Son" (1948), and
"Where Knock Is Open Wide" (1951). Lowell's "Life Studies"
sequence (1959) was, and is, the genre's most prominent land-
mark. Other poems in the genre include John Berryman's *The
Dream Songs* (1969); Frank Bidart's "Golden State" (1973) and
"Confessional" (1983); Robert Duncan's "My Mother Would
Be a Falconress" (1968); Allen Ginsberg's *Kaddish* (1960); Ran-
dall Jarrell's "The Lost World" (1965); Maxine Kumin's "The
Thirties Revisited" (1975), "My Father's Neckties" (1978), and
"Marianne, My Mother, and Me" (1989); Stanley Kunitz's
"Father and Son" (1958) and "The Testing Tree" (1971); Lowell's
"To Mother" (1977), "Robert T. S. Lowell" (1977), and "Un-
wanted" (1977); James Merrill's "Scenes of Childhood" (1962);
Adrienne Rich's "After Dark" (1966); Anne Sexton's "Division
of the Parts" (1960) and "The Death of the Fathers" (1972);
W. D. Snodgrass' "Heart's Needle" (1959); Diane Wakoski's
"The Father of My Country" (1968); and of course Sylvia
Plath's "Daddy" (1962). In all these poems, the parent-child

relationship serves as a locus for psychological investigation. In many of them it also serves as a means of representing the acquisition of poetic identity and of exploring the bounds of textuality itself. Because later writers were conscious of the Roethke-Lowell domestic poem as at least a genre in embryo, they chose to use its features, or perhaps the power of the genre was such that the features chose them. The "domestic poem" became a system of signs in which each individual text's adherence to the system and deviations within the system produced its particular literary meaning.

During Plath's trying time of 1958–59, which culminated in her visit to Yaddo and her return to England, she struggled, as we have seen, to "break into a new line of poetry" (*J* 321). As always, her method was to "read others and think hard" (*J* 302). The two male poets she read most intently, the two who most instructed her, were Roethke and Lowell. Plath understood Roethke primarily as a poet of the minimal, the vegetative, and the prerational rather than as a poet of family relationships. In spring 1959 she wrote in her journal that she had finished a "romantic iambic pentameter imitation of Roethke's Yeats poems" (*J* 299) — apparently meaning "The Dying Man" in Roethke's *Words for the Wind* (1958). She discarded her imitation, which she judged "rather weak," but in the months that followed she wrote several other poems in which, as Anne Sexton said, she tried to "out-Roethke Roethke" ("Barfly" 178): "Blue Moles," "Dark Wood, Dark Water," and "Mushrooms." At Yaddo, an old Roethkean stamping ground, Plath followed "The Colossus," her breakthrough poem, with "Poem for a Birthday," a sequence about a woman's relationship to her parents that she termed "a fine, new thing . . . Roethke's influence, yet mine" (*J* 325). She especially liked its final segment, "The Stones," which alludes to her suicide attempt and recovery. According to Hughes, she called everything she had written before it "juvenilia" ("Notes" 192). Plath began the sequence as an exercise in the Roethkean greenhouse mode: "A dwelling on madhouse, nature: meanings of tools, greenhouses, florists shops, tunnels, vivid and disjointed" (*J* 324). If the sequence as a whole often does resemble "partly digested" Roethke, as

Judith Kroll acerbically observes (91), "The Stones" succeeds in moving beyond pastiche toward Plath's own distinctive timbre and language. Thus, Roethke gave Plath vital instruction at a crucial moment in her career.

After her return to England, Roethke's influence receded. She met him once, and though she called him "the American poet I admire next to Robert Lowell" (*LH* 407), he was more impressed with her husband than with her. He spoke of a possible teaching post at Washington for Hughes but not for her (*LH* 407–8; Seager 271). Nevertheless, her poetry continued to allude to his in its imagery of shadows, echoes, trees, stone, moon, and papery feelings. The tree caught by the moon in Roethke's "All the Earth, All the Air" and "Meditations of an Old Woman" reappears in Plath's "The Moon and the Yew Tree" and "Elm"; the breathing red flowers in "The Lost Son" recur in "Tulips" and "Poppies in July"; the "shadows" that "start from my own feet" in "The Surly One" return as "a shadow starting from my feet" in "Three Women"; "the purity of pure despair" in "In a Dark Time" becomes "the O-gape of complete despair" in "The Moon and the Yew Tree"; "the moon's my mother" in "The Dying Man" becomes "the moon is my mother" in "The Moon and the Yew Tree"; and the "fixed stars" in "Her Becoming" remain "fixed stars" in "Words." Yet when Plath spoke about Roethke, she never depicted him as a domestic poet, despite the evident indebtedness of "Daddy" to his poems about his own dead father (coincidentally also named Otto). Nor does Plath's poetry overtly allude to Roethke's father poems. If John Guillory is correct in surmising that allusions indicate a lack of poetic anxiety, then we may suppose that Plath was less anxious about, and less influenced by, the vegetative/stream-of-consciousness Roethke than the domestic Roethke.

During 1958–59, Lowell's influence was even more pronounced than Roethke's. Plath met the "mad and very nice poet Robert Lowell" (*LH* 344) at Smith in May 1958 and read his poetry seriously for the first time: "Taste the phrases: tough, knotty, blazing with color and fury, most eminently sayable: 'where braced pig-iron dragons grip / The blizzard to their rigor mortis' [*Lord Weary* 3]. Oh, god, after coffee, even I feel my voice will come out strong and colored as that!" (*J* 222). We may imagine that her interest was thematic as well as formal, since Lowell, after all, was the poet who lamented, "I ask for bread, my father gives me mould" (*Lord Weary* 17). Plath read Lowell with the excitement of one who finds something she wishes to emulate. In 1959 she attended his poetry course at Boston University, along with Anne Sexton, Kathleen Spivack, and George Starbuck, and she began to write poems in the style of *Lord Weary's Castle* (1946). According to Hughes, "Point Shirley," composed in early 1959, was "a deliberate exercise in Robert Lowell's early style" ("Notes" 191), and "Suicide off Egg Rock" seems to have been another. Interestingly, Plath assumed a Lowellian style only in her poems of the sea, which Bloom associates with poetic instruction (*Map* 13–17). In those texts Plath adopted Lowell's clotted syntax, his tone of aggrieved aggression, and his vocabulary of combers, spindrift, squalls, and sluttish, rutted sea. But just as she seemed to ignore Roethke's domestic poems, so she initially ignored the domestic poems Lowell himself was publishing in *Partisan Review* and preparing for publication in *Life Studies* (1959) at the very time that she was auditing his class. Her assimilation of the Lowellian domestic poem came only later, in the annus mirabilis that ended her life. After "Point Shirley" and "Suicide off Egg Rock," Plath ceased to refer to Lowell. (An exception may be the phrase "fixed stars" in "Words," which appears in Lowell's "Inauguration Day: January 1953" as well as in Roethke's "Her Becoming"; when Frank Bidart used Plath's phrase in "Golden State," he unconsciously alluded to her precursors as well.) Nevertheless, Plath absorbed Lowell into her poetic identity. As I suggested in chapter 1, she made creativity central to her life, just as Lowell did. Beyond that, her growing desire to write poems "to be read aloud" (Interview 170) reflects Lowell's conversion to a spoken style in *Life Studies*. And her increasing use of personal material certainly was spurred by what she called Lowell's "breakthrough" in *Life Studies* (Interview 167). She could never have written "Daddy" as she did without the example of Lowell's "life studies" of his father.

Although Lowell was the American poet Plath admired most, he also made her nervous. Since she associated his authority with that of Ted Hughes (*J* 222, 229), and both of theirs with that of her father, her feelings were cathected from the start. According to Sexton, when she and Plath attended Lowell's class, they kept "as quiet as possible in view of the father" ("Barfly" 174). Not fully recognizing Plath's competence, Lowell seemed to prefer Sexton's work to hers (*J* 301) — though he ultimately reversed his opinion, ranking Plath in the company of Dickinson, Moore, and Bishop ("Conversation" 46). But at the time, as he later admitted, none of Plath's poems "sank very deep" into his awareness (Foreword xi). Plath called his response to her poems "ineffectual" and claimed not to respect it (*J* 298, 306).

Several years later Plath took revenge on her ambivalently admired mentor by choosing his nickname, "Cal," for an arrogant, insensitive character in *The Bell Jar*. In the novel, "Cal" fears to swim in the surf, preferring instead to pontificate to Esther Greenwood, who is on the verge of suicide. When Esther asks him about methods of suicide, he says, "I've often thought of that," adding that he would kill himself with his "father's gun" (*BJ* 185–86) — possible allusions to Lowell's suicidal meditation in "Skunk Hour" and to his musing on his father's "flintlock" in "Rebellion." When Esther finally entices "Cal" into the sea (poetry, eros, thanatos), he jostles her and then pushes her under (*BJ* 187); but when they begin to swim, Esther outlasts him. Her heart beats, "I am I am I am" (*BJ* 188) — one of several references to "Suicide off Egg Rock" (*CP* 115), a Lowellian poem she had presented to the master in class and that he had faintly praised as showing "a flair for alliteration and Massachusetts low-tide dolor" (Foreword xi).

Plath also took revenge on Lowell by naming one of her central suicide poems "Ariel," and by giving that title to her second collection of poetry. Lowell's nickname, "Cal," combined Caliban with Caligula (Hamilton 20). Thus, beyond intending to revise the Ariels of numerous canonical texts — Ezra (8:16), Isaiah (29:1–16), *The Tempest*, *Paradise Lost* (6.371), Eliot's "Ariel Poems," and Stevens's "The Planet on the Table" — Plath may have sought to proclaim her artistic superiority over her mentor named "Caliban." W. H. Auden had once told her that "Caliban is the natural bestial projection, Ariel the creative imagination" (*J* 77). Like the "airy spirit" of Shakespeare's play, Plath wanted to transcend her rival, the "man-animal."

Finally, and most important, Plath took revenge by surpassing Lowell in the very genre he had helped to found, the domestic poem. If the poem of instruction often takes the form of a sea shore ode, the poem of liberation frequently appears as a domestic poem. In "The Lost Son," Roethke proved he could write a sustained work in his own distinctive manner rather than in Yeats's and Eliot's style; in "Heart's Needle," Snodgrass escaped the shackles of academic rhetoric and specifically that of Lowell in *Lord Weary's Castle*; in *Kaddish*, Ginsberg justified the beat revolution against the claims of East Coast formalism; and in the "Life Studies" sequence, Lowell freed himself from the style of Allen Tate, Hart Crane, T. S. Eliot, and his own earlier texts. The Roethke-Lowell poem of severance from the parent embodies the poet's declaration of independence from the precursor. It often inaugurates the poet's major phase.

In 1959 Plath did not consciously attempt to write in the domestic poem genre, perhaps because she was not yet ready to assume her majority. Her journal entries of that period bristle with an impatience at herself that may derive from this reluctance. She may have feared asserting her "I am I am I am," which seemed to carry with it a countervailing impulse of self-retribution. But by fall 1962, when she had already lost so much, she was ready to chance tackling poetic tradition, and specifically her chief male instructors, Roethke and Lowell. In "Daddy" she achieved her victory in two ways. First, as we have seen, she symbolically assaults a father figure who is identified with male control of language. All her anxiety of influence comes to the fore in the poem: her sense of belatedness, her awareness of constraint, her fears of inadequacy, her furious need to overcome her dependency, her guilt at her own aggressivity. Since the precursors "do not do / Any more" (st. 1), she wishes to escape their paralyzing influence and to empty the "bag full of God" that has kept her tongue stuck in her jaw for so long (st. 2, 5). The father whose power she attacks is not simply Roethke or Lowell, or even Hughes or Otto Plath, but a literary character who includes reference to all of them as categories of masculine authority. Although the Daddy of poetry has already "died" (st. 2)—the fate of all published texts in Plath's postromantic perspective—the speaker must symbolically "kill" him from her own discourse. The poem ironically depicts poetry as both an aggression and a suicide. The female ephebe herself becomes a "brute" in the act of voicing (st. 10), just as have her teachers before her. But the aggression of her speech yields to the self-annihilation of language. By the end of the poem she too, like her male precursors, is "through." The speaker's textual life will be misread on innumerable occasions in innumerable ways, whereas her own misreading and miswriting of the precursors is finished. In its conclusion, the poem acknowledges its alienation from itself, confessing the transitoriness of its unbounded power.

In addition to killing the father in its fictional plot, the poem seeks to discredit the forefathers through its status as poetic act. Taking a genre established by Roethke and Lowell, "Daddy" fundamentally alters it through antithesis and parody. Like all strong poems, it transforms its genre and therefore the way we perceive the precursive examples, making them seem not fulfillments but anticipations. Thus the later work projects its anxiety retrospectively back through its predecessors. Haunted by fears of inadequacy and redundancy, it seeks to make the earlier poems seem incompetent by comparison—a kind of juvenilia in the career of the genre. In "Daddy," Plath exposed the precursors' failures of nerve and imagination. Her poem attempts to conclude the genre, to represent the final possible stroke, or at the very least to inaugurate some new and important genre, of which the whole domestic genre was but a foreshadowing.

This point comes clearer if we compare "Daddy" with two analogues, Roethke's "The Lost Son" (1948) and Lowell's "Commander Lowell" (1959). In the Freudian drama of "The Lost Son," the protagonist subjectively relives his childhood fears and fantasies. Like the speaker of the companion piece, "My

Papa's Waltz," he is still enmeshed in the family romance, remembering the father ambivalently as powerful, protective, and threatening. After locating himself at his father's grave, where he feels both grief and estrangement (in a scene that adumbrates "Electra on Azalea Path"), he descends into his unconscious, seeking, as Roethke later explained, "some clue to existence" (*Poet* 38). He encounters his death wish, his memory of his father as "Father Fear," his sexual anxieties, and finally the "dark swirl" of a blackout, after which a childhood memory of his "Papa" shouting "order" in German returns him to consciousness. Although the figure of "Papa" blends earthly and heavenly father (*Poet* 39), he also symbolizes the superego, restoring order to a psyche and a poem that had fallen into chaos. At the poem's conclusion, as the "lost son" waits for his "understandable spirit" to revive, he appears to be purged, though not cured, of the conflicts that incapacitated him.

The speaker of "Commander Lowell," in contrast, is objective, precise, and witty. His discourse reflects a detached perspective on the past rather than a psychic reimmersion in it. He portrays his father as one who threatened him only through weakness. This father "was nothing to shout / about to the summer colony at 'Matt'"; took "four shots with his putter to sink his putt"; sang "Anchors Aweigh" in the bathtub; was fired from his job; and squandered his inheritance. Whereas Roethke's poem represents a cathartic experience, Lowell's converts chaotic feelings into intellectual irony. Whereas Roethke's poem can be read as an allegory of man's relationship to God or as a model of the Freudian psyche, Lowell's remains a realistic narrative, though it does suggest the cultural and financial decline of a social class.

Plath's poem combines features of both of these precursors: Roethke's evocation of a German-speaking authoritarian with Lowell's sarcastic deflation of a man without qualities; Roethke's subjective anguish with Lowell's social comedy. Like Roethke's Papa, Plath's title character is an intimidating patriarch; like Lowell's Father, he is a buffoon ("big as a Frisco seal"). Finally, Plath's poem, like those of her predecessors, has little to do with psychological cure: the speaker's defenses remain in place.

But in a deeper sense, "Daddy" swerves sharply from its precursors, curtailing their power. It turns the psychological depth of Roethke's poem and the ironically detached surface of Lowell's poem into a fury of denunciation, an extravagance of emotion, an exaggeration of acts and effects, perhaps revealing the subtexts of both precursors. If in a sense the texts by Roethke and Lowell constitute what Ned Lukacher might term the primal scene of "Daddy," the latter poem's raw intensity succeeds in reversing the relationship, making itself resemble *their* primal scene. It unmasks Roethke's implicitly oppressive father figure as a monster and Lowell's sophisticated comedy as slapstick. It transforms the domestic genre alternately into a horror show, encapsulating every political, cultural, and familial atrocity of the age, and a theater of cruelty, evoking nervous laughter. "Daddy" takes the genre as far as it can go — and then further.

In Roethke's subsequent "Otto" (1964) his speaker is less immersed in his unconscious than previously, and in Lowell's subsequent "To Daddy" (1973) and "Robert T. S. Lowell" (1977) his speaker is less the ironic observer and more the feeling son. But neither poet moved significantly in the directions suggested by "Daddy." Neither wrote as powerful an allegory of writing or as scathing a condemnation of the patriarchy; neither became as "extreme" (Lowell, *Prose* 287). Although other poets inevitably wrote with an awareness of Plath's achievement, they tended to swerve away from her example — either explicitly, as when Bidart contradicts the end of *Ariel* in part five of "Golden State," or implicitly, as in Wakoski's studiously reflective and measured poem about her relationship with her father. But Lowell confessed a feeling of defeat in his foreword to *Ariel*, and perhaps that confession has general application: "There is a peculiar, haunting challenge to these poems. . . . In her lines, I often hear the serpent whisper, 'Come, if only you had the courage, you too could have my rightness, audacity and ease of inspiration'" (x). Lowell has been interpreted in those lines as referring to Plath's suicide, his typical evasion of her poetic achievement. But surely that evasion only masks his sense that Plath had brought the genre he created to a climax, that she had emptied the cup and then smashed it.

In her other poems of October 1962, Plath continued to revise the words of the fathers. Rather than resorting to Bloom's ratio of "daemonization," a personalized countersublime to the precursor's sublime (*Anxiety* 15), I would call Plath's particular operation *feminization*: a turning of male texts against themselves, an abduction of their language for the antithetical purpose of female inscription. In "Lady Lazarus" (*CP* 244–47), for example, she feminizes the story of Lazarus. Similarly, in the opening line of "The Jailer," "My night sweats grease his breakfast plate" (*CP* 226), she wrenches words out of patriarchal discourse (Yeats's "The night can sweat with terror," Roethke's "My shadow pinned against a sweating wall," Lowell's "animal night sweats of the spirit") and plants them in the female discourse she was devising on the spot.

In her poems of February 1963, Plath looked back on the poetic rebellion that had peaked in "Daddy"—and was displeased. Although she had devoted her last months to unloosing her creative spark and act, she found that the power she had stolen at such great personal cost evanesced as she gripped it, the voice for which she had sacrificed so much grew foreign to her ear. Fully comprehending the limits of language for the first time—its small mill of silence at the center, its inability to provide a coherent self, its fundamental inorganicity—she must have looked with horror at the sounded void of what had been her career.

"Words," like the other February poems, seems at first to have removed itself from any "system of relations" (Derrida, *Writing* 227), to be adrift on the page, staring into bare, heartless immensities. But Plath donned the guise of Melville's unencumbered traveler, who crosses "the frontiers into Eternity with nothing but a carpet-bag—that is to say, the Ego" (*Letters* 125), only in order to dis-guise the radicalness of her final struggle with literature. She now sought to free herself from the "jealous gods" (*CP* 179) in a new way. Instead of thematizing her revolt against their power, as in "Daddy," she exposed the strangeness of their medium and the vulnerability of their expression. We may find it curious that in her last two weeks she should have focused her energies on a poem about "words." Surely by this time, it might seem, she should have progressed beyond caring about poetry, should have flown directly into the red eye of mourning. When we analyze the poem, however, we realize anew that questions of poetic identity, language, and voice were not peripheral to her crisis but central to it.

"Words" (*CP* 270) once again allegorizes the poet's problematical relationship to her poetry, as Jon Rosenblatt has also observed (137–40). The ax strokes into the "wood" (st. 1) represent the poet's hewing into her psychic grammar or into her fleshly self. The reverberations stand for words, for the poetic text resulting from that mutilation. The words, imagined as "echoes" and galloping "horses" (st. 1), prove "indefatigable" but purposeless and "dry" (st. 4). Conversely, the poet's interior grammar, the source of her written words, begins to flow independently in the form of "sap," "tears," and "water" (st. 2), ultimately pooling in a deathly reflecting pond (st. 4). Even as the poem exposes the struggle of poetic creation, it expresses the alienation of poetry, the futility of texts and of the creative act.

The poem's images alter alarmingly, evading our preconceived categories with a discordant dynamism suggestive of the grotesque. Strokes become ringings, which become echoes, which become horses, which become dry words and hoof-beats (st. 1, 4). Wood transforms into sap, into tears, into water, into a mirror, into a skull, into a pool, into stars, and into a life (st. 2–4). And the life at the conclusion represents an unmasking or dis-figuring of the figure of the wood being axed (disfigured) at the beginning—though the "life" is inevitably yet another figure. In "Words," figuration seems to take on a life of its own. Simile yields to metaphor, and metaphor to metonymy. In lines 1–8, the echoes travel "like horses," and the tree sap wells "like tears" and then "like . . . / Water." But by lines 9–13 these metamorphoses seem to be epistemologically sanctioned, as in a nightmare or vision. The water establishes a mirror, covering a mobile rock that *is* a white skull. In the last six lines, the poem's initial simile ("echoes . . . like horses") assumes the status of the literal ("I encounter them on the road"), a claim that is instantly revealed as a metaphor (for "words")—and, contradictorily, as a metonym ("hoof-taps") that returns us to the initial auditory image of echoes "like horses." Furthermore, the water that aspires to the condition of mirror in lines 8–9 has accomplished its goal by lines 18–19. It reflects stars or, in the syntax of the poem, harbors stars at its bottom. The stars, in turn, mirror and harbor "a life"—the speaker's life, or perhaps preferably, the illusory life of the words on the page.

Thus "Words" deliberately exposes its status as verbal play through an endless process of figuring, disfiguring, and refiguring. This improvisational linguistic dance of arbitrary images acknowledges the *mise en abîme* of poetry. If the allegorical form itself foregrounds the signifying process, the poem's decentering of allegory further highlights the independent, discontinuous energy of language. The wood, echoes, horses, and water ultimately refer neither to natural phenomena nor to the author's psyche, but to the idea of words themselves. Plath's late poem, then, reveals itself to us, simply and completely, thematically and formally, as tropes in a tradition of troping.

Rather than celebrate the autonomy of language, "Words" expresses fear of the power language wields. The poem's speaking subject derives not from any biographical origin but from the language system of the unfolding text. Entirely determined by the figures through which she finds expression, the speaker is a linguistic being only. Her silent passivity, in contrast to the noisy activity of the entities representing language, suggests her abject weakness, "governed" as she is by the "fixed stars" of discourse. The inanimate objects, the "words," initiate and perform all the poem's actions with a will of their own. Axes stroke, echoes travel, sap wells, rock drops and turns, and so on. These busy and menacing figures are aggressive (they "stroke," "strive," and "eat") and domineering (they "establish" and "govern"). They also suggest lifelessness: an axed tree, a "mirror," a "white skull," a "riderless" horse. In the end, all of the poem's wild verbal energy winds down to stasis—underwater, in reflected light, "fixed." The frantic metamorphoses of language, portrayed as futile and redundant, yield to a fatal stillness.

"Words" reveals a severe estrangement from the writing process, implying that the poet is as determined in her linguistic
structures as in the other areas of her life. Moreover, if she
lacks freedom and power as a writer, she equally lacks it as a
reader. Her own words return to her "dry and riderless" rather
than wet with the sap of life; they have become the incompre-
hensible discourse of the other. "Words" exposes the failure of
such humanistic ideals as originality, unity, imagination, and
self-expression. The self depicted in the poem is a solitary,
diminished "I" (st. 3) encountering a world of monsters. This
bewildered speaker contrasts tragically with the "hypnotic presence" who voices "Daddy," and even with the servile yet sarcastic "I" of "The Colossus." She inhabits a linguistic world that
is inchoate, uncontrollable, and ultimately foreign to her purposes. It is a world of creatures who prey on themselves, like
Shakespeare's "monsters of the deep," and who prey on those
they dominate, like Yeats's "slouching beast" and "savage god."

Nevertheless, if "Words" shows that writing necessarily fails
to satisfy authorial desire, it also contains a logical paradox.
Since the poem questions poetry's capacity to convey meaning
and the reader's ability to decode, it invites us to distrust any
implication of authorial defeat that we may read into it—
another example of Plath's self-subverting poetics of self-doubt.
By providing us with nothing but echoes that travel "off from
the center," the poem ultimately escapes our reductive understanding, just as the speaker's chance "encounter" seems to subvert her final claim about "fixed" stars. Therefore the poem's
success as fiction undermines its fiction of failure, and its
figural variety belies its deterministic tropes.

"Words" reopens the question of the speaking subject's
power in another way as well. The poem's busy objects refer
not just to words in general but to the specific words of predecessor poems. Not as arbitrary as they may at first appear, the
images derive from the author's argument with male literary
tradition. The transumptions in "Words" impel us to recon-
sider the poem's dialectic between determinism and free play.
Have the precursors mastered the latecomer's poem, or has the
latecomer in fact taken charge of the precursors' language?

The echoing wood of the first stanza, for example, echoes Roethke's "In a Dark Time," in which the speaker hears his echo "in an echoing wood." Plath's wood additionally echoes Dante's "dark wood of my life"; Whitman's tree that "utters joyous leaves" (*Leaves* 126); Thomas's blasted tree roots and "vowelled" trees (*Poems* 10, 19); Lowell's loquacious, axed tree in "The Slough of Despond"; and finally Pound's "A Pact," which depicts Whitman's poems as newly broken wood. In addition, Plath's "pool" may recall "th' oblivious Pool" of *Paradise Lost* (1.266), while her horses and hoofbeats echo those of Hughes's "The Horses" and "The Otter." "Words," then, exemplifies the poet's final strategy of expropriating male linguistic power.

Plath gained control over literary language through a process of antithetical substitution. Although we might take this process as evidence that the history of poetry, a notoriously "ingrown art" (*J* 282), predetermined her language, we should also note that the process allowed her to alter the precursors' paradigms. Whereas Roethke's and Lowell's poems suggest a metaphysical drama—a successful or impeded "drive toward God," as Roethke said—"Words" unfolds only a drive toward the void of language. Whereas Pound can blandly claim to discover a common "sap" in himself and his poetic "father," Plath's "I" finds even her own "sap" to be "dry." Whereas Hughes makes his statuesque horses a token of mystical illumination, Plath's horses betoken alienation and loss. Plath revived the words of her male predecessors in order to transfuse them with her own antithetical ardor. Like Lizzie Borden taking an ax to the family tree, she mutilated the precursors' texts. Incomplete in themselves, they would henceforth become part of a larger intertextual poem composed by herself, with "Words" as its final strophe.

The most audacious metalepsis in "Words" occurs in its concluding lines. These lines disfigure not simply Roethke, Lowell, or Hughes, but William Shakespeare. The words in question, "fixed stars / Govern a life," echo Kent's comment in *King Lear* about the difference between Cordelia and her sisters:

> It is the stars,
> The stars above us, govern our conditions;
> Else one self mate and mate could not beget
> Such different issues.   (4.4.34-37)

Plath heavily underscored these lines in her edition of Shakespeare's plays (Smith volume). Her poem introjects Shakespeare's "stars" that "govern" into its own language system, not merely to borrow glory or to enrich its own texture (traditional explanations for literary allusion), but to provoke a dialectic, even to submerge the Shakespearean rhetoric in the Plathian. Her additions, "fixed" and "a life," appear in other passages of *King Lear*: "fix'd place" (1.4.29), "fix'd . . . course" (2.4.94-95), "lest his ungovern'd rage dissolve his life" (4.4.18), "no life" (5.3.5). The phrase "fixed stars" also occurs in Milton's *Paradise Lost* (3.481) as well as in Roethke and Lowell, demonstrating yet again just how overdetermined literary language is. Plath's transumption guarantees that henceforth "stars" that "govern" will signal Plath as well as Shakespeare — and for some readers Plath instead of Shakespeare. She put the bard's words into her own mouth and reciprocally placed her words in his.

We know that Plath had a special regard for Shakespeare, whom she viewed as the acme of the male literary tradition. He is one of the poets most frequently mentioned in her *Journals* and *Letters Home*. In *Letters Home*, Plath names him as one of the poets she and Hughes "love together" (*LH* 235), though her comments about enthusiasms shared with her husband are suspect, since they tend to reflect his preferences more than her own, or his preferences for her. In her youth, Plath responded to Shakespeare mainly with anxiety. Worried that she had not read enough of his plays, she seems to have considered reading Shakespeare an obligation on a par with learning German or shorthand (*J* 65, 241; *LH* 129, 170). At Smith she struggled for her A in Shakespeare, whereas she breezed through her other English classes. She did not save her notes from the class, a divergence from her usual custom. When she met Hughes, a man in the habit of yanking a Shakespeare volume out of the bookcase and beginning to recite (Wagner-Martin 133), her inadequate knowledge of the bard became an issue between them. During their courtship, he would test her on the subject (*LH* 235); after their marriage, he would "order" her to read Shakespeare (*J* 246); when they quarreled, they would read *King Lear* together as a way of making up (*J* 283). It seems possible that she associated Shakespeare with Hughes himself, just as she associated Hughes with her father.

Plath's feelings about Shakespeare, covered over as they were by her feelings about her husband and her father, must have been deeply ambivalent and highly cathected. We recall that she once wished that she herself might "become Shakespeare" (*J* 139), might take his place. She claimed that *The Tempest* related richly to her own "life and imagery" (*J* 223), and she seems to have allowed *King Lear* to play an equally important psychic role. She planned to name her second child "Megan Emily" if a girl: "Emily" was to honor Dickinson and Brontë as well as her father, whose middle name was Emil (*LH* 407), and "Megan" was to be pronounced "with a short 'e'" so as *not* to rhyme with "Regan" (*LH* 409). When she informed her mother of the name, Plath unconvincingly admonished her to "forget about *King Lear*" (*LH* 409). Plath must have resented Shakespeare's authority even as she admired it. She must have wanted to accuse him of inhibiting her creation of a strong text, even as his plays represented models of what a strong text could supremely be.

We may guess that *King Lear*, a study of "father against child" (1.2.121), had strong personal reverberations for the author of "Snakecharmer," "The Colossus," and "Daddy." But that personal interest, however important as pretext, transformed itself into a more direct relation when she tested her own poetic voice. As a young female poet seeking authority, she inherited a status in relation to Shakespeare that paralleled that of the three daughters in relation to their father. On the one hand, she resembled Goneril and Regan, who are "images of revolt and flying off" (2.4.91). She resembled them as perhaps they might see themselves, not as "monsters" (3.7.102) or even "tigers" (4.2.40), but as unaccommodated women, forced to deceive an authoritarian and narcissistic father in order to obtain their just patrimony. On the other hand, she resembled

Cordelia in refusing to speak the lies her father required of her, in refusing to say she loved him "all" (1.1.106), a pledge that would have prohibited her entry into adulthood through marriage, as Lynda Boose has noted (332–35). Analogously, Plath's continued self-subordination to her male precursor would have forestalled her coming of age as a strong poet. In a sense, Goneril/Regan and Cordelia are doubles of each other, the bad ephebe and the good ephebe, alike in revolt if not in virtue. To a young woman poet rebelling against patriarchal authority, a poet herself torn between impulses of destructiveness and creativity, they might well appear to be not "such different issues," as Kent says, but only different faces of the selfsame issue. *Ariel* tells of a woman poet's Cordelia-like inability to inherit her proper inheritance; and it embodies her Goneril- and Regan-like attempt to seize that inheritance by force.

Plath seized her patrimony not only through her identification with the daughter's revolt, which allowed her to steal and to alter Shakespeare's phrase in "Words," but also through her incorporation of the father himself into her own persona. In a letter, she once compared herself to Gloucester, hoping that she could achieve "new vision" like his, without an accompanying loss of sight (*LH* 229). But in her poetry she aimed even higher, her speaking subject in *Ariel* uncannily resembling King Lear. Like him, Plath's speaker grows delirious from a grief caused by love-loss. Like him, she dives inward into an intensified psychic reality: "The tempest in my mind / Doth from my senses take all feeling else / Save what beats there" (3.4.12–14). Like him, she allows herself "to feel what wretches feel" (3.4.34): victims of death camps, nuclear explosions, political oppression, and social prejudice — all the wretched of the earth. She learns to "see how this world goes" (3.4.153–54), while at the same time threatening, in her "ungovern'd" rage, to "dissolve" her life (4.4.18–19). Unhoused in the storm, deprived of her rightful place, crying after "love" that has gone (*Lear* 1.4.291; *CP* 192), she rails against the world and against her own moral "faults" (*Lear* 1.1.274; *CP* 193) until exhaustion overtakes her. In her madness, she attains a sort of reason and authority.

In *Ariel*'s world of doubles — of echoes, mirrors, shadows, and reflecting pools — Plath made her textual "I" a double of King Lear and his daughters, and she made her creating self a double of Shakespeare. As Schwartz and Bollas have observed, "something of the eery feeling we get when we read *Hamlet*, *Lear*, *Othello* and *Macbeth* . . . emerges when we read Plath's poetry" (182). If fixed stars govern her speaker's life, her authorial self demonstrated mastery over the stars at the bottom of the pool of poetry. Although Plath spent her life in the "shadow" of the father's word, power, and memory (*CP* 130, 164, 192, 227), much as Lear thought himself but a "shadow" of his past self (1.4.251), she was able to achieve a temporary release in her texts. Like Edmund in *King Lear* and Smerdyakov in *The Brothers Karamazov*, she bastardized her relation to patriarchal authority, severing the "natural" bonds between father and child, "blasting" the stars rather than being blasted by them (3.4.59), usurping the "paternal source of godhead" (*J* 223).

CHAPTER THREE

"A Woman Famous among Women"

The mother's face,
The purpose of the poem, fills the room.
—Wallace Stevens, "The Auroras of Autumn"

We think back through our mothers if we are women. It is use-
less to go to the great men writers for help, however much one
may go to them for pleasure.
—Virginia Woolf, *A Room of One's Own*

DID Sylvia Plath think back through her mothers?
Most critics have not thought so. Even those who wish to concep-
tualize her as a specifically female poet have generally portrayed
her artistic triumph as reflecting an achieved solipsism, a screen-
ing out of female as well as male influence. The split many critics describe in Plath between her sense of herself as a woman and
her self-awareness as a poet implies that she considered femininity and creativity to be at opposite poles. Tillie Olsen corrobo-
rates this viewpoint by quoting Plath's youthful comment that "a
woman has to sacrifice all claims to femininity and family to be
a writer" (30). Readers of *Letters Home* and *Journals* will remember
additional Plathian dichotomies between "domestic chores" and
"writing fulfillment" (*LH* 298) and additional complaints about
the "limitations of a woman's sphere" (*LH* 72). Although this paradigm illuminates some aspects of Plath's imaginative situation,
it obscures others and therefore needs modification—a process
already begun in Lynda Bundtzen's discussion of Plath as a
"woman creator" (94-106, 235-56) and in essays by Mary Lynn
Broe and Susan Stanford Friedman.

We may speculate that Plath both resented her feminine role
and enjoyed it; associated it with silence and, increasingly,
with verbal generativity; feared that she had to choose among

options and attempted to finesse such decisions. The one thing she did not try to do was to write a poetry that came exclusively from "inside herself," an impossible ideal. Far from isolating herself from female influence and thereby minimizing her female writing identity, she learned to subvert male ideas of female utterance, to grapple with women precursors, and to yoke femininity and creativity together — an effort that achieved one kind of climax in the aggressive and desolate poems that made her famous and another in perhaps her greatest poem, "Three Women." If at times, reflecting her education in patriarchal values, she disdained her "feminine tone" (*LH* 343), she more typically aspired to be a "woman famous among women" (*J* 260).

While Plath's growing rebelliousness toward male authority played an evident role in her creative life, her effort to locate herself within female inscription systems played an even more central and enduring one. Plath was not simply a madwoman in the attic of man's ancestral house, intent on stealing his language for her own purposes; she was also a woman residing in a house built by other women. That female house was hardly less agonistic than the other, but it possessed many features that the male house lacked. The situation of the woman poet was complicated, first of all, because she was at least partly committed to a male-dominated tradition that subjected her to a wide variety of exclusionary strategies. Joanna Russ has observed that a dominant culture normally feels comfortable with a minority representation of 10 percent or less (66–68, 76–86), and until recently women writers have indeed composed no more than 10 percent of most canons. The particular women writers chosen for inclusion have shifted from anthology to anthology and era to era, but the quota has remained constant. The token women writers authenticated the male canon without disrupting it, for as Ruth Bleier has said, "the last thing society desires of its women has been intellectuality or independence" (73). Thus, whereas male poets invent themselves under a hegemonic self-rule, female poets have been divided between two worlds: an institutionalized, androcentric culture that has defined, molded, restricted, estranged, and wasted their utterance, and an unsanctioned female culture lacking prestige and power.

Even apart from this system of dual citizenship and cultural subordination, the situation of the woman poet is complicated. Social scientists have found it more difficult to schematize the social organization of women than that of men. Whereas men's object relations often center on competition, women tend to sustain a "more total dynamic," exemplifying a wider "variety of ways of being in the world" (Jean Baker Miller 27, xii). Competition and personal integrity are only two threads; nurturance, cooperation, close friendship, growth, identification with others, kinship loyalty, desire to serve, and a regard for the group's harmony may be equally important. Therefore the strands connecting women writers to each other are likely to be even more diverse and uncertain than those connecting men writers. Although Harold Bloom and Walter Ong convincingly depict male writing as an "agon" or "contest" (Bloom, *Agon* 16–51; Ong, *Fighting* 15–115), we cannot expect to apply their paradigm to female writing without alteration. Beyond examining the ways women writers legitimate themselves in a male-dominated culture, then, we need to study the ways they situate themselves within a female culture that is, in Carol Gilligan's term, a complex "web" of social connection and individual initiative, support and rivalry (57).

In their important new work, *No Man's Land*, Sandra Gilbert and Susan Gubar do initiate such a study, finding that women writers of the twentieth century have had complex and problematic relations with their literary foremothers (1.184–205, 262–71). Plath's attitudes toward other women writers were probably more ambivalent than most. To be sure, she came to question phallocentric associations of pen with penis. Viewing patriarchal cultural as "flat" and as lacking (*CP* 177–82), she increasingly accepted and explored her identity as a "woman singer" (*LH* 256). But she did not necessarily think of herself as singing in a women's chorus. When her veneer of civilization rubbed thin in a crisis, which is to say much of the time, she frankly mistrusted all others, female as well as male. This was her dilemma: given her growing identification of herself as a woman writer, she could not feel competent without female precursors and peers near her, but given her inherent egotism, suspiciousness, and injured self-esteem, she also had difficulty feeling competent in their presence.

Most recent histories of women's writing have emphasized female strategies for opposing, subverting, and surviving the conditions of male dominance. Whereas I followed their lead in the last chapter, I now undertake to consider Plath's creative acts within the context of other creative acts by women, to study the ways Plath lays claim to her matrilineal inheritance. My account employs a method broached in the preceding chapter, as well as in my earlier work on Robert Lowell, of juxtaposing the writer's literary and family relations. This method assumes that through a process akin to transference, literary influence retraces the outlines of the initial parent-child bond. Writing unconsciously reproduces the writer's developmental history while at the same time seeking to correct, to avenge, and to supplant that history.

The forging of such connections will undoubtedly raise objections by those readers who quite understandably wish to safeguard the formal autonomy of literary discourse. Plath herself provided one sort of response to such objections when she used the terms "sublimation," "substitution," and "dialogue" to indicate the relations between her psychic and aesthetic energies (*J* 62, 281, 108). I additionally suggest that to separate the literary text from the psychosocial one is to ascribe to the institution of literature more originating power than it actually possesses, while preventing a juxtaposition that has the potential both to raise problems and to explain. Finally, I pragmatically note that much of the most illuminating recent criticism has predicated the culturally situated author as a desideratum. Even Michel Foucault in "What Is an Author?" discovered that the category of "author," like Lady Lazarus, refuses to stay dead (*Language* 113–38).

A MOTHER-DAUGHTER BOND

IT IS DIFFICULT at this late date to reconstruct the scene of Plath's early childhood. We may be certain, however, that Plath's mother, rather than her father, played the most important role of all. Freud and all subsequent students of female development have found that in our culture, the daughter's "attachment" to her mother in infancy and early childhood is the crucial and determining relationship in her life (see Freud, "Female Sexuality" and *New Introductory Lectures*; Balint; Bowlby; Chodorow; Horney). Even the daughter's subsequent cathexis of her father is simply a by-product of the earlier attachment. This general condition must have been especially pronounced in Plath's case, since her contact with her father was limited to perhaps half an hour a day (*LH* 19; Wagner-Martin 24–26). A woman hostile or ambivalent toward her father (as Plath was) is likely to have been so initially to her mother, "since the mother-relation was the original one, upon which the father-relation was built" ("Female Sexuality" 258)—though it is also true that when a father is not there enough, the daughter may idealize him or endow him with sadistic characteristics (again, as Plath did). Because in our culture a woman's ego boundaries are generally more permeable than a man's, and because a mother tends to involve her daughter in her fantasies as a subject rather than as an object (unlike her involvement of a son), the daughter never separates herself from her mother to the degree that a son does from both parents (Chodorow 108–10). The mother remains within the daughter, a crucial part of her self, her first and most enduring double.

Although we cannot literally return to Plath's childhood scene, Nancy Chodorow provides information that allows us at least to speculate on it. Drawing on clinical observations recounted in Robert Fleiss's *Ego and Body Ego*, Chodorow describes a sort of relationship that has been observed only in mothers and daughters, never in mothers and sons, fathers and daughters, or fathers and sons. In the extreme form of this relationship, the mothers were "asymbiotic" with their daughters during their pre-Oedipal stage (from birth to age three), a period when their daughters "needed symbiosis and experienced oneness with them" (100). Perhaps to compensate for unconscious hostility, however, the mothers became "hypersymbiotic" from the time their daughters began to differentiate themselves mentally and to practice physical separation:

Having denied their daughters the stability and security of a confident early symbiosis, they turned around and refused to allow them any leeway for separateness or individuation. Instead, they now treated their daughters and cathected them as narcissistic physical and mental extensions of themselves, attributing their own body feelings to them. The mothers took control over their daughters' sexuality and used their daughters for their own autoerotic gratification. As Fleiss puts it, "The mother employs the 'transitivism' of the psychotic"—"I am you and you are me"—in her experiencing and treatment of her daughter. The result, in Fleiss's patients, was that these daughters, as neurotics, duplicated many features of their mothers' psychotic symptoms, and retained severe ego and body-ego distortions. Their ego and body-ego retained an undifferentiated connection to their mother. (100)

In this context we note that Aurelia Plath described her relationship with her daughter as a sometimes "wonderful," sometimes "unwelcome" sort of "psychic osmosis" (*LH* 32). The poet herself represented the mother figure of "Medusa" (*CP* 224–26) as a jellyfish/mythic monster/vagina, who is both Freud's "symbol of horror" ("Medusa's Head" 106) and an object of ambivalent love. Like the jelly-faced, "loving and reproachful" mother in *The Bell Jar* (*BJ* 205–6), and like the mother in *Journals* who is consciously loving but unconsciously angry (*J* 269), the medusa confusingly possesses both a "lens of mercies" and an "unnerving head" (*CP* 224). Above all, she is "always there / Tremulous breath at the end of my line" (*CP* 225). Permeated by the maternal subjectivity, the speaker apotropaically declares: "Off, off, eely tentacle! / There is nothing between us" (*CP* 226). She thus implies not only that she and her mother have nothing in common but also that there is nothing dividing them (Quinn 108), that her mother has prevented her from achieving individuation. The author of *Journals* similarly complains that her mother "uses me as an extension of herself," adding, "I wish . . . I could be sure of what I am: so I could know that what feelings I have, even though some resemble hers, are really my own" (*J* 281, 282). She wants to convince herself that her mother has nothing to do with her own production of poems (*J* 281). These adult feelings indicate that Plath's self-analysis at eighteen remained accurate throughout her life: "You were frightened when you heard yourself stop talking and felt the echo of [your mother's] voice, as if she had spoken in you, as if you weren't quite you" (*J* 26).

If Plath did indeed experience the sort of relationship described by Fleiss and Chodorow, she must have felt dependent on her mother's ability to reflect back to her that she existed — and at the same time resentful of her mother's continuing power to mediate, to shape, and to claim her life and writing. She must have feared for her personhood when her mother was proximate — as did Esther Greenwood, who made a point of never living in the same house with her mother for more than a week at a time (*BJ* 140). Yet she must have feared even more being deprived of the maternal connection — again as did Esther, who wrote her fiction on her mother's paper and periodically determined to learn her mother's skill of shorthand (*BJ* 142, 144). The legacy of Plath's flawed relationship with her mother may have included her inability to be with her mother or to be without her; her construal of the maternal attachment as a "tentacle"; her double bind of need and mistrust that translated itself into an unstable ambivalence toward literary mothers; her ontological insecurity that produced creative self-doubt; and the combination of hostility and self-loathing that marked much of her emotional life. There were times when Plath seemed to free herself from this inheritance, achieving relatively independent and caring poetic speakers, as in "Three Women." But in her last nine months, beginning with the composition of "Elm," such moments rarely occurred. She was forced to construct her life and art, audaciously and resourcefully, out of the very affective conditions she could barely endure.

ALTHOUGH the literal scene of the mother-daughter relationship remains for us a permanently disappearing origin, we can observe its extraordinary textual enactment in the pages of the book the two women wrote together: *Letters Home*. This text is worth studying for its own sake. One of the most fascinating documents in the Plath oeuvre, it cries out for a seriousness of interpretation that it has rarely received. *Letters Home* is also worth studying for the light it sheds on Plath's creativity. The volume contains two overlapping but distinguishable dialogues: the one between mother and daughter preserved in the letters themselves and the one between editor-mother and author-daughter created by the volume's published form. In the first dialogue the mother's side must be inferred, since virtually none of her letters have been reproduced; apparently their recipient did not save them. In the second dialogue it is the daughter's side that must be inferred, since death has reduced her to the status of object in her mother's discourse. Within these dual dialogues we witness an uncanny interplay of signs and motives, and within that interplay a crucial sense of Plath's creative struggle: her duplicitous effort both to escape and to assume her mother's voice, to reject and to satisfy her mother's desire.

When Otto Plath died on November 5, 1940, Aurelia Plath "waited until the next morning to tell the children" (*LH* 24). As she told them of the death, her mind was already filled with plans. Her eight-year-old daughter's mind was, too. She returned from school with a "contract" for her mother to sign in which she promised never to marry again; after the signing, Sylvia behaved "briskly" and "matter-of-factly" (*LH* 25). Later, "as an exercise in courage," Aurelia Plath prevented the children from attending their father's funeral (*LH* 25). Here we glimpse the pattern the mother imposed on her daughter's emotional life: an automatic attempt to intellectualize crises and to repress negative feelings such as grief, fear, anger, and shame. If Aurelia Plath was "a remarkable woman, a true survivor," as Adrienne Rich has called her (*Woman* 231–32), a mother who "worked tirelessly" for her children despite a "painful and demeaning life" (Perloff, "Sivvy" 158), her strategies for survival exacted a considerable toll on her own emotional life and that of her daughter. Sylvia learned early to sublimate her feelings in a quest for achievement. "I *want* to go to school," she insisted on the day of her father's death (*LH* 25). She later found her identity in a drumbeat of accomplishment: "forty book reports . . . for her own enjoyment" in the fifth grade, an unbroken string of solid A's on report cards, later a scholarship to Smith, a fellowship to Cambridge, and an unending string of prizes and distinctions. During her two periods of psychoanalysis with Dr. Ruth Beuscher (in 1953 and 1958–59), Plath seemed to discover a sense of self larger than the sum of her awards and proficiencies — an adult identity capable of acknowledging a wide range of shifting emotions. But in the last months of her life she reverted to the affective constriction and deception that had previously characterized her.

Despite her mother's claim of a "psychic osmosis" — or in an effort to gain control over it — Plath generally hid her less positive thoughts and feelings from her mother, who she knew would disapprove of them. As Mary Lynn Broe has written, the two women resembled objects continually "grazing each other" but missing real intimacy ("Bond" 217). Plath told her brother Warren that she "shared really only the best parts [of her experience] with mother" (*LH* 240). We see such deception most clearly in the last year of her life, as she attempted to cope with her husband's infidelity and desertion and with the prospect of divorce. On June 15, 1962, in a period that her mother editorially characterizes as one of "marital torments" (*LH* 458), Plath wrote to her, "I don't know when I've been so happy or felt so well" (*LH* 457). But by August 27, after Hughes had left, Plath was writing of regaining "the weight and health I have lost this last six months" (*LH* 460). During the next period she struggled between an impulse to express grief and anger and an impulse to appear the courageous, decent, and self-controlled individual her mother wished her to be. Implicitly, the mother would have rejected the angry, uncontrolled, and suffering Sylvia — the real Sylvia — as indeed the mother rejects her posthumously, as we shall see.

Two themes appear in the letters Plath sent to her mother at this time. First is an unwillingness to encounter her: "I haven't the strength to see you for some time. . . . I cannot face you again until I have a new life" (*LH* 465). In contrast, Plath almost begged her sister-in-law, whom she had never met, to visit her. She clearly perceived her mother as a source of tension or disapproval, whom she could bear to see only in her strength, never her weakness. The second theme is Plath's desire to stifle her feelings and to perform an "exercise in courage" that would meet with her mother's approval (and therefore her own). For in her emotional difficulty, she had reverted to her mother's structure of achievement and willpower, reification and repression; she had returned to her childhood status, half-formed, emotionally dependent and short-circuited.

At several points in mid-October 1962, Plath rejected her mother's advice to avoid expressing her anguish in her poetry. In one memorable letter Plath wrote: "Don't talk to me about the world needing cheerful stuff! What the person out of Belsen — physical or psychological — wants is nobody saying the birdies still go tweet-tweet, but the full knowledge that somebody else has been there and knows the *worst*, just what it is like" (*LH* 473). In another she added: "Now stop trying to get me to write about 'decent courageous people'— read *Ladies' Home Journal* for those! . . . I believe in going through and facing the worst, not hiding from it" (*LH* 477). But the triumph of her art, in which she found her power by "facing the worst," was not paralleled in her life. For in life she attempted to follow her ·mother's advice and example. Aurelia Plath, at her husband's death, had refused to show grief or anger — though anger at her husband's dictatorial and self-destructive behavior seethes between the studiously objective lines of her preface to *Letters Home*. Her daughter, similarly, sought to suppress her outrage and sorrow at the death of her marriage. Just as she insisted to her mother that "we've been doing quite well" (*LH* 456) when in fact she and her husband were on the verge of separation, so she continued to take an optimistic tone after the separation, even when this ploy forced her into curious contradictions. Several letters in mid-October show her seriously examining her loss: "It is hurtful to be ditched" (*LH* 467); "the loneliness here now is appalling" (*LH* 467). But her characteristic strategy is to deny: "My only problems now are *practical* "

(*LH* 469); "I am fine in mind and spirit" (this concluding a letter of conspicuous desperation) (*LH* 470); "I am *glad* this happened *now*" (*LH* 475); "I can truly say I have never been so happy in my life" (*LH* 488); "I have never been so happy. . . . Everything is such fun" (*LH* 491–92). The point here is not simply that Plath was telling her mother what her mother wanted to hear, but that she had incorporated her mother's own strategy of denial. She was telling herself what she too wanted to hear.

Finally, as her mother puts it, Plath's "courage began to wear thin" (*LH* 486). In her last letter it is clear that the emotional self-deception could not continue: "I just haven't written anybody because I have been feeling a bit grim — the upheaval over, I am seeing the finality of it all, and being catapulted from the cowlike happiness of maternity into loneliness and grim problems is no fun. . . . I shall simply have to fight it out on my own over here" (*LH* 498). Exactly one week later she was dead. Painfully alone at the end, she had a self that was filled only when it included her mother, but a mother capable of sharing only positive feelings and accomplishments. Bereft and partial, she sought to repeat the trick that had worked so well for her at twenty: a symbolic death of the fractured and empty self, followed by psychotherapeutic sessions that would help her to create a new, independent, replenished self. But the maneuver failed this time. She replicated not her twenty-year-old self, the Lady Lazarus who came back from the dead, but the metaphor behind that metaphor: her father, a man divorced from feeling, without purpose except "the book" or "the chapter" he obsessively worked on (*LH* 13), who unconsciously willed himself to death.

Any reader of *Letters Home* must be struck by the insistent tone of self-praise that permeates the pages. The volume describes a world measured out in "A's," fellowships won and renewed, acceptance letters, compliments bestowed, applause, victories, triumphs — and, of course, the reverse: the fellowships lost, the rejection slips that are the gaping abyss that keeps the epistolary heroine stepping high, climbing resolutely. This is a world mutually created by the author and the reader of the letters, Sylvia and Aurelia Plath. The insistent paradigm is that of a poor, defenseless, and innocent young girl who, against all odds and her own expectations, triumphs through pluck, luck, and her natural but hidden superiority. The exemplary image is of Sylvia Plath, ending a difficult year of teaching "spoiled bitches" at Smith (*LH* 330) by measuring out the degrees of her triumph: "I was amused at my last day of classes to get applause in the exact volume of my own feelings toward every class: a spatter at 9, a thunderous ovation at 11 which saw me down two flights of stairs, and a medium burst at 3" (*LH* 341). The pattern, whether it involves applying for a grant, submitting a manuscript, teaching a class, or courting a husband, remains constant: inflation of the object (the most prestigious foundation, the best magazine, the biggest, most desirable man); deflation of the probabilities (I know I have no chance); and ultimately a surprising, immensely gratifying attainment of the goal. Over and over again, week after week, Plath and her mother shared these hopeless struggles and miraculous victories. The surprise never wore off, and the successes never satisfied for very long.

Sylvia Plath was born and raised to be an overachiever. Her mother, in her preface to *Letters Home*, carefully mentions first her own "double promotion" in grade school and then Sylvia's promotion (*LH* 4, 29). The quest for such promotions never ceased; and when Sylvia in any sense flunked a course — as in the failure to secure admission to Frank O'Connor's creative writing class that contributed to her first suicide attempt, or the failure of her marriage ten years later — she found herself in deep trouble. Showering her gifted daughter with praise for success throughout her life, Aurelia Plath proved a receptive audience for her daughter's endless recountings of trials and victories, though hardly of defeats. By omitting many personal and trivial passages, *Letters Home* allows this motif to stand out, but the motif organizes the letters even when they are read in their entirety. Plath's striving is simply the *donnée* of her discourse; one cannot read her letters without being implicated in their repetitive drama of struggle and reward, invisibility and recognition. That drama is in a sense Aurelia Plath's creation, describing the limits of her interest and imagination. If Plath's poetry and fiction represent her own fantasy life, her career represents that of her mother. "The high school years were such fun," Aurelia Plath writes in her introduction, almost as if she meant her own (*LH* 38). Perhaps sensing the oddity, she adds, "I'd taste [Sylvia's] enjoyment as if it had been my own." Near the end of her life, Plath complained to her brother that her mother "identifies much too much with me" (*LH* 472), and of course she wrote elsewhere about the fearsome maternal "clutch" and "tentacle" (*J* 280; *CP* 226).

Aurelia Plath's praise contained two key elements that subtly affected its character. First, the praise was directed at what her daughter achieved, never at what she was. Sylvia Plath's compulsive discourse of personal success implies that the mother's approval depended on her continued achievement. This was probably a conspiracy into which mother and daughter entered unknowingly. But its effect surely ran counter to the conscious desires of both participants. Rather than making the daughter more secure, each word of praise from the mother, each word of self-praise by the daughter, had the unintended result of making the daughter less secure. For the precariousness of each success raised the question whether it could be duplicated, and the psychic importance of each success reminded her that her value was contingent. Walking that tightrope of conditional acceptance, she must inevitably, eventually slip. Nowhere does one find an indication that Sylvia Plath was loved for herself. Mother and daughter shared a remorseless moral universe in which people were judged on the basis of what feat they performed or what use they served. Every accomplishment and every compliment only made Plath more aware of the inherent worthlessness of her inner being.

The second key element was that Aurelia Plath never gave unqualified praise. She was always keen to correct, to reprove, and to improve. While she did not make her daughter feel incompetent, neither did she allow her to feel fully competent. She forced her to occupy ambiguous space, to be always on approval. The daughter's descriptions of her teaching, child raising, travel plans, liberal politics, and writing arrangements often have a defensive air, as if preparing in advance for her mother's anticipated objections. In one of Aurelia Plath's last letters to her daughter (December 4, 1962; Smith ms.), she characteristically refrains from mentioning anything personal and instead delivers an almost angry lecture on how to forward Christmas boxes, how to read poems before a working-class audience, how to make the move to London, the necessity of furnishing the Devon house before renting it, the immortality of Frost's poetry, and so on. The editing of *Letters Home* similarly reveals Aurelia Plath's need to withhold complete acceptance. For example, she is willing, even eager, to make minor corrections in her daughter's letters. When her daughter in haste or perhaps ignorance writes of "the Brandenburg Concerto" (*LH* 188), the mother inserts a scholarly "[a]" to correct the egregious "the." When her daughter scrambles syntax or omits a preposition, the mother stands ready to make the necessary change, and always in ostentatious bracketed italics, never silently—though she silently crops whole sentences and paragraphs at will. She frames the letters with a personal essay that runs to thirty-six pages. She constantly appends information to her daughter's discourse, much of it unnecessary: for example, the exact nature of Auden's objection to Plath's poems ("[*Auden called them facile*]" [*LH* 315]). And she often suggests the unreliability of her daughter's narration: "Actually the girl in question was not suicidal" (*LH* 64); "her magnifying a situation all out of proportion" (*LH* 96); "actually, this emphasis on her lack of funds may have been an exaggeration" (*LH* 461); and so on. Indeed, everything Aurelia Plath ever wrote about her daughter includes this questioning of her veracity: see, for example, her letter to Harper & Row opposing the publication of *The Bell Jar* in the United States (*BJ* 309–10); her inserted disclaimer in *Journals* (*J* 266); and her essay "Letter Written in the Actuality of Spring."

Aurelia Plath's urge to correct her daughter, even after death, raises the question of her real feelings toward her. Certainly she was conscious only of loving her daughter and of intending *Letters Home* as a tribute to a young writer of genius. But just as Aurelia Plath seems ambivalent toward her husband in her introduction to the book, selecting details that make him appear deceptive, high-handed, and destructive, yet all the while maintaining an ostensibly nonjudgmental tone, so she seems ambivalent toward her daughter in the body of the book. Her editing supports Plath's observation in her journal: "I wasn't loved, but all the signs said I was loved" (*J* 269).

The ambivalence appears most clearly in Aurelia Plath's eloquent but curiously double-edged editorial comments in the final fifty pages of *Letters Home*. For example, her preface to the last nine letters concludes in this way:

> Feeling she needed a backlog of funds to prepare for the sterile periods every writer dreads, she had earlier sent out *The Bell Jar* for publication, stipulating that it appear under a pseudonym in the firm belief that this would fully protect her from disclosure.
>
> By the time the novel appeared in the London bookstores, she was ill, exhausted, and overwhelmed by the responsibilities she had to shoulder alone — the care of the children, the bitter cold and darkness of the winter, and the terrible solitude she faced nightly.
>
> Despite the strong support of her friends, her sure knowledge of the importance of her new writing, her deep love for the children, supportive letters from her beloved psychiatrist Dr. B., the hope of a reconciliation with Ted, and endless offers from her family to help her weather her crisis — her tremendous courage began to wear thin. (*LH* 483–86)

Despite the touching sympathy of these sentences, it is possible to detect two hidden agendas in them: first, to denigrate *The Bell Jar*, the novel Aurelia Plath thought "the basest ingratitude" (*BJ* 310); and second, to absolve herself and others of responsibility for her daughter's suicide. We are left to contemplate the conundrum of what "tremendous courage" might be required of a person surrounded by the "strong support" of friends, the "hope of a reconciliation" with her husband, and "endless offers" of help from her family. Of course, these phrases constitute a tissue of half-truths. Plath had cut herself off from her friends (as Alvarez makes clear in *The Savage God*), had reduced her family relations to the merest superficiality, and had no interest in a reconciliation with Hughes. The "hope" of a reconciliation projects Aurelia Plath's own desire rather than her daughter's (or perhaps the phrase was stipulated by Hughes). Mother and daughter had become virtual strangers to each other at the end. The daughter was going her own way, violating her mother's wishes by publishing *The Bell Jar*, writing the poems of *Ariel*, refusing to reconcile with her husband, and refusing to come home to the United States.

Yet if Plath had struck out for freedom, she could not really handle it. It left her feeling inadequate and desolate. Her letters of "desperation" in September and October 1962 resemble Hart Crane's demanding and hysterical letters to his mother over many years. Her superficial letters of November, December, and January and then her week-long silence in February are perhaps equivalent to the years in which Crane refused to communicate at all with his mother. Both cases manifest a similar pattern: a tension-filled hypersymbiosis, leading to physical separation, followed by suicide and the return of the mother to take over the literary remains of the child, in an attempt to "make right" the memory of the relationship. In both cases we see a neurotically intertwined parent and child, a struggle for dominance, and an ultimate failure of the child to sustain an independent adult life. Aurelia Plath, like Grace Crane, must have felt her child's repudiation deeply, hence her effort to disguise it to herself and to others through her publication of the letters, carefully selected to show her daughter's expressions of affection for her, carefully edited to vindicate her own role.

In its consequences for her art, Sylvia Plath's relationship to her mother undoubtedly outweighed her relationship to her father. Because her mother was consciously affectionate but unconsciously skeptical, Plath from an early age felt the need to invest herself in her texts: "I felt if I didn't write nobody would accept me as a human being. Writing, then, was a substitute for myself: if you don't love me, love my writing and love me for my writing" (*J* 281). In her last years, as she felt frustration at being unable to achieve "separateness and individuation" in life (Chodorow 100), she increasingly sought to achieve them in her art. One way she attempted to split from her mother was to portray her negatively in *The Bell Jar*. Esther Greenwood's recovery begins when she can admit to her psychiatrist that she hates her mother (*BJ* 244). Plath made a similar admission to her own psychiatrist in 1958 but was never able so much as to hint at such feelings to Aurelia herself. Plath covered her tracks by dismissing *The Bell Jar* as a "potboiler" (*LH* 472, 477), but its artistry and power suggest that it contains desires she found herself unable to act on in life. Another way she sought to achieve autonomy was to criticize her mother in her journals (while continuing to flatter her in her letters home). Plath's final and most important method of individuation, as Marjorie Perloff has also suggested ("Sivvy" 170–75), was to create a figure of herself in her late poems that bears little resemblance to the optimistic overachiever she projected in real life. Rather than being self-controlled, rational, and strong, her textual "I" is angry, frightened, uncertain, and given to destructive emotional states. Plath began the last poem she ever wrote with the assertion, "The woman is perfected" (*CP* 272). Thus it seems evident that her conflicted relationship to her mother helped to determine the character of her most powerful writing: its project of self-creation deferred from life to text.

In addition, Aurelia Plath's identity as a secretary and a teacher of secretaries intensified her daughter's confusion about her own identity. Although *The Bell Jar* portrays Esther's mother as encouraging her to acquire secretarial skills, *Letters Home* reveals that it was Plath herself who asked her mother to teach her those skills. Plath undoubtedly requested the assistance because she knew that it would please her mother, while refusing actually to learn the skills because they symbolized her death as a writer. It may be no accident that she frequently called her mother "Mummy." Learning secretarial skills stood in relation to her mother as learning German did to her father. Plath obsessed about both, especially when in psychological trouble, but could master neither. Although Aurelia Plath apparently composed the first draft of Otto Plath's treatise "Insect Societies" (*LH* 12), she, her husband, and her daughter all continued to conceive of her role as secretarial and his as authorial. Sylvia Plath must have begun by deciding that if authorship was inherently male, she would play the male role,

choosing Shakespeare, Yeats, Eliot, Roethke, and Lowell as her
poetic masters. Yet, as we have seen, this determined entrance
into the tradition of male inscription induced a massive
conflict. For she knew herself to be a woman; and beyond that
fact, her relations with her father, and eventually with her husband, were unsatisfactory. Her father dominated her and the
other family members, then rejected them by dying. Her husband similarly dominated her, then deserted her. Each retained
a lien on her creativity. Although as a girl Plath had fantasized
that her mother might work for *her* as a secretary (*LH* 103), during her marriage she insisted on functioning as her husband's
secretary, laboriously typing his manuscripts and circulating
them to publishers. In life, then, she set out to play both "feminine" and "masculine" roles, identified as secretarial/domestic
and authorial, while in art she set out to become a "masculine"
author. But instead of sustaining and challenging her, the male
literary tradition dominated her and threatened to reject her.
She determined to obliterate it first, as we have seen: when she
explodes, "Daddy I have had to kill you" (*CP* 222), it was
"daddy-poetry" as much as any autobiographical figure that
she meant. Her alternative, more adaptive solution to her problem was to redefine authorship as a female activity. Thus the
most articulate "voice" in her most female-identified poem belongs to a secretary-poet who argues that women are the natural creators (*CP* 177–79).

   In addition to her other functions, Aurelia Plath modeled
both audience and voice for her daughter. Sylvia Plath wished
to be loved for her words, and her mother faithfully read her
words, commented on them, and taped them to the walls of
her house. But she also displayed an unsettling will to power
over her daughter's texts. The daughter could never be sure
her words were actually her own. She feared that her mother
would "use" or "appropriate" them (*J* 281), just as she used and
appropriated her emotional life. Furthermore, the mother's discourse provided an ambiguous image of voice that the
daughter wished both to duplicate and to transcend. Even
more than the mother's role as verbal transcriber rather than
originator, her contradictions as reader and writer interfered

with Sylvia Plath's ability to trust the literary women who eventually took her mother's place.

During her second period of psychoanalysis, which culminated in the artistic self-discovery of late 1959, Plath asked
herself: "What to do with your hate for . . . all mother
figures? What to do, when you feel guilty for not doing what
they say, because, after all, they have gone out of their way to
help you?" (*J* 271). As we have seen, Plath's attachment to her
biological mother remained highly cathected and ambivalent.
She figured her as "Trouble-Making," as a "Medusa," as a
"hag" (*J* 167; *CP* 224-26, 70). Aurelia Plath seemed to offer
emotional sustenance but was "somehow not there" (*J* 286);
she gave mixed signals of ambition and sycophancy; and she
set career and domesticity at odds with each other, alternately
endorsing the primacy of one and then the other. Her denial of
emotional security during the earliest stages of childhood may
have provided the impetus for her daughter's life project, and
her emphasis on the importance of literature probably directed
the project's final form. Yet the mother's strict sense of propriety narrowed her definition of what literature might achieve;
her desire for control deterred her from giving her daughter's
efforts more than "guarded praise" (*J* 223); and her intolerance
of failure prevented her from accurately mirroring her
daughter's strengths and weaknesses. Thus Plath's filiation
with her mother inhibited the very creative activity it sparked.
On the one hand Plath needed to sense her mother near her in
order to feel whole. But on the other hand she wanted to "keep
clear" of her mother (*J* 261); she found that only expressing
"hostility" toward her mother could free her from the "Panic
Bird" in her heart and her typewriter (*J* 267); and she commanded the "mother of mouths" to "keep out of my barnyard"
so that she herself stood a chance of "becoming another" (*CP*
133).

Plath expected to have the same confusions in her relations
with the various mother figures in her life, and she did. "*Who
am I angry at?*" became a key question for her in 1958-59 (*J* 272).
Beyond being angry at the male conservation of power, she was
angry at "all the mothers I have known who have wanted me to

be what I have not felt like really being from my heart." For
Plath, the image of the mother — the literary mother as well as
the biological mother — involved competition, envy, misunder-
standing, and a desire to control, mixed with more supportive
traits of attention, help, and guidance. Unlike her biological
mother, Plath's female precursors were fully adequate, but that
adequacy posed a problem of its own, since it seemed to leave
little room for her own efforts. She regarded her creative mothers with a bifurcated emotional response. Although they often
appeared nurturing and even saintly, they also claimed what
Dickinson called "the power to kill" (poems 358, 754). Plath,
who was vulnerable because she loved them, had to be contin-
uously on guard.

If Plath rebelled against male tradition by feminizing its
tropes and thematizing her transgressive utterance, she gradually learned to accept female tradition while continuing to preserve herself against its bondage. As she matured, she increasingly compared herself with women writers rather than with
men. At first these comparisons made her "jealous . . . , green-
eyed, spite seething" (*J* 185), but by the end of her life they may
have consoled her. In early 1958 she wrote in her journal that
she saw no reason she should not "surpass" at least Isabella
Gardner and Elizabeth Bishop (*J* 189). Later she habitually
compared herself with Adrienne Rich (*J* 212, 219, 294, 296,
298). At a time when Rich was still composing "universalist"
poems, Plath was experimenting with just the kind of discourse that Rich would later term necessary: writing that
defines "a female consciousness which is political, aesthetic,
and erotic, and which refuses to be included or contained in
the culture of passivity" (*On Lies* 18). Plath's biographer writes
that she "sought out women as friends and mentors and long
admired the writing of Virginia Woolf, Marianne Moore, Stevie Smith, Elizabeth Bishop, and Anne Sexton" (Wagner-Martin
12). Plath's journals and letters attest to this growing interest in
women's writing. Exempting her patrons Olive Higgins Prouty
and Mary Ellen Chase, the women novelists she most often in-
voked were, in order, Virginia Woolf, Emily Brontë, Mavis
Gallant, and Jean Stafford. The women poets she most com-

monly mentioned were Marianne Moore, Adrienne Rich, Elizabeth Bishop, Louise Bogan, Emily Dickinson, and May Swenson (Axelrod, "Literary Relations").

I believe that Plath affiliated with two of these writers in particular: Virginia Woolf and Emily Dickinson. She lavished intense, ambivalent, and luminous attention on Woolf, whom she discussed more frequently than any other novelist, male or female. Conversely, her comments on Dickinson were brief and perfunctory, while her poems engaged in a ceaseless dialogue with her. Plath adopted divergent strategies to deal with the two literary mothers who most deeply penetrated her artistic identity. But if Woolf and Dickinson often made Plath struggle, they also offered her satisfying images of female creativity. Once, in "Three Women," she even achieved the kind of autonomous self-development in relation to them that she sought but never attained in relation to her mother.

DAEMONIZATION

PLATH took Virginia Woolf as a model very early in her career. She undoubtedly considered Woolf the greatest woman writer of the century. But beyond that appeal, she must have identified her own emerging life pattern with the one she saw in Woolf. Woolf too suffered loss at an early age; she too had a writer-father who was remote and demanding; and she too had an ambivalent, "obsessed" relationship to her mother, who remained an "invisible presence" in her life and art (Woolf, *Moments* 80; cf. Rosenman 3–71).

Moreover Woolf, like Plath, suffered through periods of intolerable mental pain. Woolf reputedly attempted suicide at thirteen; had a second breakdown at twenty-two; took a lethal dose of Veronal at thirty-one; had recurrences of mental illness from her early thirties on; and drowned herself in the river Ouse at the age of fifty-nine. When Plath at twenty tried to drown herself at Nauset Beach and then took an overdose of sleeping pills, she clearly had Woolf in mind. Nine months before, she had written in her journal: "I am a conglomerate garbage heap of loose ends — selfish, scared, contemplating devoting the rest of my life to a cause — going naked to send clothes to the needy, escaping to a convent, into hypochondria, into religious mysticism, into the waves . . . the colossal wave, sweeping tidal over me, drowning, drowning. . . . Why did Virginia Woolf commit suicide? Or Sara Teasdale or the other brilliant women?" (*J* 61–62). Several years later she confirmed the connection to Woolf: "But her suicide, I felt I was reduplicating in that black summer of 1953. Only I couldn't drown" (*J* 152). Whereas Woolf had weighted her coat pocket with a large stone before walking into the Ouse, Plath depicted Esther Greenwood diving repeatedly into the water only to pop up each time "like a cork" (*BJ* 191). Plath may well have been thinking about Woolf again during the black autumn and winter that ended her life. At the end of *A Writer's Diary*, which Plath knew well, Woolf describes her fears of a German invasion. To avoid the humiliation and torture that would await them, Woolf and her Jewish husband planned to gas themselves in their garage: "I reflect: capitulation will mean All Jews to be given up. Concentration camps. So to our garage" (323). In her own last months, Plath figured herself as a Jew at "Dachau, Auschwitz, Belsen," a being who melted to a "shriek" (*CP* 223, 246); and then she realized the metaphor by gassing herself in her kitchen oven.

If Plath thought of herself as Woolf's inheritor on the basis of their lives, she must also have noted the correspondence in their creative outlook. Woolf too felt in her "fingers" the "weight of every word"; she too equated "writing" with "living" (*Writer's Diary* 344, 347). For both Woolf and Plath, the text figuratively assumed the dimensions of a living person, while the self became a reader/writer — or nothing. During her final dark night, Woolf complained in her diary that "the writing 'I' has vanished. . . . That's part of one's death" (323). In her suicide note to her husband she wrote: "I can't fight any longer. . . . You see I can't even write this properly. I can't read" (Bell 226). Plath similarly discovered during her dark times that "the words dissolve and the letters crawl away" (*J* 298). She describes Esther Greenwood in her madness as being unable to write or read. In her last poem, "Edge," she depicts her "I" as "dead," its pitcher of words "empty" (*CP* 272). Woolf heard voices at the end; Plath did not; but for both of them suicide was intimately connected to the cessation of their textual voice. Plath intuited this similarity. As an adolescent, she wondered whether both her writing and Woolf's were a "sublimation" of "deep, basic desires" (*J* 62). Probably so, but I think that for both of them writing also *was* a basic desire: desire for creativity, for an erotically charged relationship to self-objects. When that "seething," "embarrassing" desire failed to sustain them (*J* 62), when the scrolling text momentarily halted, so did they themselves fail.

Plath first encountered Woolf in Bradford High School and Smith College, where Woolf was one of the few women writers admitted into the curriculum. Plath later recalled those occasions as involving a shock of recognition: "I love her — from reading *Mrs. Dalloway* for Mr. Crockett — and I can still hear Elizabeth Drew's voice sending a shiver down my back in the huge Smith classroom, reading from *To the Lighthouse*" (*J* 152). At Cambridge University, where David Daiches lectured eloquently on Woolf, Plath took pleasure in being considered "a second Virginia Woolf" (*LH* 230). She confided to her journal that she felt somehow "linked" to Woolf (*J* 152). In early 1957, just before moving back to the United States to teach at Smith, she bought the "blessed" *Writer's Diary* (*J* 152) and a set of Woolf's novels, which she read intently for months. She wrote in her journal that "Virginia Woolf helps. Her novels make mine possible" (*J* 168).

Even at this early stage, however, Plath was beginning to view her precursor ambivalently. She described herself as being similar to Woolf in that she was "overvulnerable, slightly paranoid," and yet different in that she was "so damn healthy & resilient" (*J* 152). The latter feeling was probably more wish than reality. Plath continued: "Only I've got to write. I feel sick, this week, of having written nothing lately. The Novel got to be such a big idea, I got panicked" (*J* 152). Thus, thoughts of Woolf and her novels made Plath feel "healthy" but also "overvulnerable," "paranoid," "sick," and "panicked." Woolf was a kindred spirit, but she was also one of the "Big Ones" who released the Panic Bird in Plath's heart (*J* 152). Plath's divided reaction to her precursor, conditioned by the ambivalent structure of her bond with her mother, typified her reflections during these formative years. In a letter to her mother, for example, she claimed that reading Woolf's diary empowered her, but her sentence reveals that it also enfeebled: "I get courage by reading Virginia Woolf's *Writer's Diary*; I feel very akin to her, although my book [a now-lost autobiographical novel] reads more like a slick best-seller" (*LH* 305). Woolf's prose exposed the "slick" and shallow nature of her own. In a similar vein, she wrote to her mother that Woolf's novels provided "excellent stimulation for my own writing" (*LH* 324), while she confided to her journal that they put her off. She anxiously wished she could be "stronger" than Woolf (*J* 165).

One of the crucial passages concerning Plath's desire to discover her voice through and despite Woolf's occurs in the *Journals* in mid-1957:

Last night: finished *The Waves*, which disturbed; almost angered by the endless sun, waves, birds, and the strange unevenness of description — a heavy, ungainly ugly sentence next to a fluent, pure running one. But then the hair-raising fineness of the last 50 pages: Bernard's summary, an essay on life, on the problem: the deadness of a being to whom nothing can happen, who no longer creates, creates, against the casting down. That moment of illumination, fusion, creation. . . . That is the lifework. I underlined & underlined: reread that. I shall go better than she. (*J* 164)

We can decipher two conflicting codes here. First, we note Woolf's desperate involvement in Plath's inner drama of "the deadness of a being . . . who no longer creates" yet who attempts to create nonetheless. Woolf's character Bernard raises the issue of imaginative self-actualization so powerfully that Plath segues without a pause from reflecting on Woolf's fiction to contemplating her own artistic hopes and fears. But second, we note the disparity between Woolf's achievement and Plath's aims: "I shall go better than she." Plath also felt competitive toward Woolf. At this point Plath seems to have had an ambiguous relationship to her precursor: she felt nurtured by Woolf (the good mother), awed by Woolf (the too-powerful mother), and endangered by Woolf (the bad mother). In this discussion of *The Waves*, we glimpse the beginning of Plath's effort to separate herself from a literary progenitor who could evoke such strong and conflicting emotions in her. Thus she concludes the passage by pronouncing Woolf's writing "too ephemeral" (*J* 165). Like a Bloomian strong poet, or like the inveterate player of zero-sum games that she was, Plath sought to enhance herself by diminishing Woolf. If she was to win, the precursor had to lose.

By 1959, the year Plath discovered her distinctive poetic voice, she was in full-scale revolt against her predecessor, a revolt that required her to misread Woolf as a minor novelist who merely "flits" about, throwing a "gossamer net" over her subjects (*J* 306). Having just finished reading Woolf's "tiresome" *The Years*, Plath dismissed not only that novel but virtually the entire oeuvre: "That is what one misses in Woolf. Her potatoes and sausages. What is her love, her childless life, like, that she misses it, except in Mrs. Ramsay, Clarissa Dalloway? Surely if it is valid there, she should not keep losing it to lighting effects" (*J* 307). Only a few years earlier Plath had praised Woolf because she "cooks haddock and sausage" (*J* 152); now she condemned her novels for lacking "potatoes and sausage." The metaphors derive from Woolf's last words in *A Writer's Diary*, which Plath, perhaps unconsciously, tried to turn against her: "I think it is true that one gains a certain hold on sausage and haddock by writing them down" (351). Recalling Plath's enduring equation of creativity with orality, we may suspect that the real issue for her was not the inclusion or exclusion of "sausages" from Woolf's prose, but rather the anxiety this master chef provoked in her sous-chef. By this time Plath was defining her literary task in opposition to her precursor's accomplishment: "I MUST WRITE ABOUT THE THINGS OF THE WORLD WITH NO GLAZING" (*J* 305). Although we do not have Plath's journals for her last years, her letters for that period numbly include Woolf along with Auden, Eliot, Lawrence, and Spender as emblems of a hidebound English high culture that had little to offer her (e.g., *LH* 369, 381, 397–98). If Woolf initially functioned for Plath as a "blessed" spirit and a source of "stimulation," she ultimately became just another canonical statue standing in her path, another depriving mother.

To UNDERSTAND the causes of Plath's disenchantment more precisely, let us loop back to 1958, when she was still in the floodtide of her mentorship. She wrote in her journal: "I felt mystically that if I read Woolf, read Lawrence (these two, why? their vision, so different, is so like mine) I can be itched and kindled to a great work" (*J* 196). In this passage, Lawrence seems to stand synecdochically for male writing. His stature was perhaps enhanced because Plath was writing an assigned paper on him for Dorothea Krook at Cambridge, and besides, he was Ted Hughes's favorite novelist. Woolf, on the other hand, seems to stand for female writing—that marginally situated, less prestigious tradition to which Plath herself wished to belong faute de mieux. A week later, Plath returned to the theme of Lawrence and Woolf as twin exemplars, and perhaps as prefigurations of the writers that she imagined her husband and she might become:

How does Woolf do it? How does Lawrence do it? I come down to learn of those two. Lawrence because of the rich physical passion — fields of forces—and the real presence of leaves and earth and beasts and weathers, sap-rich, and Woolf because of that almost sexless, neurotic *luminousness*—the catching of objects: chairs, tables and the figures on a street corner, and the infusion of radiance: a shimmer of the plasm that *is* life. I cannot and must not copy either. (*J* 199)

In this entry we observe not Gilbert and Gubar's "anxiety of authorship" but rather Bloom's "anxiety of influence" transposed to the world of women's writing. Plath warns herself that she "must not copy" Woolf, ironically copying Woolf's own futile warning to herself that she "must . . . not copy another" (*Writer's Diary* 347). Plath's self-injunction indicates that the possibility of weakly repeating Woolf looms as a real threat, since her own writing also exhibits "neurotic luminousness," catches "objects," and evokes "the plasm that *is* life." Plath makes Lawrence a relatively simple trope for Hughes, whose work she also identified with "woods and animals and earth" (*LH* 235).

But if she makes Woolf a trope for herself, she also makes her
a rival, an image of what she is not. "What is my voice?" she
had asked herself earlier, answering "Woolfish, alas, but tough"
(*J* 186). Although Plath's textual "I" would eventually achieve
a Woolfian "glitter" (*CP* 239), she would seem more anguished
than luminous; though she would catch objects, she would
catch them on "hooks." And rather than seem almost sexless,
Plath would increasingly place female generativity at the center of her imaginative vision.

Several interesting points arise here. Plath is content to let
Hughes reduplicate his precursor, Lawrence, but she herself refuses to "copy" either Lawrence or Woolf. She reveals that she
is unconsciously willing to relegate Hughes to the status of a
weak writer who identifies himself too closely with his precursor, while she reserves for herself the status of a strong writer.
Additionally, we note a complication in Plath's depiction of
Woolf. Although Woolf may capture a "plasm that *is* life," she
lacks a requisite toughness or earthiness. This is almost the
negative image of one of Woolf's stereotypes about herself—
especially in *A Room of One's Own*, where she critiques her
fiction, under the pseudonym of Mary Carmichael, as being
altogether too material (84–98). Plath's misprision of Woolf is
the crucial thing for us to consider: her wish to compose a countersublime to her precursor's sublime. Plath represented the
swerve in terms of her own ability to include the "things of the
world" in her texts as opposed to her precursor's "glazing" (*J*
305), but that distinction only disguises a more fundamental
difference. Plath's portrayal of Woolf as an ivory-tower aesthete
surely owed something to the commentary of her teachers Elizabeth Drew and David Daiches. More recently, critics like
Alice Kelley, Brenda Silver, Susan Squier, Pamela Transue,
and Alex Zwerdling have convincingly demonstrated Woolf's
textual engagement with the world. Plath's commentary on
Woolf is feeble, however, not because it reflects the critical judgment of her day but because it subserves Woolf's own depiction
of her texts as a dialectic between "inner" and "outer," or "luminous" halo and "external" fact (*Writer's Diary* 136; *Common Reader*
154). Whether Woolf or Plath prefers one pole or another at

any particular time matters less than Plath's fealty to Woolf's postromantic epistemology. Plath's repetition represents an exquisite evasion: first, because the distinction she attempted to draw between herself and her predecessor unites rather than divides them; and second, because Plath did not care deeply about the conflict between "glazing" and "things of the world." What was she trying to prevent herself from seeing by means of this evasion? I believe we can answer this question by considering an issue both writers cared about very deeply indeed: anger.

In the transitional year of 1959, Plath asked herself in her journal, "What to do with anger?" (*J* 305). Several short paragraphs later she commented, "Reading V. Woolf's *The Years*." The question of what to do with anger is more than fortuitously connected to Woolf, for it is one of the central issues in all of Woolf's work. That Woolf's answer to Plath's question, "What to do with anger?" differed so radically from Plath's own may begin to explain the later writer's ultimate sense of severance from her precursor. I have seen no evidence that Plath read Woolf's *Three Guineas*, though the connections she suggests among patriarchy, fascism, and war in "Daddy" and "Three Women" reflect the essay's central insight. But she certainly knew *A Room of One's Own*. She bought a cloth-bound edition in 1957 and kept it with her until her death, along with seven other Woolf volumes (*The Voyage Out, Jacob's Room, Mrs. Dalloway, The Waves, The Years, Between the Acts*, and *A Haunted House* [all at Smith]). Yet she seems not to have read *A Room of One's Own* with great enthusiasm, since it is unmarked. Plath shared with her mother the habit of underlining, bracketing, and annotating the books she read closely. She marked essays as well as poetry and fiction; indeed, key works of intellectual prose dropped to the bottom of her mind, where they remained (as James said of Dickens's novels). *A Room of One's Own*, however, seems to have dropped so low that it became inaccessible. Plath never mentioned it in her journals, letters, or essays. Although there is no way to ascertain her attitude toward this essay, we may speculate that she knew what was in it, at least vaguely, and perceived it as a threat.

I would posit two explanations for Plath's lack of receptivity to *A Room of One's Own*, one possibly superficial and the other profound. The superficial explanation is that when she bought the volume in Cambridge in 1957, during her first year of marriage, she resisted its radical commentary on the position of women writers "under the rule of a patriarchy" (*Room* 33). We recall that Woolf begins her essay—the first half of which was initially presented at Newnham College, Plath's own college—by contrasting the meagerness of "Fernham" (Newnham) with the abundance of male "Oxbridge." In the succeeding sections of the essay Woolf expands on the theme: "Why did men drink wine and women water? Why was one sex so prosperous and the other so poor? What effect has poverty on fiction?" (25). Such questions may have unnerved the newly married Plath at a time when she did not wish her own prospects to be described so bleakly and, further, when she did not wish to conceive of the literary world as patriarchally ordered. Although her marriage story of late 1956, "The Wishing Box" (*JP* 204–10), with its portrait of an impoverished female imagination, expressed a Woolfian pessimism, Plath generally repressed such knowledge until the final year of her life. In the mid-1950s she wished to succeed in the world as it was, and not simply as a writer but as a woman as well. She did not analyze the standing social organization too closely, fearing the alienation such scrutiny might bring. She was, in fact, ideologically committed to just the patriarchal rule that Woolf questioned. Woolf wrote sardonically that "women have served all these centuries as looking-glasses possessing the magic and delicious power of reflecting the figure of man at twice its natural size" (35). In her marriage, Plath frequently functioned as a magic mirror reflecting her husband at twice his natural size. To have read Woolf's essay with seriousness at this stage of her life would have threatened Plath's ego, which (like all egos) wished to conserve itself in its current configuration. Yet the author of "The Wishing Box" must have experienced the truth of Woolf's analysis daily and might have found some relief from suffering had she allowed herself to recognize its power openly. Woolf discredited what was false in Plath in the 1950s, discredited the ways Plath was false to herself, and Plath was probably attracted to the essay for that reason, though even more strongly frightened away.

A Room of One's Own includes a second element, however, that Plath would have found even more disturbing. I believe it is this element that kept her from ever turning to the essay, even after her dreams of reflecting the magnitude of man at twice his natural size had ended. Woolf in *A Room of One's Own* is deeply antagonistic to the kind of writer Plath would become. On the surface, Woolf seems hospitable to the young woman writer of the future. She begins and ends by speaking of the need of the woman writer to have "money and a room of her own" (4) — an idea that certainly spoke to Plath's condition, especially in her impoverished and harassed last six months. Woolf ponders "how unpleasant it is to be locked out; and how it is worse perhaps to be locked in" (24). She means here that women are locked out and men locked in, but Plath increasingly found herself to be both at once: locked out from male tradition and locked in to her subservient role by a patriarchal "jailer" who fed her only a "ghost ration" (*CP* 226-27) — or as Woolf would have it, a luncheon of water, custard, and prunes (*Room* 17). Woolf commiserates throughout her essay with women writers who like the Manx cat lack a tail (tale/phallus), who are forbidden the "safety and prosperity" of male tradition while suffering the "poverty and insecurity" of their own lot (24).

Yet despite such sympathetic gestures, Woolf's essay effectively disqualified Plath as an artist. Woolf wrote that "the artist's mind must be incandescent. There must be no obstacle in it, no foreign matter unconsumed" (58). Plath must have realized, if she read this, that Woolf would have disapproved of her own work. For Woolf assumes that anger destroys literary inspiration. Woolf is really of two minds on the issue. "Who shall measure the heat and violence of the poet's heart when caught and tangled in a woman's body?" she movingly muses about Shakespeare's imaginary sister Judith — who finally kills herself in despair (50). It is possibly not coincidental that Plath called Esther Greenwood "Judith" in her initial plans for *The*

Bell Jar (Smith ms.). Yet Woolf goes on to privilege "incandescence" and to disallow "heat and violence." Plath had probably inferred Woolf's position from her portrayal of Mrs. Ramsay, Lily Briscoe, and especially Clarissa Dalloway, who struggles so heroically against her own hatred. But in *A Room of One's Own* Woolf expresses herself propositionally: Anne Finch's poetry amounted to nothing because her mind was "distracted with hates and grievances" (62), Margaret Cavendish's work was similarly "disfigured" by rage (64), and so was Charlotte Brontë's (73). Plath must have wanted to close the book when she read such statements — or perhaps she refrained from opening the book precisely to avoid reading them. For in her own writing she frequently felt what Woolf would dismissively have called "anger tugging at her imagination and deflecting it from its path" (76). As we have seen, "What to do with anger?" was Plath's key personal and creative question. To have disavowed that anger would probably have forced her not to write. Similarly, she conceived of herself as a woman who must choose between conciliating men and rebelling against them. Yet Woolf ordained that the great creative mind neither rebels nor conciliates (77). Rather, it is "androgynous, . . . resonant and porous," "it transmits emotion without impediment," it is "undivided" (102). Plath's mind was indeed resonant, but not porous: it let foreign matter in and out only with difficulty. And though Plath's art is nothing if not a transmission of emotion, those emotions are characteristically cathected, impeded, and divided.

Woolf summarized her position in this way: "It is fatal for anyone who writes to think of their sex. . . . It is fatal for a woman to lay the least stress on any grievance; to plead even with justice any cause, in any way to speak consciously as a woman" (108). Adrienne Rich, Elaine Showalter, and Jane Marcus have all remarked on Woolf's debilitating need in *A Room of One's Own* to deny her femaleness and her anger. Rich criticizes Woolf for adopting "the tone of a woman . . . who is *willing* herself to be calm" (*On Lies* 37). Showalter argues that Woolf creates a female space "that is both sanctuary and prison. Through their windows, her women observe a more violent masculine world in which their own anger, rebellion, and sexuality can be articulated at a safe remove" (*Literature* 264). And Marcus wishes that Woolf had acknowledged her anger rather than burying it, because "anger is *not* anathema in art; it is a primary source of creative energy" (94). Alex Zwerdling has countered that "the whole literary climate of Woolf's time fostered the kind of detached, controlled, impersonal esthetic theory she adopted" (247). Zwerdling's point is well taken, but it should be noted that few of the male modernists seem to have repressed "grievance" to quite the degree Woolf did: think of Pound, Eliot, Hemingway, or Wyndham Lewis, for example, or Allen Tate challenging the philosopher William Barrett to a duel.

However that may be, Woolf's exclusion of aggressivity and gender identification from fiction must have had a negative impact on Plath. Plath regarded Woolf as the most authoritative spokeswoman women writers had. She probably magnified Woolf's importance, both because her mother had trained her to overestimate maternal authority and because Woolf's position eerily replicated Aurelia Plath's own. Aurelia Plath programmatically suppressed negative emotions, which she tended to interpret as "basest ingratitude" or want of "courage" (Ames 215; *LH* 486). According to one story, Plath believed that her mother "had never wanted her to become a woman, but rather to remain a neuter creature dependent upon her" (Butscher 170). Furthermore, Woolf's essay duplicated the didacticism, if it transcended the style, of Aurelia Plath's discourse. And what it prescribed was a kind of writing that no one could do so well as Woolf herself. Thus, Woolf's self-regard inhibited the development of Plath's own.

Just as Plath felt rejected by men's tradition, she now found herself rejected by women's tradition. And this latter rejection must have hurt even more than the other, for it was directed at her not as an unavoidable function of her sex but because of the kind of woman she was. Woolf sarcastically imagined a literary work of the future that resembled "a horrid little abortion such as one sees in a glass jar. . . . Such monsters never live long" (*Room* 107). She thereby conjured up and dismissed the author of *The Bell Jar* three years before her birth. The Plath who wrote in rage rather than calm, who was painfully aware of being female in a male-dominated world, who insisted on expressing grievances and pleading for just causes—this Plath found herself discredited by the very person she hoped would defend and sustain her. It would have helped could she have rejected Woolf's point of view, as Adrienne Rich was eventually to do, but Plath was too complexly involved with Woolf, too unsure of her own identity, too skeptical about her own creativity, and just too young to confront Woolf directly. Rather, she continued to pay homage, though with mounting reservations, to a literary mother she secretly and guiltily knew disapproved of her work. Woolf concludes her essay, which ostensibly advocates thinking "back through our mothers" (79), with an odd perception of its alternative significance: "There is no arm to cling to, we go alone, our relation is to the world of reality and not only to the world of men and women" (118). Sylvia Plath must have read those words, if she read them at all, with a chill of recognition. Her precursor offered no arm to cling to, wished her to go alone.

The problem for the writer, as for the person, is not simply that one will never live so long nor see so much as those who went before; the problem is also that the giants of the past may prove hostile. Although Plath opened the "vaults of the dead" in order to find support (*J* 165), she uncovered only another threat. "What to do with anger?" became transformed to "How to rebury the dead?" Yet if she reburied them, she would have no force capable of acknowledging her authority. She was illegitimate either way, with precursors or without them. Thus Woolf did not simply make Plath's novels "possible," as the young writer had hoped (*J* 168), she also made them impossible. Plath chose to ignore *A Room of One's Own* because it contained the intolerable secret that she received the "boot in the face" from her mothers as well as her fathers (*CP* 223). Like Woolf, she was an "Outsider" but without a Woolfian "Society" to join (*Three Guineas* 106); like Dickinson, she was "nobody" (poem 288); like Lowell, she was "unwanted" ("Unwanted"). Throughout her career, Plath underwent an enduring crisis of authority, the authority not simply to write but to be. Her relationship to her mothers—to Virginia Woolf as well as to Aurelia Plath—contains the mortal struggle with herself that was so crucial to her life and art and that may account for their continuing power over us. Plath asks, Do I exist? And if I do, as what? A freak, pariah, syphilitic? A "traitor, sinner, imposter" (*J* 61)? Or a person of worth?

Plath's relationship to Woolf demonstrates that it can be a more difficult and painful thing to think back through one's mothers than Woolf implied. For there are mothers who exact a horrendous "price" for their "care and influence" and who withhold their love if the price is not paid (*BJ* 263). Plath turned to Woolf as an intermediary who might absorb and replace Aurelia Plath—a better parent whose eloquence, intellect, and sympathy would supersede those of the original. Yet she chose an individual who demonstrated many of the traits she recognized as maternal: a need to control and to withhold, a wish to reprove, and a reluctance to grant autonomy. What was consciously an effort to achieve revenge or rescue was unconsciously an effort to duplicate the precise outline of her prison. Much as before, Plath found herself trapped in ambivalence—in need of just the strategies of duplicity, rebelliousness, acquiescence, and rage that she had honed from childhood.

PLATH revised Woolf primarily in the pages of *The Bell Jar*, though also in her short fiction and in her poem for voices, "Three Women." In the novel, Plath's response combines obedience with disobedience. Just as she fulfilled Aurelia Plath's wish that she achieve literary distinction and betrayed that wish by revealing feelings she should have kept hidden, so she enacted Woolf's desire for a female fictional tradition and subverted that desire by writing a novel brimming with "hates and grievances," noncooperation between the sexes, and bitter laughter (*Room* 62, 101, 94). Despite the subversion, if we ask the Plathian question, "Did she escape?" (*CP* 225), the answer is no. Although Woolf's program in *A Room of One's Own* offered Plath ambiguous support at best, Woolf's fiction penetrated her imaginative life. *The Bell Jar* reveals and conceals Woolf's

presence more strongly than either writer might have thought
or wanted.

According to Lois Ames (209), Plath wrote an early draft of
her novel in 1957—just when she was reading through Woolf's
oeuvre. She then let it sit for four years. In 1961, after a sleep-
less night during which she was "seized by fearsome excitement" at seeing "how it should be done" (Plath, quoted in
Ames 211), she rapidly wrote the novel over again. With her
remarkable ability to turn every writing activity into a transgression, she pretended to the Saxton Fellowship trustees in a
series of fake progress reports that she was composing the
novel in 1962, but in fact she had completed it late the previous
year (Smith mss.). Terming *The Bell Jar* an "apprentice work"
(Ames 213), she published it in January 1963 under an assumed
name.

The names one chooses for oneself are always significant,
and that is especially true of a writer like Sylvia Plath, who
thought that her names for things absorbed her identity. Publishing her novel pseudonymously—in secret from her mother,
who would have disapproved, and so to speak in secret from
her literary mothers as well—she chose the cognomen "Victoria Lucas." What meaning might that name have had for
her, and what might it tell us about her motives in writing *The
Bell Jar*? "Victoria" suggests victory—yet another instance of
Plath's conception of experience as a battle. One of the first
stories she ever published, in 1947, was called "Victory." Like
Thoreau in a well-known and curiously revealing passage of
Walden (chap. 2), she needed to "put to rout all that was not life,
. . . to drive life into a corner." "Victoria" may signify that her
novel represented a triumph over her enemies or over doubts
that she could write a novel. The text itself testifies to Plath's
association of fiction with revenge. At one point Esther Greenwood decides to "spend the summer writing a novel. That
would fix a lot of people" (*BJ* 142).

Plath also seems to have connected the name "Victoria" with
Queen Victoria and therefore with maternity, with the past,
and with a life devoted to mourning. In "Morning Song" the
"I" describes herself as being "floral" in her "Victorian night-

gown" (*CP* 157). Plath probably thought of her domesticated, widowed mother as Victorian, and she may also have thought of Virginia Woolf—born in what Lowell called "Victoria's century" (*Life Studies* 89) and the daughter of an eminent Victorian—as Victorian. Plath undoubtedly intended an ironic contrast between the name's connotations of nostalgic propriety and the grim, funny, and shocking modernity of *The Bell Jar.* She may have been suggesting, perhaps unconsciously, that the novel represented the flowering of Aurelia Plath's own stunted aspirations for success, creativity, and voice. And she may have been implying a relationship between Virginia Woolf and herself as well. She may have conceived the novel as both a victory *by* Woolf, the patron saint of female novelists, and a victory *over* Woolf, the scourge of women writers who emphasize "grievance" and speak "consciously as a woman" (*Room* 108).

This latter possibility looms large when we consider the similarity in the names Victoria Lucas and Virginia Woolf. One might even trace the etymology backward from "Lucas" through "Lupus" (wolf) to "Woolf." "Victoria" begins with the same two letters as "Virginia" and ends with the same two letters. Both first names have an identical number of letters, as do the two last names (and Plath's own last name). As I noted in chapter 1, such considerations mattered to Plath, whose conception of "self" was heavily rhetoricized. Interestingly, she used "Victoria Lucas" as her heroine's name as well as her own authorial name in the typed draft of the novel—a striking example of her difficulty in separating biographical identity from textual immanence. Only a query from her editor made her realize the oddity of the duplication, at which time she changed her heroine's name to "Esther Greenwood" (Smith ms.). In the published novel Esther names her own fictional heroine "Elaine" (*BJ* 142), but in the typescript Victoria names her heroine "Virginia." Thus, as in Freud's case study of the Wolf Man, a Woolf seems to be hiding in the Greenwood. In both typescript and published version, Esther/Victoria composes her novel after feeding a "virgin" sheet into her typewriter (*BJ* 98)—just as Woolf observed stories developing in her "virgin" mind (*Writer's Diary* 100). The adjective may suggest Plath's associa-

tion of fiction with Virginia Woolf as well as with sublimated
sexual desire. But the latter connotation indicates that even if
Plath wanted to think back through her mother, the very act of
writing marked for her a transition from virginal daughter to
experienced woman. In writing she cut the umbilical cord,
creating a looser bond that allowed for a sense of competence
and autonomy.

Although *The Catcher in the Rye* served as *The Bell Jar*'s struc-
tural model (Wagner-Martin 187), *Mrs. Dalloway* functions as
the more essential, if less obvious, parent text. *The Bell Jar*
differs from *Mrs. Dalloway* in several ways. Reflecting its debt to
American realist tradition, it transforms the precursor's high
ironies into satire. It also offers a superficially different protagonist. Esther Greenwood is an American late adolescent, self-
conscious about her sex and seeking to negotiate a passage to
adulthood without any "ritual" to support her (*BJ* 290); Clarissa
Dalloway, conversely, is a middle-aged, upper-middle-class
Englishwoman firmly ensconced in a social web. Esther is the
kind of person who steps on as many feet as possible as she exits
a theater and who achieves a catharsis by giving herself permission to "hate" (*BJ* 51, 244); Clarissa struggles nobly against
"hatred," which she pictures as a "monster grubbing at the
roots" (*Mrs. Dalloway* 17). Within this system of differences, however, *The Bell Jar* undertakes to retell and to revise *Mrs.
Dalloway*'s fundamental story. Like its precursor, it examines a
woman's place, choices, and suffering in a patriarchal culture,
posing self-annihilation as one possible antidote to pain. We
recall that Shakespeare's Hamlet considers suicide in a dazzling
variety of languages and then effectively commits it in silence:

> Had I but time — as this fell sergeant, death
> Is strict in his arrest — O, I could tell you —
> But let it be.   (5.2.347–49)

Conversely, both Clarissa and Esther mutely anticipate suicide
and then eloquently reflect on it, Esther as she recovers from
her attempt, Clarissa when she learns of the death of her
double, Septimus Smith. Borrowing Harold Bloom's metaphor
of "daemonization" from *The Anxiety of Influence* (99–112), we

might call Woolf's novel the "daemon" of *The Bell Jar*, the divine incubus that gave it birth. Plath acknowledged the power of her daemonization by incompletely repressing it. Just as she chose to live across an ocean from her mother yet continued to correspond regularly, so she wished to separate from her precursor while avoiding abandonment.

Almost all critics have assumed that *The Bell Jar* is, in the words of Eileen Aird, "largely autobiographical" (98). In a provocative reading, Lynda Bundtzen has disturbed the universe by calling the novel "closer in form and style to allegory than autobiography" (112). She suggests that it allegorically depicts three aspects of femininity: "the woman's place in society; her special creative powers; and finally, her psychological experience of femininity" (113). Unfortunately, Bundtzen's analysis ultimately develops into an exposure of Esther's — and Plath's — "repressed desire to be a male" (140). The allegory becomes a version of autobiography after all, and one modeled on Freud's androcentric notion of the castration complex at that. Without questioning the presence of autobiographical and allegorical codes in *The Bell Jar*, I propose that we study a third code: the intertextual. "Esther Greenwood" reflects not only Plath's actual and fantasy life and her sociological concerns, but her involvement with literary history. To perceive the wonderful and unwelcome osmosis of Woolfian and Plathian texts, let us read the characters of Clarissa and Esther as an interlocking system of repetition and difference. We may take encouragement from Jean Starobinski's comment that decipherers "have a free range: a reading which is symbolic or numeric or systematically attentive to a partial aspect can always bring to light a latent depth, a hidden secret, a language within a language" (124). Even if our reading fails, there will remain to us, as Starobinski consolingly concludes, "the constant attraction of the secret, of anticipated discovery, of steps astray in the labyrinth of exegesis" (124).

Clarissa Dalloway, recuperating from illness, initially appears "very white" and fragile as a bird (*Mrs. Dalloway* 4). Married to a dullard "who could not bring himself to say he loved her; not in so many words" (179), she has a perpetual sense of

"being out, out, far out to sea and alone" (11). She can recall
only one moment of passionate contact in her life, a girlhood
kiss from her friend Sally Seton. Even motherhood has proved
unrewarding, since Clarissa feels "unmaternal" (290). Nor has
she fully recovered from the Great War, which "had bred in
them all, all men and women, a well of tears" (13). In her "solitude" (181), she feels "invisible" to others (14). She had refused
her first admirer, Peter Walsh, because he would not have
granted her "a little licence, a little independence" (10), yet
even married to Dalloway, she feels submerged: "This being
Mrs. Dalloway; not even Clarissa any more; this being Mrs.
Richard Dalloway" (14).

Esther Greenwood resembles Clarissa in that she too is isolated, uncertain, and emotionally "empty" (*BJ* 3). If Clarissa
imagines herself alone in a vast solitude, Esther figures herself
as "a small black dot": "It's like watching Paris from an express
caboose heading in the opposite direction—every second the
city gets smaller and lonelier and lonelier, rushing away from
all those lights and that excitement at about a million miles an
hour" (*BJ* 20). If Clarissa feels dangerously "out to sea," Esther
has to work to keep her "head above water" in conversation (*BJ*
66) and eventually tries to kill herself by swimming out into the
ocean (*BJ* 188–91). If Clarissa has suffered from the Great War,
Esther is grieved by the Cold War, metonymically represented
by the electrocution of the Rosenbergs. Even more "invisible"
than Clarissa, Esther feels that she resembles "the negative of
a person I'd never seen before" (*BJ* 11); she is a "secret" even
from herself (*BJ* 176). Whereas Clarissa can at least recognize
in her mirror the "pink face of the woman who was that very
night to give a party; of Clarissa Dalloway; of herself" (*Mrs.
Dalloway* 54), Esther observes in her mirror only a "big, smudgy-
eyed Chinese woman," a "sick Indian," or a "conglomeration
of bright colors" (*BJ* 22, 133, 208).

Like Clarissa, Esther resents men for dominating her but cannot alter their behavior. She complains that Buddy Willard, who
resembles a humorless Peter Walsh, "was always trying to explain things to me and introduce me to new knowledge" (*BJ* 79).
He proposes by asking her, "How would you like to be Mrs.

Buddy Willard?" (*BJ* 109), echoing Clarissa's comment about "being Mrs. Dalloway; not even Clarissa any more." Buddy confidently repeats his mother's maxim that "What a man is is an arrow into the future and what a woman is is the place the arrow shoots off from" (*BJ* 83); he insists in a "sinister, knowing way" that after Esther has had children she will forget about writing poetry (*BJ* 100). The other men she meets are at least equally destructive, except for one who lethargically falls asleep in her company. Marriage to any of the men depicted in the novel would mean cooking, cleaning, and washing from morning to night; it would mean going about "as a slave in some private, totalitarian state," a "dreary and wasted life for a girl with fifteen years of straight A's" (*BJ* 99-100). With twice her husband's wits, she would have "to see things through his eyes — one of the tragedies of married life," as Clarissa says (*Mrs. Dalloway* 116).

The Bell Jar preserves these tensions about marriage to the very end, neither repressing nor resolving them. Like the "unmaternal" Clarissa, Esther feels herself to be "unmaternal and apart" (*BJ* 265). As in *Mrs. Dalloway*, lesbian love almost becomes a viable alternative — Esther's psychiatrist tells her that what one woman sees in another is "tenderness" (*BJ* 262) — but it does not. After her analysis, Esther affirms that she has become her "own woman" (*BJ* 266), implying the strength to avoid what Clarissa calls the tragedy of married life, yet we know that as she composes the narrative she is indeed a wife and mother. Although the nature of that marital existence remains provocatively uncharacterized, Esther's offhand comment about cutting plastic starfish "for the baby to play with" (*BJ* 4) resonates ominously with her prediction that "if I had to wait on a baby all day I would go mad" (*BJ* 265). If Esther, like Plath herself, wishes to be both a housewife and a professional writer, the social arrangements of her time compel her to choose. The novel's comedic ending, which implies both marriage *and* a writing career, coexists uneasily with the novel's acute depiction of a war between female desire and cultural expectations. Although Esther wishes to think of herself as having been "born twice," as Teresa De Lauretis (173-83) and Judith Kroll (104-5) have noted, she also figures herself as a

"patched" and "retreaded" tire, ready to blow again (*BJ* 290).
Her narration of past conflict thus points toward an even
greater explosion to come, down the road she cannot foresee —
a time and place Plath later represented twice and destroyed
twice, first in the idealized marriage novel she composed and
burned in spring 1962 and then in its debunking revision, the
lost satire titled *Double Exposure*.

Both Clarissa and Esther confront death, though in different
ways. Clearly, Clarissa has contemplated suicide in the past
and continues to consider it. When she learns of the stranger
Septimus Smith's suicide, she recalls a time when she said to
herself, "If it were now to die, 'twere now to be most happy"
(*Mrs. Dalloway* 281). "Even now," the text continues, "quite often
if Richard had not been there reading the *Times*, so that she
could crouch like a bird and gradually revive, send roaring up
that immeasurable delight, rubbing stick to stick, one thing
with another, she must have perished" (281–82). Clarissa as-
suages her suffering through her capacity for invention in
everyday life. "Heaven only knows why one loves it so, how one
sees it so, making it up, building it round one, tumbling it,
creating it every moment afresh" (5). She also finds consolation
in the way her "incompatible" fragments of self coalesce into
"one centre, one diamond, one woman" when plunged into
"the very heart of the moment" (54–55). Thus the reciprocal
activities of "making a world" and "making oneself" save her
(114, 81), activities that occur paradigmatically in the giving of
a party. Significantly, Clarissa's party text and the novelistic
text conclude simultaneously in a moment of pleasurable self-
confirmation: "For there she was" (296).

Whereas Clarissa experiences self and world as an eternal
"ebb and flow" that occasionally coalesces into a "centre" (*Mrs.
Dalloway* 12, 54), Esther suffers from a rigidly polarized conception of experience that prevents her from achieving a unified
or satisfying sense of self or world. One moment she resembles
the "Pollyanna Cowgirl" Betsy at heart (*BJ* 7, 27); the next
moment the cynical, "dirty" Doreen is a "secret voice" speaking straight out of her own bones (*BJ* 27, 8). Everywhere she
looks, she sees sets of mutually exclusive "twins" (*BJ* 40): vir-

ginal June Allysons and sexy Elizabeth Taylors (*BJ* 49), men
named "Attila" and "Socrates" (*BJ* 60), "people who had slept
with somebody and people who hadn't" (*BJ* 96). She constructs
these dichotomies to stabilize a shifting and confusing cosmos,
yet they in turn construct, fix, and menace her. Images of pri-
sons, barbed wire, manacles, and enclosures proliferate in her
discourse, just as images of space, fluidity, and flight proliferate in Clarissa's. Whereas Clarissa equates London with life,
Esther associates New York with an Eliotesque wasteland of
"cindery dust" (*BJ* 1), with a Conradian "jungle" of moral inver-
sion (*BJ* 13), with a Puritan hellfire in which one is "burned
alive" along the nerves (*BJ* 1). Unlike Clarissa, whose sense of
dispersal yields to an instant of pleasurable definition, Esther
moves from strangulating pairs of fixed definitions to attempted
suicide. This event paradoxically allows her to bury her rigid
way of knowing and to make a new world hypothesis. In the
end, she juxtaposes her indubitable subjective presence—"I
am, I am, I am" (*BJ* 289), perhaps an echo of Woolf's own "I
am I" (*Writer's Diary* 347)—with the dense unfathomability of existence: "All I could see were question marks" (*BJ* 290). Now resembling Clarissa, she claims to feel "surprisingly at peace"
and "open to the circulating air" (*BJ* 257). Yet Esther's last metaphor of self brings this peripeteia into question. As noted, she
figures herself as a patched tire (*BJ* 290)—an inanimate object
that, like the "I" in "Daddy," has been "stuck together with
glue" (*CP* 224).

Both Clarissa and Esther symbolically undergo their death
by means of a double, who represents, enacts, and purges their
suicidal impulse. Septimus Smith, whose story interlaces with
Clarissa's, replicates her experience in more extreme terms.
Even more than Clarissa, Septimus feels alone, loveless, confused, guilt-ridden, and imaginatively thwarted. He has experienced loss in the war firsthand, whereas her own losses were
abstract. His ideas, though crazed, correspond to her own:
"First that trees are alive; next there is no crime; next love, uni-
versal love" (*Mrs. Dalloway* 102). In one sense his "message" (126)
is the opposite of Clarissa's party, but in another sense it is identical: self-transformation through an "embrace" with otherness

(281). The text reinforces the two characters' correspondence through verbal echoes. Just as Clarissa feels "far out to sea and alone," so Septimus resembles a "drowned sailor" who has gone "under the sea" (104); just as Clarissa reiterates "Fear no more the heat of the sun" from *Cymbeline*, so Septimus thinks "fear no more" when he is about to kill himself (211). Septimus is Clarissa without her ability to perceive, to create, and to connect, without her languages and mediations. Unlike her (but like Esther Greenwood), he can no longer "feel" (130–31) or discover "meaning" (133).

Although they never meet, Clarissa and Septimus are a part of each other, each one expressing the other's hidden significance. Clarissa believes that "to know her, or anyone, one must seek out the people who completed them" (*Mrs. Dalloway* 231). When she learns of Septimus's death, she understands his motives intuitively, for he is simply one of her selves. She first thinks, "Oh! . . . in the middle of my party, here's death" (279). Septimus's suicide is the obverse that reveals the hidden nature of her own "offering" to life. She accurately guesses that he chose to die because "life is made intolerable, they make life intolerable, men like that" (281), men like Dr. Bradshaw and Dr. Holmes (precursors of Plath's inept Dr. Gordon). But as she continues to cogitate, Clarissa understands in a deeper way why the young stranger had "flung it away" while the rest of them would go on living a while longer:

A thing there was that mattered; a thing, wreathed about with chatter, defaced, obscured in her own life, let drop every day in corruption, lies, chatter. This he had preserved. Death was defiance. Death was an attempt to communicate; people feeling the impossibility of reaching the centre which, mystically, evaded them; closeness drew apart; rapture faded, one was alone. There was an embrace in death. (281)

Just as Clarissa is "completed" by Septimus, so he is completed by her in this passage, for she articulates the meaning in his mute act, the meaning he himself seemed not to understand. At this moment we cannot tell which of the two is the more heroic, Septimus or the middle-aged hostess who "felt somehow very like him — the young man who had killed himself"

(283). She "felt glad that he had done it; thrown it away," for he embodies a force similar to the one Robert Lowell identified in Plath, the voice that whispers, "Come, if only you had the courage, you too could have my rightness" (Foreword x). Ultimately it may take more courage to bear living with Richard Dalloway than to impale oneself on rusty spikes, but for the moment Septimus is for Clarissa a hero of negation, just as she herself embodies the Stevensian passion for yes that underlies every no. '

In a similar way, Esther Greenwood encounters her death through the suicide of Joan Gilling. Esther and Joan lead parallel lives. They come from the same town; have attended the same church and college; have dated Buddy Willard; attempt suicide; and recover at the same hospital. Yet they also rival each other. When Joan seems to be making the faster progress, Esther regards her with envy: "I gathered all my news of Joan into a little, bitter heap, though I received it with surface gladness. Joan was the beaming double of my old best self, specially designed to follow and torment me" (*BJ* 246). The two characters seem halves of the same whole: when one waxes, the other wanes; when one chooses to live, the other dies. Like Clarissa and Septimus, they inhabit a world of interdependent signs. Contemplating her sexual and attitudinal differences from Joan, Esther thinks, "Her thoughts were not my thoughts, nor her feelings my feelings, but we were close enough so that her thoughts and feelings seemed a wry, black image of my own" (*BJ* 261). Ultimately, in spite of reservations, Esther thinks that she "would always treasure Joan. It was as if we had been forced together by some overwhelming circumstance, like war or plague, and shared a world of our own" (*BJ* 268).

In one sense, Joan duplicates Septimus Smith's function. Like Septimus, Joan has experienced disaster firsthand — "war or plague," in Esther's words — and gives the image of that horror back to the double who has also experienced it. After Esther loses her virginity, and perhaps as a result of that act of separation, Joan hangs herself — a method of suicide Esther herself had once contemplated. Joan enacts Esther's death impulse just as Septimus enacts Clarissa's. Yet in another sense Joan

functions as Septimus's virtual opposite. She attaches herself to
Esther parasitically, embodying both the "beaming" image of
Esther's salesman self and the "black" image of her secret self
(*BJ* 246, 261). More closely resembling Richard Dalloway than
Septimus Smith, she symbolizes the animal life with which one
must cohabit (she reeks of horses), rather than the pure soul
destroyed by a world of flesh. Furthermore, whereas Septimus's
suicide becomes "part" of Clarissa's life-enhancing party,
Joan's suicide contrasts with Esther's recovery. Rather than
Septimus *and* Clarissa, we read Joan *or* Esther. At her friend's
funeral, Esther wonders "what it was I thought I was burying"
(288), implying that it is a portion of herself that she inhumes —
the wish to die, which in this novel is not a transcendent "defiance" and "embrace" but a last, alienated gesture. Whereas
Clarissa celebrates Septimus's death as a transumptive echo of
her own love of life, Esther conceives of Joan's demise as a
"shadow" or reversal of her own resurrection (*BJ* 288–89). We
witness here the textual pattern common to each author:
Woolf's wish to balance, to add, and to unite; Plath's need to
defeat, to divide, and to conquer.

We might well suppose that these conflicting sign systems
were at work in the writers' psyches as well as their texts — that
Woolf's suicide was a transcendent "embrace," whereas Plath's
was simply an angry shutting of the heart. But we must bar the
impulse to literalize relations between biography and art. Inscribed texts include distorted and even reversed images of
authorial psyche; lived experience alternately reflects and
defies the text. I believe that for Woolf and Plath alike, suicide
represented a release from intolerable pain and a termination
of the signifying process — "signifying" in the double sense of
"purveying meaning" (as a text signifies something) and "having standing" (as a person is significant). Plath's death was
more a repetition of Woolf's than a contradiction. Since Woolf
in *A Room of One's Own* foretold and sought to prevent Plath,
and since Plath in *The Bell Jar* strongly misread her foreteller,
the two writers' life histories as well as their texts interpene-
trated. When the young Plath asked herself, "Why did Virginia Woolf commit suicide?" (*J* 62), she was really asking,

"What can I do to avoid the same fate?" In having Esther "bury" rather than incorporate Joan, Plath may have been striving to inter her own Woolfian aspect and destiny. Plath's speaker may have hoped that she was burying Woolf's presence in her text. "Virginia," after all, was Victoria Lucas's name for her otherness. But like Madeline Usher, Woolf continued to breathe, and she finally returned to embrace her kin. Plath's subject and text were too highly compacted of the image of the precursor to resist.

Plath did indeed think back through her mothers, more so than she even knew. And the most prominent progenitor of all—the writer who showed her what it meant to be a powerful female creator, the writer whose rhetorical acts incorporated her life and whose death doubled her words—that literary mother was Virginia Woolf. Consciously or unconsciously, Plath substituted Woolf's textual immanence for her mother's empirical reality and, like Lily Briscoe, found her motive for existence in the creative enterprise—a salve for life's injury. According to Bloom's revisionary ratio of "daemonization," an "intermediary being, neither divine nor human" enters into the adept (*Anxiety* 15). Plath similarly opened herself to what she believed to be a power associated with Woolf, a power intended to ward off or transform the power of the biological mother. She then attempted to resist that intermediary being, becoming in effect the daemon's daemon. As a result, the texts of the two writers interact across time. I believe that Plath is most influenced by her precursor in the passage describing the myriad "question marks" at the end of *The Bell Jar* (290). Speaking through Esther, Plath abandons her characteristic struggle for "sure" knowledge and accepts Woolf's reality, which consists of an "incessant shower of innumerable atoms" (*Common Reader* 154). At this moment of near synonymity—but even in the moments of Plath's resistance and denial—we might say of Woolf what she herself says of Clarissa Dalloway: "She survived; . . . part of people she had never met; being laid out like a mist between the people she knew best, who lifted her on their branches as she had seen the trees lift the mist, but it spread ever so far, her life, herself" (*Mrs. Dalloway* 12).

SEPARATION

WHEN Sylvia Plath wrote poetry, a host of female presences hovered about her. The eleven historical "rivals" she mentioned in her journal make a good beginning list: Sappho, Elizabeth Barrett Browning, Christina Rossetti, Amy Lowell, Emily Dickinson, Edna St. Vincent Millay, Edith Sitwell, Marianne Moore, May Swenson, Isabella Gardner, and Adrienne Rich (*J* 211-12). To those names we might add some others: Sara Teasdale, Elizabeth Bishop, and Anne Sexton, for example. But of all women poets, Emily Dickinson was undoubtedly the germinal influence—the one poetic "giantess" (*J* 212) who achieved a stature equivalent to Woolf's in prose fiction. Plath studiously avoided mentioning Dickinson in essays written in high school, college, graduate school, or later life; she did not teach her precursor's poems at Smith or keep a volume of her work in her permanent library, and she referred to Dickinson only perfunctorily in journals and letters. Whereas she obsessively read Woolf in order to learn from her and to surpass her, she seems to have repressed Dickinson, possibly fearing that she had already learned too much from her and could never surpass her. If Plath did indeed feel influenced by Dickinson, she must have experienced a powerful contradiction between that dependency and her need for autonomy.

Since Aurelia Plath writes that she considered Dickinson her "new bible" (*LH* 5), we can easily fathom her daughter's reluctance to displace Dickinson, or even to appear to do so. For one thing, given Aurelia Plath's stringent adherence to standards, she would probably continue to prefer her "bible" to her daughter's revisions of it. But even if the mother's use of the term "bible" was hyperbolic, it remains significant that she chose to introduce her daughter's posthumous collection of letters by reference to the Amherst poet. In the reading regime she established for her young daughter, Emily Dickinson "was a constant" (Aurelia Plath, Talk). Later, she sent her daughter to college in Northampton, a stone's throw from Dickinson's hometown. Whether Aurelia Plath intended it or not, Sylvia Plath established a lifelong identification with Dickinson. As early as September 1951, Eddie Cohen, her most insightful early correspondent, compared her to Dickinson (Indiana ms.). In April 1953, four months before her first suicide attempt, she wrote three poems in conscious imitation of Dickinson's style: "Admonition," "Parallax," and "Verbal Calisthenics" (*LH* 110–11). When she became pregnant in 1961, she decided that if her baby was a girl she would name her "Megan Emily," partly in honor of the poet (*LH* 407). And in the flush of her October 1962 exuberance, four months before her death, she boasted to her brother that she was the first woman poet A. Alvarez had taken seriously "since Emily Dickinson" (*LH* 476). If we agree with Bloom that the meaning of a poem can only be another poem, we begin to suspect that Plath's poetry "means" Dickinson's. Certainly her poetic ambitions were entwined with those of her predecessor.

I believe that Dickinson played three interrelated roles in Plath's creative economy. First, she functioned as Plath's poetic mother, replacing the biological mother with whom she was associated. Second, she was Plath's poetic child, since Plath regarded her texts as children and wished to name her child "Emily." Finally, she was Plath's poetic double, whose struggle for voice portended, permeated, and rivaled Plath's own. The younger poet seemingly projected all the considerable ambivalence she felt toward her biological mother onto her poetic mother/child/double. As in a symbiosis, Plath enacted Dickinson's repressed desire on the stage of her own life and texts. At the same time, she attempted to separate herself from Dickinson by refusing to read her or to speak of her, a futile *dédoublement*, since Dickinson was already present in her purpose and utterance.

Charles Newman's early essay "Candor Is the Only Wile" initially established the affinities between the two poets by interweaving their verses and arguing that "Emily is in many way the beginning, and Sylvia the culmination of the movement whereby the imagination, sated with the abstraction of myth, is driven back to the concrete" (29). Subsequent critics (for example, Blessing, Diehl, Gilbert, Lane, Ostriker, Walker, and Watts) have taken it for granted that Plath's poetry reveals

"the impact Dickinson's work continues to exercise" today
(Diehl 186). Joyce Carol Oates, however, has recently countered that "of course" Dickinson has "no heirs or heiresses"
(824). She reflects that "in the minuteness of their perceptions
and the precision of their images one might think of Marianne
Moore, Elizabeth Bishop, the early Anne Sexton, and, certainly, Sylvia Plath, but so far as the development of American
poetry is concerned, Emily Dickinson really leads nowhere
since she herself is the highest embodiment of the experi-
mental method she developed. Genius of her kind is simply in-
imitable" (824). I believe that in Oates's reduction of influence
to mere imitation and in her insistence on kicking an intimidating predecessor upstairs, we observe a classic example of the
disclaimer that validates what it intends to deny. In the pages
that follow, we shall have reason to follow almost precisely the
course that Oates indicates leads "nowhere": from Dickinson
to Moore, Bishop, Sexton, and Plath. It is, in fact, a main
route of female poetic influence in the United States.

Although she remained indebted to Dickinson to the end of
her life, Plath achieved degrees of independence in her major
texts of 1958–63. Unlike her Dickinsonian poems of 1953, (*LH*
110–11), which Marjorie Perloff has rightly called "remarkably
clever imitations" ("Sivvy" 163), the later poems attempt to
complete Dickinson antithetically, a relation Bloom terms "tes-
sera." They read Dickinson in such a way as to suggest that the
precursor did not dare enough. In her most famous poems,
Plath subverts the predecessor's rhetoric through programma-
tic intensification. Whereas Dickinson's speaker calls her father
a "Burglar! Banker—Father!" or an "Eclipse" (poem 49; letter
261), Plath's calls hers a "panzer-man" and "devil" (*CP* 222–24);
whereas Dickinson's speaker terms her home a "soft . . . prison" (poem 1334), Plath's tells of being "drugged and raped" by
her "jailer" (*CP* 226–27); whereas Dickinson evokes nature as a
"haunted house" (poem 1400), Plath enumerates its death's-
heads and hooks (*CP* 155, 160, 168, 193, 239, 268); whereas Dickinson personifies Death as a "kindly" courtier (poem 712), Plath
personifies him as a masturbating "bastard" (*CP* 254–55); and
whereas Dickinson speaks in elliptical ways of "heavenly hurt"

and "bandaged moments" (poems 258, 512), Plath exposes
specific, bloody injuries — a "flap" of skin, a "thumb stump"
(*CP* 235–36).

Plath's misprision of Dickinson suggests that she thought
back through her poetic mother not simply to find support but
also to hold an adversary at bay. We might infer that Plath was
simply franker about rivalry than other women writers have
been, or that she was more steeped than others in a drama of
struggle and destitution, sacrifice and theft. Whatever our
interpretation, it is clear that competition energized her creativity, especially in moments of great stress. Her interior
conflict was that she needed Dickinson and her other female
precursors near her to permit her words to count as meaningful utterance, but that she also needed to have them away from
her in order to open up a space that was hers alone. As noted
previously, this kind of double bind uncannily reconstitutes
her relationship to her biological mother — a woman to whom
she wrote every day but whom she was constantly warning to
keep her distance, a woman with whom she shared an uncomfortable "psychic osmosis" (*LH* 28). On the one hand, Plath
feared that her poetic mothers would absorb her identity:

> From the mercury-backed glass
> Mother, grandmother, greatgrandmother
> Reach hag hands to haul me in.   (*CP* 70)

On the other hand, she feared they would withhold their nurturance entirely, leaving her abandoned on the beach like the
little girl in "Ocean 1212-W." Thus, for much of her career she
was uncertain where she stood, sustained in ways that did not
fully satisfy, beleaguered in ways she could not understand,
and unable to adopt a single, consistent attitude.

In the pages that follow, I shall suggest that Plath's adult
career encompassed three manifestations or voices in relation
to the female poetic tradition. First appeared the transitional
poet of 1957–59, who struggled with the verbally playful and im-
agistically precise poetry of Dickinson, Moore, and Bishop.
Then appeared two distinct emanations vying for authority: a
powerful but archaic voice, ambivalent about femaleness and

trapped in a cycle of rebellion and suffering (the voice of "Daddy," "Medusa," and "Edge"); and an equally powerful innovative voice, positive about femaleness and exploratory in its approach to experience (the voice of "Three Women," "By Candlelight," and "Ocean 1212-W"). The trapped voice intensified the rhetoric of anguish she found in Dickinson, Teasdale, Millay, and Sexton; the exploratory voice, while still connected to Dickinson, achieved a degree of autonomy denied Plath's other voices. Time and circumstance erased this latter poetic immanence before it could fully establish itself. Perhaps its emergence so frightened and maddened the archaic voice as to induce it to preserve itself through suicide. Yet the third voice, insisting on a fundamental association between female identity and creative power, has left its trace like a ghost image on the screen, a phantom of a future that never was. We encounter it not as we might discover a photograph of a dead parent taken as a young child, but as we might dream, in the chill of the night, of a dead child grown to maturity.

LET US STUDY each of Plath's three manifestations in turn, searching for its hidden character. We begin with two key poems from her transitional period of 1957–59, "Mussel Hunter at Rock Harbor" and "Metaphors."

"Mussel Hunter" (*CP* 95–97), Plath's longest and most ambitious poem of 1958, belongs to a genre that Constance Rourke labeled "small compass" poetry (267). Originating with Emily Dickinson, the genre came to Plath through the mediation of Marianne Moore and Elizabeth Bishop. Plath's speaker in "Mussel Hunter," attending to what Dickinson termed "minor Things" (poem 985), contemplates the shellfish of Cape Cod, much as Dickinson's speaker contemplates an avian visitor in "A Bird came down the Walk" (poem 328), Moore's speaker an anteater in "The Pangolin," and Bishop's speaker a tremendous fish in "The Fish." "Mussel Hunter" partly attempts to explode this "small compass" tradition and partly wishes to return it to its Dickinsonian origins, against the macerations of Moore and Bishop. Plath characteristically "daemonizes" the poems of Moore and Bishop. She seeks to reveal their thinness, to expose them as weaker than they might at first appear. It is as if Plath is proclaiming, "I can do as child's play what you have worked so hard to achieve, and what is more, I can correct the mistakes that you have so carefully disguised." In regard to Dickinson, however, Plath's poem might be taken as an instance not of "daemonization" but of "tessera," which Bloom calls the characteristically American revisionary ratio. In this mode of revision, "a poet antithetically 'completes' his precursor, by so reading the parent-poem as to retain its terms but to mean them in another sense, as though the precursor had failed to go far enough" (*Anxiety* 14). Rejecting the intermediaries Moore and Bishop, Plath restores the "small compass" poem to its American source in Dickinson, only to reveal Dickinson's own failure of nerve.

In "A Bird came down the Walk" (poem 328), Dickinson's "I" commences her discourse with a disturbing image:

> A Bird came down the Walk—
> He did not know I saw—
> He bit an Angleworm in halves
> And ate the fellow, raw.   (*Poems* 156)

Her secrecy—"He did not know I saw"—suggests the presence both of revelation and of guilt, implying that the speaker is not only viewing an exterior creature but also catching a glimpse of her own unconscious. In watching a creature who "bit an Angleworm in halves," she seems to witness impulses of devouring violence, perhaps even of sexual aggression. When she offers the bird a crumb in stanza four, he behaves "like one in danger, cautious," though the syntax is ambiguous and the phrase may refer to the "I" as well, thereby reinforcing the analogy between bird and self. With this act of communion, the poem's disturbing images vanish, along with the bird itself, who "unrolled" his feathers

> And rowed him softer home—
> Than oars divide the Ocean,
> Too silver for a seam—
> Or butterflies, off Banks of Noon
> Leap, plashless as they swim.

On one level of significance, the poem is a brief Dickinsonian journey to chaos, in which the speaker spies on her unconscious self, cautiously offers it a crumb of recognition, and is momentarily freed from guilt and fear by the encounter, which she then represses (perhaps healthily) in a flood of tranquilizing metaphors.

Moore established her poetic identity through poems in which an uncharacterized "I" similarly focuses minute attention on somewhat anthropomorphized animals. Moore's speaker, however, uses the occasion to imply a coherent set of values rather than to plumb her unconscious. "The Fish," with its portrait of a mussel shell "opening and shutting itself like / an / injured fan" probably contains the most apposite local analogue to Plath's "Mussel Hunter," but let us consider instead a more typical poem, "The Pangolin," which foreshadows not only "Mussel Hunter" but Bishop's "The Fish" and "The Armadillo" and Lowell's "Skunk Hour" as well. In contrast to Dickinson's "A Bird came down the Walk," Moore's "The Pangolin" inspects its animal in great detail, using, as Marie Borroff has explained (109–20), language characteristic of popular science magazines:

> Another armored animal — scale
> lapping scale with spruce-cone regularity until they
> form the uninterrupted central
> tail-row! This near artichoke with head and legs and grit-
>   equipped gizzard,
> the night miniature artist engineer is,
> yes, Leonardo da Vinci's replica —
> Impressive animal and toiler of whom we seldom
>   hear.   (*Poems* 117–20)

The emphasis here is on vivid and interesting details rendered concisely and wittily. These particulars derive not from a fictive encounter with the creature, as in Dickinson's poem, but frankly from books and journals: Richard Lydekker's *Royal Natural History* and Robert T. Hatt's article "Pangolins" in *Natural History*. Despite the surface objectivity of Moore's description, subjective social commentary occasionally obtrudes, as in: "a splendor / which man in all his vileness cannot / set

aside." Even the purely informational passages contain a latent
judgment: the pangolin receives sympathetic attention because,
unlike human beings, it gracefully "draws / away from danger." Thus Moore moralizes and aestheticizes the Dickinsonian animal poem, turning it into a reflection on beauty and
ugliness, peace and war, right behavior and wrong. The most
repressed of major American poets, she removes all disturbing
personal elements from the Dickinsonian animal poem and
makes of it not a journey to chaos but a laudation of order.
Whereas Dickinson's poem explores, however gingerly, the
frightening and the unknown, Moore's poem—with its image
of an "armored animal" that rolls itself "into a ball"—forcefully
defends against all that is dangerous. It erects a barrier of language against the social turmoil without and imposes a deco-
rum forbidding mention of psychological turmoil within.

Bishop's "The Fish" returns the genre from Moore's natural
history library to Dickinson's fictive world of individual encounters, but the poem keeps most of Moore's repressions intact. Bishop's "I" catches a "tremendous fish" and carefully
aestheticizes him. The pattern of his dark brown skin

> was like wallpaper:
> shapes like full-blown roses
> stained and lost through age.
> He was speckled with barnacles,
> fine rosettes of lime.   (*Poems* 42–44)

Like Moore's pangolin, the fish assumes moral qualities,
though he is hardly the pacific creature Moore's was. Sporting
a "sullen face," a "weaponlike" lip, and five pieces of fishline
hanging "like medals with their ribbons," he resembles a general who has gone through many battles. Like the pangolin,
however, he embodies dignity and fortitude; he too defends
against chaos, though more aggressively than his predecessor.
Like Dickinson's, Bishop's speaker attempts to achieve a redemptive transaction with the observed creature, but in this
poem the moment fails—or so it seems to me. Bishop's "I"
stares into the fish's face until

> Everything
> was rainbow, rainbow, rainbow!
> And I let the fish go.

Although the language eloquently suggests that the "I" has received grace through her aesthetic and moral perception, she has received it essentially in isolation: the fish has all along impassively refused to return her gaze. Whereas Dickinson's speaker has confronted something in herself and in otherness, Bishop's has neither discovered an unknown psychic truth nor made contact with the natural world. In freeing the fish, she has simply confirmed her aesthetic and moral figurings.

There can be no doubt that Plath had both Moore and Bishop on her mind when she composed "Mussel Hunter at Rock Harbor" in May or June 1958. In January of that year she had written in her journal, "No reason why I shouldn't surpass . . . even the lesbian and fanciful Elizabeth Bishop in America. If I sweat the summer out" (*J* 189). But it was Moore who was the more immediate model, or target, of her poem. Thinking of Moore as Bishop's poetic "godmother" (*J* 321), she seems to have wished to share the godmother or to capture her for herself. Plath first met Moore in April 1955, when the elder poet served as a judge of a college poetry contest in which Plath was a cowinner. Even at that meeting, Plath pretty clearly hoped to elicit the kind of support and friendship that Moore had earlier given to Bishop, when the latter was a student-poet at Vassar. Plath wrote to her mother that she "took to Marianne Moore immediately," congratulating herself on having bought a volume of Moore's poetry so that she could "honestly" praise some favorite poems (*LH* 168). She added that Moore resembled "someone's fairy godmother incognito"—implicitly revealing the wish that the elder poet might serve as her own. It is surely significant that at this time Plath was using "Marcia Moore" as her pen name (Wagner-Martin 118).

Nevertheless, Moore eventually assumed a Januslike identity in Plath's eyes: not only a potential godmother but also one of the "aging giantesses" of poetry (*J* 212), one of those colossal figures who restrict and inhibit rather than help and guide.

Moore enters Plath's discourse more often as a judge than as an inspiration (*J* 154, 235, 241, 251; *LH* 168, 296–97, 340, 341), and in that role she ominously appears as Hughes's "loyal supporter" rather than Plath's own (*LH* 341). But when Plath sat down to compose "Mussel Hunter," Moore certainly still represented a positive ideal. She was a successful woman poet describing the natural world in an independent, even idiosyncratic voice. On May 1, 1958, Plath wrote in her journal that she felt "tugs toward writing at every itch applied by reading Marianne Moore, Wallace Stevens, etc." (*J* 221). She wanted to surmount her artificial, rigid style and to write poems about "the real world, its animals, people, and scenery" (*LH* 347). Sometime in late May or early June, she composed "Mussel Hunter at Rock Harbor" in Moore's own syllabic verse form. She explained to her brother Warren: "This is written in what's known as 'syllabic verse.' . . . I find this form satisfactorily strict (a pattern varying the number of syllables in each line can be set up, as M. Moore does it) and yet it has a speaking illusion of freedom" (*LH* 344). On June 10, Plath and Hughes visited Moore in Brooklyn, and Plath pronounced her "lovely" (Smith ms.). A few days later Plath mailed her a packet of poems, including "Mussel Hunter," in the hope that Moore would write a letter of recommendation supporting her for a Saxton fellowship. It may not be too far-fetched to speculate that Plath wrote the syllabic-verse animal poem in order to seduce the famous poet, hoping to win her approval through the flattery of imitation.

The stratagem failed, as any sensitive reader of both poets might have anticipated. Moore wrote an unenthusiastic response in which she termed Plath's poem "too unrelenting" (Smith ms.). Taking the letter to be a brutal rejection, Plath called it "queerly ambiguous, spiteful" (*J* 251) and worried that Moore might have ruined her chance for the fellowship (which in fact she did not receive). She bizarrely attributed Moore's "spitefulness" to the fact that she had sent her a carbon copy rather than the original; she crossed Moore off her list of potential "fairy godmothers"; she never again wrote to her or mentioned her in positive terms; and she did not continue with her experiments in syllabic verse. "Mussel Hunter" became not her "star piece" (*J* 244), the long-sought inauguration of a mature style, but a sport in her canon, an experiment abandoned.

In her cool answer to Plath, Moore almost certainly was not objecting to having received a carbon copy; her comment on the copy's clarity reads like an attempt to be ingratiating. Rather, she must have been repelled by the poem itself. Plath, in her sometimes astonishing blindness, could not discern the radical discrepancy between her art and Moore's, a divergence made all the more obvious by the superficial similarities. The animals, the observer, even the verse form of "Mussel Hunter" are analogous to those of a Moore poem, but everything that matters is utterly different. Rather than model her voice flatteringly on that of her precursor, Plath had subverted all the tenets that make a poem like "The Pangolin" possible. Plath's poem seems designed to reveal the limitations of Moore's art, to demonstrate an effortless attainment of a power forever beyond the precursor's grasp. Plath had the effrontery and naïveté to send this very poem to Moore, expecting her approval. The whole incident — a comedy of manners really — demonstrates Plath's obliviousness to her own motives and ignorance of her developing poetic strength. She sought to barter her treasure for a pittance and failed — as if the Indians had been refused when they offered to sell Manhattan for a string of beads.

In "Mussel Hunter at Rock Harbor" (*CP* 95–97), the speaking subject recalls a visit she made to the seashore one morning to collect mussels. Her discourse does not so much describe the scene as characterize herself through her mode of description. In the first stanza Plath's "I" could almost pass for Moore's or Bishop's: solitary, objective, and attentive to design, color, and light. She seems an aesthete/moralist observing the natural phenomena. But by the second stanza the poem begins to swerve from the Moore-Bishop formula back toward Dickinsonian origins. The speaker reveals aims that escape confinement in aesthetic and moral categories: "I'd come for / Free fish-bait." Undermining her initial self-characterization as one who had come "to get the / Good of the Cape light," this admission exposes the hint of criminality hidden in her opening

assertion that she "came before the water- / Colorists came."
Furthermore, Plath's "I" notices the kinds of things that
Bishop's and especially Moore's ignore. She *smells* where they
fastidiously see, and she uses a diction they would find quite
foreign: "I smelt / Mud stench, shell guts, gull's leavings." Little wonder that Moore could not prevent herself from making
comments like "Don't be so grisly" and "I only brush away the
flies" (Smith ms.). In substituting her own tropes for Bishop's
and Moore's, Plath was repressing and rejecting her immediate precursors, returning to the spirit of the opening stanza
of "A Bird came down the Walk."

If Plath's language has a Lowellian violence, her seascape is
a Swiftian terrain of alienation and debris (see Fabricant
24-54). Its representative image is the "husk of a fiddler-crab"
on which Plath's speaker fixes her stare (st. 10-12): a "samurai
death mask" whose innards have been "bleached and blown
off." Unlike the nature portrayed by Moore and Bishop, this
landscape lacks redemption. Whereas Moore's "The Fish" describes a mussel shell delicately "opening and shutting" like a
fan, Plath's poem portrays its mussel shells as having swung
"shut" at the human presence (st. 3)—something like the
tightly closed "valves" of Dickinson's "The Soul selects her own
Society" (poem 303). Unable to connect imaginatively with her
surroundings, Plath's "I" stands "shut out, for once, for all"
from the "absolutely alien" order (st. 8). She feels rejected by a
scene seemingly riddled with Dickinsonian "abysses," Lowellian "voids," Swiftian "deserts," and Frostian "desert places."
Like the ghostly "stranger" Dickinson describes in "What mystery pervades a well!" (poem 1400), Plath's nature remains a
"wary underworld" known only by a "name it / Knew nothing
of" (st. 3, 9). Plath's "I" discerns in the animal kingdom neither
Moore's "model" of exactitude and grace nor Bishop's visionary "rainbow." Neither, however, does she quite attain
Stevens's "mind of winter" ("The Snow Man") or Lowell's "description without significance" ("Shifting Colors"), though
those conditions come closer than do the affirmations of
Moore and Bishop. Rather, Plath's speaker reluctantly admits
the coldness and blankness of the scene to her eye, the un-

bridgeable cleavage between the natural "otherworld" and her own ideational categories.

Since she cannot understand the crab husk she inspects, she must speculate about it in terms that actually project her own possible identities rather than the crab's. She calls it a "recluse," "suicide," or "headstrong Columbus" (st. ii). Opposed to Moore's moral and aesthetic self-assurance and Bishop's poignant need to discover a bond with nature that the facts belie, Plath proposes an epistemology of multiple choice whose uncertainty quotient surpasses that of her Dickinsonian/Hawthornean/Jamesian predecessors, since all her offered choices seem false. The natural object, described only in inapplicable metaphors, remains forever concealed, ungrasped by human knowledge. Plath's poem ends not in affirmation or communion but in frank acknowledgment of estrangement and in an obsessive will to discern death everywhere. Combining Woolf's consolatory image of the waves' ebb and flow (in *The Waves*) with Whitman's shockingly deidealized vision of "wash'd up drift," which convinces him that he has "not really understood anything" (in "As I Ebb'd with the Ocean of Life"), Plath's "I" watches mutely as "bellies pallid and upturned" ride "the waves' dissolving turn / And return" (st. 13).

If Plath denies Moore's and Bishop's portrayal of the animal kingdom, she corrects and completes Dickinson's trope. In "A Bird came down the Walk," Dickinson discovers the repellent violence of both nature and psyche. She then represses the uncovered horror with metaphors that permit culture and consciousness to reincorporate nature and the unconscious. In "Mussel Hunter at Rock Harbor," conversely, Plath refuses to suppress her dark insight. The poem leaves us with the iconic image of a "crab-face" fronting the "bald-face sun" (st. ii–13). "Face," for Plath, implies corporeal being, just as "effacing" implies suicide (as in "Tulips"). Yet a face is also a nothingness, for without imaginative interiority it is but a pasteboard mask. "Mussel Hunter" thus evokes one of Plath's obsessional themes: the deathliness of a being who lacks creative fulfillment. "Shut out" of her world (st. 8) as Dickinson's "I" was once shut out of heaven for singing too loud (poem 248), identifying herself with the "husk of a fiddler-crab" (st. 10) as Dickinson's stiffened "I" once called herself a husk without a kernel (poem 1135), Plath's speaking subject directly confronts the imaginative void, the failure of linguistic desire. Her imagery of shells and husks recalls Pound's lament in Canto VII for the "thin husks I had known as men," who speak "words like the locust-shells, moved by no inner being." Yet in Plath's poem, unlike Pound's, no "live" poet-hero appears to revitalize the dry pods. Plath's poem evokes without evasion the dreaded alter ego "to whom nothing can happen, who no longer creates" (*J* 164).

Significantly, "Mussel Hunter at Rock Harbor" takes place beside the sea, which Plath associated with the writer's "poetic heritage" and "moment of illumination" (*LH* 345; *J* 164). For Plath's speaker, however, the visit to the ocean is transgressive, marked by a feeling of apartness rather than the more traditional "feeling of an indissoluble bond, of being one with the external world" (Freud, *Civilization* 65). Overtly thanatotic, Plath's seascape encompasses a "dead low" tide, "cratered pool-beds," grimacing "skulls," and "dissolving" waves (st. 2–3, 12–13). If, like Whitman's sea in "Out of the Cradle," it whispers "death," it does not do so seductively. Small wonder that Plath's "I" approaches this sea reluctantly, "on the bank of the river's / Backtracking tail" (st. 1–2). Plath's imagery suggests that her poetic heritage menaces rather than nurtures her, that she remains as creatively destitute as the husk of a Prufrockian crab, and that she receives no inspiration from the "old men" and "medusas" who inhabit the deep (*CP* 92, 224).

From this standpoint, the poem's crucial parent poem is none of the ones we have thus far considered but Dickinson's "I started Early—Took my Dog—" (poem 520). In that poem Dickinson's "I" encounters a "Tide" who "made as He would eat me up—." The sea pursues the fleeing woman

> Until We met the Solid Town—
> No one He seemed to know—
> And bowing—with a Mighty look—
> At me—The Sea withdrew—   (*Poems* 254–55)

The sea here acts even more aggressively than in "Mussel Hunter." Both poems (like so many "voyage" and "seashore" poems of the past two centuries) adumbrate Frye's "myth of dissolution" (20). More specifically, both evoke the belated poet's fear of drowning in the sea of poems already written. Whereas for Dickinson that sea is male and malevolent, for Plath it is sexually undifferentiated and "alien" (st. 8). Female as well as male, it destroys not by assault but by indifference, impersonally "dissolving" the beings that attempt to "perform their shambling waltzes" on it (st. 13).

Plath must have sensed in Dickinson her strongest precursor and most mothering mother. Yet she rewrote the forerunner's texts in order to edit out their implications of visionary success. Dickinson's "I" escapes the sea's attack by returning to a "solid" domestic world where she belongs and the sea does not, thus demonstrating her power if not to subdue, then to outwit it. Plath's "I" finds herself shut out of a seascape that remains "beyond" her "guessing" (st. 6), a figure of the self-doubting imagination. In both "A Bird came down the Walk" and "I started Early—Took my Dog—," Dickinson's "I" transcends her creative demise, whereas in "Mussel Hunter at Rock Harbor" Plath's "I" simply encounters hers—and in a characteristic maneuver makes a poem of the occasion. If Moore was too polite a poet for Plath to have much transaction with (as Moore instantly recognized), Bishop and even Dickinson also held something back. Plath needed to affront the disaster that Bishop only denied (except in late masterpieces like "In the Waiting Room" and "One Art"). Plath needed to experience fully the "Zero at the bone" that Dickinson named (poem 986) but often fled. Although written more than a year before Plath's breakthrough at Yaddo, "Mussel Hunter" prophesies the progress of her career. She would scrutinize dangerous scenes in dangerous ways. What her vision cost her is apparent; what she gained is her art.

IN ADDITION to the poem of "small-compass" observation, Dickinson excelled in a second, complementary mode, the riddle poem. Moore did not write in this mode precisely, though she did compose texts that are replete with allusive codes, fables, and verbal play. Bishop did write riddling poems, such as "The Man-Moth," "The Monument," and "12 O'Clock News." Plath worked the vein too, in such poems as "The Thin People," "Words for a Nursery," "Mushrooms," "You're," "Words heard, by accident, over the phone," and the poem we shall be studying closely, "Metaphors."

Riddle, as Dickinson practiced it, reveals not only the unstable relation between words and phenomena but also that between words in one context and words in another. Like the observational poem, the riddle poem reveals the linguistic order's attempt to grasp the natural order and the natural order's uncanny ability to slip out of the grip. But the riddle poem highlights the powers and limits of language even more than those of observation. It reveals the holes with which the linguistic act is "riddled," the spaces dividing writer from reader and signifier from signified. Although the riddle's conclusion enacts an apparent closure of those spaces (by allowing the reader finally to make "sense" of the semantic problem), that closure is always only apparent, for the conclusion creates new and unbridgeable gaps of its own. Dolores Dyer Lucas has observed that whereas metaphor unites ideas and joke severs ideas, riddle remains "deliberately obscure, having an element of conscious deception. . . . It is ambiguous, neither separating nor uniting, but transitional in nature" (14).

As we know, Dickinson's texts consistently display a reticence about naming, a preference for the "apparently cryptic notation" (Anderson xii). Her circumlocutions, periphrases, omissions, enigmatic allusions, idiosyncratic punctuation, and multiple variants all testify to her skepticism about the value or possibility of unitary reference. Riddle, then, does not simply exist as a distinct poetic genre for Dickinson but "haunts" her every utterance. Some Dickinson texts, however, present themselves very specifically as riddles to be solved: poems like "It sifts from Leaden Sieves" (poem 311), "I like to see it lap the Miles" (poem 585), and "Further in Summer than the Birds" (poem 1068). In one sense the apparent solutions to these puzzles—the snow (poem 311), a train (poem 585), and a cricket (poem 1068) — matter much less than the problem they pretend to clear up: the language of the poem. The riddle poem demonstrates the superiority of linguistic system to the actual world of referents and the independence of the signifier from the signified. What in one context is flour or fabric in another becomes snow (poem 311); what in one context is a horse in another becomes a train (poem 585). In another sense, however, the solution proves crucial, since it changes the character of the linguistic system into which it is introduced. The solution actually expands rather than reduces the text's indeterminacy: a poem that at first seemed to be about a horse now becomes a poem about either a horse or a train, and the poem oscillates unstoppably between those alternative significances. By placing the text in increased doubt, the "solution" subverts our desire for interpretive stability — precisely the desire it deceptively promised to satisfy. Furthermore, as Lucas suggests, one can never decide with assurance among the competing significances that the "solution" itself may contain. Although Dickinson told a correspondent that "Further in Summer than the Birds" refers to "My Cricket" (letter 813), subsequent commentators have discovered a plenitude of metaphysical significances in that apparently simple analogy: man's alienation from nature (Yvor Winters), a pagan nature rite (Charles Anderson), a parodic Christian mass (Marshall Van Deusen), the nothingness at the heart of visible presence (Sharon Cameron), uninterrupted death (Cynthia Wolff), and so on.

For Dickinson, then, the riddle poem was a form of linguistic play, exposing both the plurisignative nature of language and the inability of language to convert otherness to itself. Moreover, riddle enacted Dickinson's personal drama of disguise and revelation, which may have originated in her ontological insecurity and her consequent anxiety about the legitimacy of her utterance (see Mossberg, Pollak, or Wolff). That the riddle's solution renders the poem more opaque rather than less implies that the poet's intention was not to tell the truth, even in a slant fashion, but to communicate the undesirability or impossibility of undeceptive statement: "The Riddle we can guess / We speedily despise" (poem 1222). Dickinson, like

Shelley, regarded poetic language as both a veil and a rending of the veil, but her rending disclosed only an additional fold. Like the minister in Hawthorne's parable, she never emerged from behind her veil. Thus the deep-structure answer to all of Dickinson's riddles is the question of language itself, a question that presented itself most keenly to a woman who would not be understood and who had the wit to speak "in Circuit" (1129). Although riddle in recent centuries has become a form of child's play, in ancient times it was a test of wisdom: for Dickinson it was both.

Plath too liked to speak in riddles, as we can tell from the message she sent home during a winter holiday in 1953:

BREAK BREAK BREAK ON THE COLD WHITE SLOPES OH KNEE ARRIVING FRAMINGHAM TUESDAY NIGHT 7:41. BRINGING FABU-LOUS FRACTURED FIBULA NO PAIN JUST TRICKY TO MANIPULATE WHILE CHARLESTONING. . . . YOUR FRACTIOUS FUGACIOUS FRAN-GIBLE SIVVY. (*LH* 101–2)

What Mary Lynn Broe calls a "riddling atmosphere" (*Poetic* 44) pervades Plath's discourse. Her wish to tell the truth (as a dream may tell the truth of the unconscious) attached itself to her need to camouflage (as a dream tells the truth in disguise). Like Dickinson, she preferred to speak obliquely: "My poems do not turn out to be about Hiroshima, but about a child form-ing itself finger by finger in the dark. They are not about the terrors of mass extinction, but about the bleakness of the moon over a yew tree in a neighboring graveyard" (*JP* 64). She thought of her poems as "deflections" that would be under-stood by a "relatively few" decoders (*JP* 65). The decoders, however, ultimately discover only further ciphers. Plath in-tuited the wild dispersal of linguistic meaning and, perhaps as a legacy from her training in the New Criticism, composed texts that purposely resist disambiguation. Her paradoxical drives to light and to veil parallel Dickinson's. The two poets shared a struggle for voice that involved duplicity as a tactic, perhaps because both endured a painful personal history of in-timacy withheld or breached, privacy invaded, and the right to speak placed in question. By composing cryptograms, they established an apparent connection to others and achieved the standing of public utterance, while at the same time preserving their privacy and avoiding the reprisal that direct communication would have invited. But beyond those personal motives, they spoke in riddles because they sensed that that was all language could ever come to: a game, a test of wits, a deceit. They wrote riddles to demonstrate the impossibility of untying them.

"Metaphors" (*CP* 116), which Plath composed toward the end of her apprentice period in March 1959, stands as her exemplary riddle poem. It evinces a Dickinsonian skepticism about the value or possibility of unambiguous communication while enacting a Dickinsonian drama of distance and apparent disclosure. Yet Plath swerves away from her precursor in several important respects. First, her riddle refers not to external phenomena such as snow, a train, or a cricket, but to the "I" herself: "I'm a riddle." Whereas Dickinson explores the capacity of language to represent and to disguise the world, Plath explores its capacity to reveal and conceal a self. As it happens, "Metaphors" inscribes a fictive rather than an autobiographical being, since Plath herself, unlike her speaker, was not pregnant at the time. The important point, however, is that for Plath the riddle of identity takes precedence over the riddle of the natural world. A second, related difference is that whereas Dickinson's poems describe a relatively stable scene comprising objects in metonymic relation to each other (for example, a horse or train moving effortlessly across the land), Plath's poem comprises images (an elephant, a melon, a house) that bear no intrinsic connection to each other. The images function only as contrastive metaphors for the poem's single constant, its "I." Thus, whereas Dickinson superimposes mutually exclusive but internally coherent systems of reference on each other (a galloping horse, a speeding train), Plath juxtaposes arbitrary images so as to represent a single, coherent subject-object (a pregnant woman). A third difference is that whereas Dickinson's child's play typically establishes an ambience of aesthetic wonder, "Metaphors" communicates a sense of humiliation (a "melon strolling on two tendrils"), grotesquerie (an "elephant" woman), instrumentality (a "means"), capitalist reification ("money's new-minted in this fat purse"), sexual powerlessness ("boarded the train there's no getting off"), and pain ("I've eaten a bag of green apples"). Beneath the humor of Plath's imagery, we discover very little real pleasure: only lines 4 and 5 contain images that could easily be interpreted as positive. Indeed, in the last two lines even the humor vanishes, displaced by an anxious awareness of remorseless fate.

Additionally, "Metaphors" swerves from Dickinson — and from Moore, Bishop, and Woolf as well — by focusing attention on women's reproductive life. It is true that Dickinson occasionally implies a powerful sexual and affective need, in language that Plath liked to echo. Whereas Dickinson writes of being "hungry, all the Years" (poem 579), Plath writes of being "hungry, hungry" for burgeoning love (*J* 131; *CP* 23). Whereas Dickinson writes of turning, "tenderer," to another woman's heart (poem 309), Plath describes love, especially for other women, as being a form of "tenderness" (*BJ* 262; *CP* 269). Nevertheless, Dickinson rigorously excludes pregnancy, childbearing, and child rearing from her androgynous texts. Moore and Bishop generally repress eroticism as well as reproductivity. All three poets refute Whitman's notion that he might appropriately encapsulate female experience in the assertion that "there is nothing greater than the mother of men" ("Song of Myself"). Although Virginia Woolf limns a memorable mother in *To the Lighthouse*, she too tends to exclude sexual passion, pregnancy, and childbearing from her discourse — perhaps because, as Elaine Showalter has suggested (*Literature* 271-76), her husband and sister conspired to eliminate them from her life. In contrast, Plath vividly evokes heterosexual desire in "Stone Boy with Dolphin," "Wreath for a Bridal," and the early *Journals*; depicts lesbian feeling in *The Bell Jar*, "Lesbos," and the later *Journals*; and inscribes the monologues of an angry, abused wife in "The Jailer" and the lost manuscript, *Double Exposure*. Beginning with her first pregnancy in 1959, Plath's poems oscillate between representing motherhood skeptically ("Metaphors" and "Morning Song") and as redemption ("By Candlelight" and "Nick and the Candlestick"). Her poems disdaining barrenness ("Barren Woman," "Elm," "The Bee Meeting," and "Amnesiac") incontestably contradict the position Lowell attributes to her in *History*: "I hate marriage, I must hate babies" (135).

In actuality, Plath's texts express feelings about marriage and babies that are as complex, mobile, and charged as the contrasting perspectives contained in her great work, "Three Women." In her depiction, children are at once incomprehensibly other, performing acts the "I" cannot fathom (as in "Sweetie Pie and the Gutter Men" and "Balloons") and strangely emblematic of the self's creativity—poems with a human face (as in "By Candlelight" and "Three Women"). Whereas female as well as male tradition has generally opposed motherhood to literary creation, Plath sought to associate them (*LH* 478, 493). As we shall see in the discussion of "Three Women" later on, Plath posited the unity of "making in all its forms" (*JP* 64): children, bread, paintings, buildings, and poems. In one of her sustaining tropes, she figured successful texts as living beings with "lungs" and "heart"—progeny nurtured by their author's "mother-love" (*CP* 142). Although her castigation of barrenness at times reflects her personal rivalries with the childless Assia Gutman (Wevill) and Olwyn Hughes, it more generally voices her recurrent fear that she might prove imaginatively "empty" (*CP* 157). In "Metaphors," however, she portrays the reverse: a "big" woman boarding an inexorable train (*CP* 116). Prophesying her own unalterable future as a mother of both children and texts, the poem suggests first the amusement and then the chill she felt as she contemplated that destiny.

Finally, and relatedly, whereas Dickinson's riddle poems contrast language and reference, "Metaphors" evokes the incestuous doubling of discourse and author. For Dickinson such doubling was an occasional theme, as in the poem that begins "This was a Poet—" (448), in which "this" may refer to either poetic text or authorial figure. For Plath the organic connection between her self and the text that would "speak of her" (*CP* 142) was a crucial trope. She did not feel alive except in the act of text creation, perhaps because text as a transitional object recalled her feelings of pre-Oedipal oneness with her mother, perhaps because only text could defeat the mortality she feared so strongly. She craved the satisfaction, the self-discovery, and the endurance that written language could provide. She wanted to "leave" her "mark" (*JP* 175). We see this set of desires expressed quite clearly in "Metaphors." The title alone tells us that the self of the poem is composed of language, as does the initial assertion: "I'm a riddle in nine syllables." Seen from a linguistic perspective, the text itself utters the poem. The first line, like all the lines, has nine syllables; moreover, the poem as a whole functions as a nine-syllable riddle, with each line constituting a single syllable. As in Barthes's "The Death of the Author" (*Rustle* 49–55), the black-and-white of writing has drawn all the vitality out of the author, who may function symbolically as the absent "you," the speechless, inessential other. Seen from a humanist perspective, however, a fictive woman speaks the poem. She figures each month of her pregnancy as one syllable in a nine-syllable term or "sentence." She understands her experience as a system of signs, a grammar of feelings. From whichever perspective we regard this poem, we see that the relationship supporting the structure is the one between linguistic and organic existence. The "I" says, in effect, "I'm a succession of metaphors." In this poem, as in all of Plath's work, we witness an unsettling of boundaries, an exchange of energies between author and script.

"Metaphors" announces the beginning of Plath's poetic maturity just as the counterpart poem, "Words," announces its end. These poems suggest that for Plath the making of metaphors was life. Each time the making subsided, life itself waned, pain increased, and the desperately scattered and fragmentary author could renew her quest for a never achieved wholeness only by resuming the metaphor-making process. In one sense, the Dickinsonian riddle genre mastered Plath by speaking through her, by embedding itself in her discourse. In another sense, Plath mastered the genre by metaleptically inscribing within it her own obsessive theme of the doubleness of self and text. She entertained all the contradictory significances contained in one of her key words, "figure" (*CP* 216, 249, 261, 278, 300, 309): poetic trope and bodily frame; truth and lie; prophecy and memorial; design and cognition. For her, it was not so much a case of an empirical identity sustaining a poetic immanence as of each one creating and destroying the other.

LET US TURN now from Plath's poetry of verbal and epistemo-
logical play to what I earlier called her second voice or manifes-
tation, which articulates a rhetoric of anguish, bereavement,
fear, and anger. Since even the most intense poetry is governed
by "the very nature of the signifier" (Foucault, *Language* 116) as
well as by the discursive codes made available by culture, when
Plath came to write a poetry of extreme subjectivity she inevitably, if paradoxically, relied on prior texts to guide (and to contest) her. Again she summoned Emily Dickinson, whose voice
had also plumbed "the extremes of experience" (Gelpi 225).
Plath sought to make her own poems press against their linguistic medium and the tradition of utterance in such a way as to become a dissembling image of what John Irwin calls the author's
"other self" (20).

Dickinson excelled in the poetry of loss because, as Sharon
Cameron has said, "in Dickinson's cosmology loss is the most ir-
reparable phenomenon and confers the greatest transfigura-
tion" (138–57). Much as Freud's grandson acted out his mother's
daily departures by repeatedly throwing a reel of string over the
side of his cot and then pulling it up again (*Beyond* 14–17), so Dickinson wrote dozens of poems to express her anxious awareness
that "A loss of something ever felt I" (poem 959). Yet whereas
Plath above all feared the departure of the beloved other, Dickinson most dreaded the forfeit of consciousness. Unlike Plath,
she actually seemed to prefer losing the other to achieving emotional relation, for the act of loving includes just the variety of
loss that she found most intolerable—the loss of individual
awareness and identity. As Freud wrote, "At the height of being
in love the boundary between ego and object threatens to melt
away" (*Civilization* 66). Perhaps to obviate that particular danger,
Dickinson chose not to represent romantic attachment in the in-
dicative mood. Although Charles Newman, in his valuable but
sometimes misleading essay on Dickinson and Plath, has written that "no American poet of her era treated the theme of love
with more candour than Emily Dickinson" (26), in fact Dickinson figured love primarily in terms of difference and deferral (as
Albert Gelpi, Suzanne Juhasz, and Melinda Rosenthal have

noted). Conserving her integrity by rejecting intimacy, she repeatedly evoked the failure of love, in such well-known poems
as "There came a Day at Summer's full" (poem 322), "I measure every Grief I meet" (poem 561), "I cannot live with You"
(poem 640), and "My life closed twice before its close" (poem
1732).

We might speculate that beyond threatening the separateness of the ego, heterosexual love quite specifically endangered
Dickinson's writing career. Since her culture conceived of a
wife as the husband's lesser partner, for whom domestic obliga-
tions were primary, Dickinson felt that she must refuse the
"soft Eclipse" of marriage (poem 199). She therefore portrayed
unfulfilled love, at least in the context of female-male relations,
as a necessary and even rewarding martyrdom. In "There
came a Day at Summer's full," for example, the "I" understands renunciation as a process of crucifixion and resurrection, in which a romantic couple's earthly "Calvaries of Love"
lead to an eternal "Marriage" in heaven. In "I measure every
Grief I meet" and "I cannot live with You," the speaker denies
herself that simplistic consolation but does take a "Piercing
Comfort" in observing the "Calvary" of others, enigmatically
calling her own "Despair" a "White Sustenance." In "My life
closed twice before its close," the speaker accepts her two love
losses so thoroughly that she actually looks forward to a "third
event," which she disconcertingly terms "all we know of
heaven." In such poems, we participate in what Cameron
describes as a process of "elevating the moment of loss to
supremacy" (143), or what Dickinson herself calls a "hallowing
of Pain" (poem 772). It is as if the "I" could best know love
through refusal; or as if she decided, with Faulkner, that
"between grief and nothing, I will take grief"; or as if she discovered, with Freud, Lacan, and Derrida, that separation and
absence underpin adult consciousness. Knowing the object of
desire by that which pained her, defining the self by that which
resisted its incorporation, Dickinson willingly sacrificed affective relation for intellectual power.

With the composition of "Elm" (*CP* 192–93) in April 1962,
the Dickinsonian love-loss convention began to regulate Plath's

texts as well. Interestingly, the convention's textual appearance preceded by almost three months Plath's shocked discovery of her husband's infidelity. As we have seen before, her poems frequently anticipated rather than reflected her empirical existence: "The Snowman on the Moor" prophesied with astonishing accuracy a pivotal quarrel with her husband four years later (see Butscher 310–12), "Metaphors" prefigured her first pregnancy, and "Edge" evoked her death. Although Plath's poems and journals apparently had the power to influence their author's experiential text, her fiction did not: when she wrote "Elm" she was also composing the idealized novel about marriage that she later incinerated in disgust.

In "Elm," Plath again appropriates Dickinson's strength by means of a "tessera," an antithetical completion. Dickinson's love-loss poems, driven by ambivalence, include compensatory gestures, whereas "Elm" and Plath's subsequent poems expose the "hurt" and the "pain" of abandonment (CP 203, 241) without defenses. Newman claims that Plath suffered from "an inability to accept love," unlike Dickinson, who was perpetually rejected (44). I believe that something like the opposite is true. Plath's texts and what we know of her life both suggest the image of a person who readily accepted love. What she could not handle was its withdrawal. Her psychotextual economy differs from Dickinson's in this way: for Dickinson, romantic love signifies loss of ego, whereas lovelessness conserves the ego; for Plath, love signifies completion of the ego, whereas lovelessness perpetuates a mortal injury. It is no accident that the most frequently occurring active verb in Plath's poetic vocabulary is "to love," while in Dickinson's it is "to know." Far from regarding marriage and authorship as being in conflict, Plath wished to view her happy marriage and her creative drive as being in league: "The joy of being a loved and loving woman; that is my song" (LH 277). Since she married a poet partly in order to marry herself to poetry, the breaking of that bond put utterance itself at risk. Therefore, in Plath's poems of parting the pain is unmitigated and the damage uncontrolled. If Dickinson uses love-loss as a way to wall out greater losses, Plath stumbles through love-loss as through a portal to ruin.

In "Elm," the feelings of privation are so devastating that they provoke a disturbance in the relation of subject to speech. The woman of the poem listens dumbly as the eponymous tree outside her window verbally taunts her:

> Love is a shadow.
> How you lie and cry after it.
> Listen: these are its hooves: it has gone off, like a horse.
>
> (st. 3)

Freud, in reporting the Wolf Man's nightmare of wolves staring from a tree outside his window, remarks that "a high tree is a symbol of observing, of scoptophilia" (*Case Histories* 229). In Plath's psychomachia, the elm scoptically observes and analyzes the inarticulate woman, appearing almost sadistically stimulated by the woman's grief. Just as in a Freudian case history, the analysand (the woman) has ceded linguistic and interpretive power to the analyst (the tree). Nevertheless, the woman's psychic conflicts soon invade and "possess" the elm's speech (st. 9), transforming the tree from a detached observer to a subjective double. The resultant discourse exposes the elm-woman's obsessive search for "something to love" and her failure to recapture "the faces of love, those pale irretrievables" (st. 10, 12). Far from being a "White Sustenance," her despair is "tin-white, like arsenic" (st. 5). It "petrifies" (turns to stone, terrifies, paralyzes, kills) a head already filled with "faults" (lines of fissure, moral transgressions) (st. 14). Whereas Dickinson's poems of parting symmetrically balance opposites, such as "Sustenance" and "Despair" (poem 64) or "heaven" and "hell" (poem 1732), the elm-woman knows only "the bottom" (st. 1). "Incapable of more knowledge" (st. 13), she owes less to Dickinson's ambivalent meditations on love-loss than to her fearful descriptions of a consciousness that "Finished knowing—then—" (poem 280). Plath's "voice of nothing" (st. 2) metaleptically recovers the precursor's "numb intelligence" (poem 965), her "nothing with a tongue" (poem 1385).

In crossing Dickinson's portrayal of love-loss with her intimations of self-extinction, Plath turned from the Moore and Bishop line of Dickinsonian inheritance to a competitive tradition that leads from Dickinson to Sara Teasdale, Edna St. Vincent Millay, and Anne Sexton. Whereas Moore and the earlier Bishop and Plath diluted Dickinson's "drop of Anguish" (poem 193), avoiding her "Boundaries of Pain" (poem 644), Teasdale, Millay, Sexton, and the later Plath willingly downed the bitterest medicines and journeyed to the darkest interiors. Millay asked:

> And must I then, indeed, Pain, live with you
> All through my life?—sharing my fire, my bed,
> Sharing—oh, worst of all things!—the same head?—
>
> (*Poems* 734)

Sexton similarly described swallowing a daily "teaspoon / of pain" (*Poems* 547), and Plath too wrote of living on "arsenic" (*CP* 192), of waking each morning to "pain" (*CP* 241). It was Teasdale who generated this alternative line of Dickinsonian inheritance by disambiguating the precursor's rhetoric of loss, and it was Teasdale who most directly influenced Plath's change of direction in "Elm." In such early poems as "Erinna," "But Not to Me," "Winter Night," "Union Square," "Twilight," "Spring Night," and "I Shall Not Care," Teasdale insistently mourned the absence of a love object—as Millay would subsequently do in "Ashes of Life," "Kin to Sorrow," and *Fatal Interview*, and as Sexton would do, after Plath's death, in *Love Poems* and *45 Mercy Street*. Teasdale prized the genre to such a degree that she sought to memorialize it in her anthology of women's love lyrics, *The Answering Voice*, which included both Dickinson's "My life closed twice" and Millay's "Ashes of Life."

In Teasdale's early poems of love-loss, the bereaved speaker can neither alleviate nor transcend her suffering. Refusing all consolatory gestures, she perceives the failure of love as an injury that will ultimately prove fatal. As Teasdale's career progressed, these laments gradually merged into meditations on suicide:

> Bitter and beautiful, sing no more;
> Scarf of spindrift strewn on the shore,
> Burn no more in the noon-day light,
> Let there be night for me, let there be night.

> On the restless beaches I used to range
> The two that I loved have walked with me—
> I saw them change and my own heart change—
> I cannot face the unchanging sea.   ("To the Sea")

We find in such a poem neither a "White Sustenance" nor a desire for a "third event" but simply, in the wake of two intolerable losses, the wish for oblivion. In another late poem, Teasdale wrote that "Rebellion against death, the old rebellion is over" ("The Old Enemy"). In a similar vein, Dickinson had once attested, "It don't sound so terrible—quite—as it did— / I run it over—'Dead,' Brain, 'Dead'" (poem 426); Millay would write of "Death's shadow beside my own" ("Journal"); Sexton would ask, "What am I hanging around for?" ("Lessons in Hunger"); and Plath herself would conclude, "We have come so far, it is over" ("Edge").

It is not irrelevant to our discussion that Teasdale killed herself by taking an overdose of pills shortly before a nurse was scheduled to come to her room, an act parallel to Plath's own half-mistaken suicide thirty years later. Each death followed the removal of a beloved other: Teasdale had divorced her husband (Ernst Filsinger) and had drifted from her mentor (John Hall Wheelock), whereas Plath had separated from her husband and mentor (Ted Hughes). Teasdale and Plath seem to have shared a common affective structure, a system of signs in which the death of love uncovered a wish for death. Even as a very young woman, Plath had acquired Teasdale's key volume, *Dark of the Moon*. She seems to have considered Teasdale a role model along the lines of Virginia Woolf. Furthermore, she viewed the suicides of both writers as integral to their creativity—as a final silence that somehow authenticated their struggle for words. A year before her own first suicide attempt, she contemplated her artistic aspirations in terms of Woolf and Teasdale: "Why did Virginia Woolf commit suicide? Or Sara Teasdale or the other brilliant women? . . . If only I knew how high I could set my goals, my requirements for my life!" (*J* 62). Later, however, as Plath came to identify her poetic talent with her marriage, she rejected Teasdale as a possible model: "My voice is taking shape, coming strong. Ted says he never read poems by a woman like mine; they are strong and full and rich — not quailing and whining like Teasdale or simple lyrics like Millay; they are working, sweating, heaving poems born out of the way words should be said" (*LH* 244). On another occasion, she wrote that with her husband's help she would avoid becoming either an "abstractionist man-imitator" or, conversely, a "bitter, sarcastic Dorothy Parker or Teasdale" (*LH* 277). If Plath meant the latter adjectives to apply to Teasdale as well as to Parker, she misrepresented her, but the important point is that Hughes had sanctioned a way of being a poet that denied the woes and challenges of influence. He implied that Plath, as a female poet married to a male poet, could singularly transcend the limitations of both traditions. This vision of solipsism and dependency held her for five and a half years, from 1957 to 1962. In spring of 1962, however, as Plath found her marriage unraveling, the poetic identity that Hughes had given her began to unravel as well. She returned to those "brilliant women" she had previously idolized and rejected. She realized that Hughes had been mistaken, that her voice developed best not in the context of her special relationship to him but in the context of other poets. It had been a shared delusion to think she was unique. She was a poet like others, bearing the burden of the past and compelled to utterance by the anxieties of authorship and influence, by the affiliation complex. To hold oneself apart from the process of literary history was simply to deprive oneself of words, which may have suited Hughes's hidden agenda for his wife but certainly not her conscious aims for herself.

Beginning with "Elm" in April 1962, Plath reactivated her connection to Teasdale. Her late poems echo Teasdale's images of solitary nature (moon, trees, cloud, stars, fog, birds, sky, shadows, night, pools, wind, sea) and Teasdale's themes of loneliness, grief, and death. We may speculate that Plath had two distinct motives in revising Teasdale: she sought access to Dickinson's complex grammar of feelings by means of the intermediary's comparative simplifications, and at the same time she wished to explore more fully Teasdale's own characteristic association of love-loss with death. By echoing Teasdale,

Plath acquired lyrical powers that had heretofore remained just beyond her grasp. Whereas Teasdale wrote, "My window is starred with frost" ("A Winter Night"), Plath wrote, "The frost makes a flower, / The dew makes a star" ("Death and Co."); whereas Teasdale complained, "The moon is cruel" ("A Winter Night"), Plath lamented, "The moon, also is merciless: she would drag me / Cruelly" ("Elm"); whereas Teasdale compared love to a "cry forever / Lost as the swallow's flight" ("Deep in the Night"), Plath compared the heart to a "cry" that flaps out of a tree, looking "for something to love" ("Elm"); whereas Teasdale described a visit by physicians named "Pain and Death" ("Doctors"), Plath described a visit by salesmen named "Death and Co." ("Death and Co."); whereas Teasdale wrote of hearing "the sea" in the trees ("The Sea Wind"), Plath wrote of hearing "the sea" in an elm ("Elm"); whereas Teasdale depicted eyes that "call and call" ("I Know the Stars"), Plath depicted men who "call and call" ("Lady Lazarus"); whereas Teasdale sought to recover an "innermost Me" from her "scattered selves" ("Sanctuary," "The Crystal Gazer"), Plath sought to recover a "queen" or "virgin" from her "dissolving selves" ("Stings," "Fever 103°"); and whereas Teasdale wrote of being as "self-complete as a flower or a stone" ("The Solitary"), Plath wrote of being as "perfected" as a night "flower" or a stone pitcher ("Edge"). In her late poems, Teasdale wrote obsessively of intolerable mental pain, just as Plath did herself.

Perhaps Plath's clearest appropriation of Teasdale's language and imagery occurs in "Elm," which echoes one of Teasdale's most poignant love-loss poems, "Spring Night":

> The park is filled with night and fog,
>   The veils are drawn about the world,
> The drowsy lights along the paths
>   Are dim and pearled.
>
> Gold and gleaming the empty streets,
>   Gold and gleaming the misty lake,
> The mirrored lights like sunken swords
>   Glimmer and shake.
>
> Oh, is it not enough to be
> Here with this beauty over me?

My throat should ache with praise, and I
Should kneel in joy beneath the sky.
O, beauty are you not enough?
Why am I crying after love,
With youth, a singing voice and eyes
To take earth's wonder with surprise?
Why have I put off my prize,
Why am I unsatisfied,—
I for whom the pensive night
Binds her cloudy hair with light,—
I, for whom all beauty burns
Like incense in a million urns?
O, beauty, are you not enough?
Why am I crying after love?   (*Poems* 49)

In her copy of the poem (in Oscar Williams's *Little Treasury of Modern Poetry*, at Smith), Plath vigorously underscored Teasdale's key question, "Why am I crying after love?" This verse—together with Millay's near repetition of it in "Macdougal Street," "What can there be to cry about that I should lie and cry?"—helps to generate the comment of Plath's elm to its auditor: "Love is a shadow. / How you lie and cry after it" (st. 3). Furthermore, Teasdale's question, "Why am I unsatisfied?" seems embedded in the elm's inquiry, "Is it the sea you hear in me, / Its dissatisfactions?" (st. 2). More generally, "Elm" rewrites Teasdale's park "filled with night and fog" as a rural landscape of "night" and "clouds," while transforming the predecessor's beauty that "burns" into an "atrocity of sunsets." Recalling the overdetermination of literary language, we realize that while "Elm" may appear to come "directly from inside" Plath herself, as Suzanne Juhasz says (*Naked* 101), it achieves this effect by carefully transuming the discourse of the predecessors.

   "Elm" and "Spring Night" work in concert to subvert the consolatory impulses in Dickinson's poetry of love-loss. As I have suggested, Dickinson's speaker in "I measure every Grief I meet" (poem 561) relieves her "larger Pain" by discovering an almost Whitmanian kinship with strangers:

   A piercing Comfort it affords
   In passing Calvary—

> To note the fashions — of the Cross —
> And how they're mostly worn —
> Still fascinated to presume
> That Some — are like My Own —

In "I cannot live with You" (poem 640) and "My life closed twice" (poem 1732), the "I" takes pleasure in her very capacity for feeling: "Despair" becomes a "Sustenance." Teasdale's "I," conversely, remains isolated not only from her lover but from the rest of humanity and from herself, concluding in frank bafflement: "Why am I crying after love?" Plath's woman in "Elm" similarly fails to take comfort in others' suffering or her own. Her only companion is her double, the tree, an instrument for translating her abysmal, presymbolic "cry" (st. 3) into what "Spring Night" terms a "singing voice." Teasdale occasionally portrays terrible pain as the instigator of language: "I had to take my own cries / And thread them into a song" ("Song Making"). Modeling on her predecessor, Plath in "Elm" abandons her earlier equation of a loving marriage with "singing joy" (*LH* 235) and instead identifies loss with the "release" of her poetic "energy" (*LH* 467). She does not, however, take comfort from the identification, for the loss of love leaves her defenseless against her internalized "punitive aggression" (Freud, *Civilization* 128).

WHEN PLATH came to write her great poems of October 1962, a different and even more powerful set of Dickinsonian texts supported and challenged her endeavor. We know that the precursor did not always evade the implications of her vision. In such poems as "There's a certain Slant of light" (poem 258), "I felt a Funeral, in my Brain" (poem 280), "After great pain, a formal feeling comes" (poem 341), "It was not death, for I stood up" (poem 510), and "One need not be a Chamber — to be Haunted" (poem 670), she developed a poetics of death that has humbled her posterity, male as well as female. While in "Daddy" Plath vanquished a minor Sexton poem called "My Friend, My Friend" (as Heather Cam has shown) and wrestled with the more substantial "The Truth the Dead Know" and "All My Pretty Ones," she also revised Dickinson's depictions of "my Father's House" and "that Pause of Space which I call 'Father'" (poem 824; letter 418). But "Lady Lazarus" represents her strongest misprision of Dickinson during this period. Interpreted along these lines, "Lady Lazarus" (*CP* 244–46) is less concerned with suicide than with Dickinson's poetry about suicide. This significance becomes overt in the poem's assertion, "Dying / Is an art" (st. 15). Even when, following her first suicide attempt, Plath wrote that she felt "like Lazarus" (*J* 99), her discourse already interwove personal and textual threads. Her memory of "being dead" and rising "up again" leads through references to "scars" and a "marring mark" to an explicit meditation on the problematics of resurrecting the self by rhetorical means: "I identify too closely with my reading, with my writing" (*J* 99). Often feeling that somatic life was synonymous with death whereas creative "work" offered the promise of "salvation" (*J* 178), she troped on death and rebirth in "Lady Lazarus" to suggest the way art might double and supplant death-in-life, might defeat death. But within that fantasy of poetic immortality lay another awareness, of the deathliness of a process that converts organic and psychic life into black marks on a page. Dickinson shared Plath's interest in being "raised from oblivion," like Lazarus in the Book of John (poem 1560; see also poems 216, 258, 491, 598, 608, 984, 1530, and 1731). She too sought the survival of consciousness through art, and she too may have sensed the ironies embedded in that effort. So when Plath inscribes herself as Lady Lazarus, she may be representing not only her attempt to make her own bones live again in textual form but her ability to raise Dickinson from the dead as well.

While death undoubtedly occupies a central position in all poetry, Dickinson particularly excelled in the art of "dying." As Joanne Feit Diehl has written, Dickinson was tempted by death as a way "to obviate the frustrations of experience" and was repelled by it as a source of "defeating silence" (18). Even more than the final termination, she dreaded the daily deaths of consciousness, as the following quatrain suggests:

> The dying, is a trifle, past,
> But living, this include
> The dying multifold—without
> The Respite to be dead. (poem 1013)

Teasdale and Millay rewrote the poem of dying by simplifying it, while Plath's friend Sexton brought it to one kind of hyperbolic conclusion in *All My Pretty Ones* (1962) and subsequent volumes. Lowell once commented that in Plath's "half-dozen supreme, extreme poems," she "learned" from Sexton (*Prose* 287), a judgment that would have pleased Plath, who prided herself on her ability as a student. In "Lady Lazarus" she in effect boasts that she has bested all her rivals in the "art" of "dying." Whereas Dickinson questioned whether she had "the Art", to express death and absence (poem 701), Plath confidently affirms, "I do it exceptionally well" (st. 15). Self-reflexively pondering her position as a latecomer in an overpopulated profession, Plath's "I" insists, "I've a call" for this art (st. 16), just as she exclaimed in her journal, "This is my call, my work" (*J* 196). As so frequently in Plath's canon, the underlying motive of "Lady Lazarus" is the need for self-legitimation. In addition to rebelling against the patriarchal forces of the past who sadistically exert control over her, she must revise the matriarchal presences who, through their affective and rhetorical power, both generate and inhibit her. The speaking subject of "Lady Lazarus" makes a space for herself by revealing the inadequacy of the mothers' voicings, by rising like Lazarus from the ashes of their scripts.

Plath does preserve the sense of suffering so central to Dickinson's texts, and even the imagery of a mineralized self. Her "pure gold baby" (st. 23), for example, reinscribes Dickinson's "quartz contentment," "marble feet," and "children, made of Gold" (poems 341, 510, 588). But unlike her forerunner, Plath fully releases her aggression. Her protagonist shrieks (st. 24) where Dickinson's only sobs (poem 588); and she emerges from fires that recall those of Eliot, Celan, and Lowell rather than anything in Dickinson. Indeed, Plath's cry to Herr God, Herr Lucifer, "I turn and burn" (st. 24), specifically evokes the claim of Lowell's speaker that God or Lucifer will "turn / The bier and baby-carriage where I burn" (*Lord Weary* 45), while her titular trope reflects the plea of another Lowell speaker for "blessings on my burning head / Until I rise like Lazarus from the dead" (*Lord Weary* 22). Just as the writing subject of Plath's *Journals* calls herself "burned and reburned," "kindled to a great work" (*J* 184, 196), so the speaker of "Lady Lazarus" proclaims:

> Out of the ash
> I rise with my red hair
> And I eat men like air.   (st. 28)

This conclusion reverses Dickinson's characteristic laments that "Dying annuls" her "power to kill" (poem 358) or, conversely, that she has "the art to kill, / Without—the power to die" (poem 754 variant). Whereas Dickinson's language suggests limitation and failure ("annuls," "but," "without"), Plath's asserts success ("I rise," "I eat"), implying that her textual surrogate, unlike Dickinson's, has the art of both dying and killing.

Dickinson, embarrassed by the covert aggressivity of her words, attributes her poetry to a male "Owner" or "Master" (poem 754)—possibly one of the powerful men in her life (Edward Dickinson or Thomas Wentworth Higginson), possibly her own imaginative capacity envisioned as a male (like "Tim" in poem 196). For much of "Lady Lazarus," Plath similarly portrays her creative self as the "opus" of a male "Doktor" (st. 22–23)—possibly one of the powerful men in *her* life (Otto Plath or Ted Hughes), possibly the male-identified side of herself (her "buried male muse" [*J* 223]). In the poem's conclusion, however, the speaker escapes her role of male possession, assuming an autonomous identity capable of eating men like air. Whereas Dickinson's "I" typically weakens as the text progresses ("letting go," "finished knowing," "could not see," "without the power"), Plath's "I" resurrects herself by means of her ferocious alphabet.

The status of "Lady Lazarus" as metapoetic contest explains its metaphors of performance and audience: the protagonist's "strip tease" for a "peanut-crunching crowd" and her "theatrical" comeback (st. 9–10, 17–18). The poem acknowledges the theatricality of voice as well as the erotic component of art, demonstrating an acute awareness of itself as performative act and an anxiety about reception. Plath must have felt herself to be playing on a major stage, in competition with one of the great performers of the past, who also (as it happened) used the theatrical metaphor in such passages as "we — are dying in Drama— / And Drama—is never dead—" (poem 531). Plath was not simply thinking back through her mother, she was accusing the mother of failing to bring her secret code of rebellion into the open. Rather than borrow the masks and stilts of a "tragedy" envisioned by men (*J* 30; *CP* 117), Plath revolted against such conventions. I believe that the images of self-exposure in the poems of October (Lady Godiva, strip tease, bathing, and so on) have less to do with Plath's revelation of private details than with her libidinized sense of her newfound voice, her feeling that finally, after many years of "patching masks" (*J* 102), she was disclosing her speech at its strongest and most dangerous. In her October poems Plath felt naked and vulnerable, uncertain as to the attractiveness of the "figure" she presented. While she loved the voice that might heal the injury to her ego, she also felt doubtful that this voice, even at its most powerful, would prove powerful enough; she questioned her legitimacy as a poet at the very time that she made good on her aspiration; she exposed the contradictory cultural signs that surrounded and penetrated her; she feared that her revolt against men only masked a more profound trouble in herself; and she sensed the limitations of the voice that revolted, knowing that the triumph of that voice meant the defeat of other voices she also possessed, voices more perdurable, more encompassing, more capable, more liberated, if not from her civilization, then from the forces that would drive her mad.

Reading Plath's very last poems, written in January and February 1963, we might almost think she ceased to swerve from Dickinson at the end, so thoroughly do those texts correspond to the "formal feeling" described in "After great pain" (poem 341). If Dickinson inscribes a self at the far edge of utterance, a marmoreal being "like tombs" or "like a stone," Plath evokes her twin, a being like "rock" or like a "pearl" (*CP* 266, 271). In

"Edge" (*CP* 272–73), Plath's final poem, we read not of a "cere-monious" but of a "perfected" woman, not of a "quartz content-ment" but of a "smile" etched in stone, not of a heart grown "stiff" but of a corpse in a stiffening garden, not of feet that "go round" but of feet that have "come so far." In "After great pain" the poetic voice, unable to "bear" its witness any longer, be-comes attenuated, dislocated, and stupefied; in "Edge," the voice has already left the body, like the recording of a deceased woman being played at her own funeral. In remarkably similar vocabularies, both poems address the triad of crises that Harold Bloom associates with poetic crossings: death, the death of love, and death of the creative gift (*Stevens* 403).

Thus, in her final poem Plath seems to have abandoned "tes-sera," or correction, for something else. But what is it? Bloom's sixth and last revisionary ratio is "aprophrades," or the return of the dead, in which the ephebe's poem is held open to the pre-cursor, making it seem to us "not as though the precursor were writing it, but as though the later poet himself had written the precursor's characteristic work" (*Anxiety* 15–16). In "Edge," Plath may have sought to win her career-long agon with Dickinson, her mother's "bible," by appearing to have written Dickinson's poems. Conversely, since the relations among women poets are so remarkably complex, Plath may have been acknowledging her place in the web of connection, accepting her fate as the precursor's prophecy. She may even have been adopting Dickinson's "letting go" of voice as her own, echoing and then hypostatizing the predecessor's trope. Whatever her motives, Plath in her final weeks seems to have relented from her pro-ject of separation. She seems to have symbiotically reunited with her literary mother at the far edge of words.

GENERATIVITY

To GLIMPSE the Plath that might have been, let us back-track from the tropical depression of her last nine months to the quite different poetic climate of the period just preceding "Elm." From October 1961 to March 1962, Plath wrote in-tensely about mothers and motherhood, perhaps because she herself gave birth to her second child during that time. The period begins with an ambivalent representation of maternal power in "The Moon and the Yew Tree." In *The Bell Jar*, however, Esther Greenwood chooses to become a mother herself, while in its sequel, "Mothers," she bonds with two other young mothers, though refusing to join an oppressively pious "Mother's Union" (*JP* 10–19). "Three Women," together with the subsequent "By Candlelight" and "Nick and the Candlestick," climaxes Plath's effort to rethink maternity. In writing "Three Women," the longest and most ambitious poem in her oeuvre, Plath evades not only the demon of maternal disapproval (the mother who thought her daughter should have "sunk like a stone" [*JP* 25]), but the threat of male rejection (the father and husband who were "not-there" for her [*J* 279]), and the self-defeat of her own skepticism toward women (the feeling that "women in numbers" disturbed her [*J* 33]). The poem encodes Plath's unlearning of two key childhood lessons: that creativity was identified with masculinity and that even "the mothers" thought her work not "good enough" (*J* 271).

"Three Women" was a major departure for Plath. Composed for presentation on BBC radio, it attributes three alternating monologues to women undergoing birth or miscarriage in a maternity ward. While all three share features with Plath herself, none is a specular image; each possesses her own individuated "range of emotions" (Wagner-Martin 199). Beyond their alterity, the voices are remarkably independent. They do not reflect obsessively on the past, do not define themselves in terms of their difference from oppressors, and do not privilege men through either hostility or dependence. Although the second woman calls the earth a "vampire" (*CP* 181), apparently a malignant mother imago (Schwartz and Bollas 197; see also *J* 280), none of the three names her mother or father, and only the second alludes to her mate. If the women do at times experience the helplessness and self-injury that Susan Gubar attributes to Plath's texts about female creation ("Page" 256–58), they also make decisions, consent to change, experience joy, and exert control over their discourse. Indeed, they inhabit a magical arena of young women's authority. The traditional female governance of the nursery in this case permits a revolutionary institution of female linguistic power.

Plath herself assumes an unprecedented degree of autonomy in "Three Women." First, she denies the prestige of the phallus, refusing either to subordinate female experience to the desires of males or to trivialize motherhood by idealizing it. "Three Women" refashions the unfortunate "creature without a penis" of the Freudian text ("Female Sexuality" 259) into a being who appears satisfactory and whole. Whereas Freud wrote of male penis and female "jealousy" ("Anatomical Distinction" 192), Plath's second voice asserts that it is men who are "jealous" of female anatomy (*CP* 179). Whereas Freud depicted childbirth as a poor substitute for a penis ("Anatomical Distinction" 195), Plath's poem celebrates childbirth as a "great event" that allows women to achieve feelings of creativity and power. Whereas Lacan regarded the phallus as a signifier and Ophelia as Hamlet's cry of "O phallus" (*Ecrits* 285–90; "Desire" 23), Plath's speakers seem to regard their wombs as signifiers. Refusing to entertain Freud's premise that what a girl "wants" is a penis ("Anatomical Distinction" 191), these speakers imply that it is men who are wanting. "Three Women" places women at the center of the symbolic order, substituting a trinity of female originators for the male myth of origins. By positing female norms of experience, anatomy, and language, the poem subverts the patriarchal assumptions that frequently regulate Plath's texts, even her poems of revolt.

Plath pulls free from the mother's hypersymbiosis as well. Surely the woman who advised her daughter to write about "decent courageous people" would not wish to "appropriate" these frightened, angry, conflicted, and self-assertive monologues (*LH* 477; *J* 281). If Plath achieved only an illusory independence in "Medusa," she attained a more authentic separation in "Three Women" by inventing female voices that speak beside, rather than against, the mother. In a complementary sense, however, Plath's voices also speak *for* the mother. Nancy Chodorow, revising Freud, argues that women value childbearing not as a substitute for a penis but as an occasion to recover their pre-Oedipal feelings of oneness with their mothers (201).

In a parallel way, Plath restores her mother's voice—the "one mouth" she "would be tongue to" (*CP* 132)—through giving birth to voices of her own. She recovers a oneness by creating characters (in both senses of the term) with whom she feels united. Thus, in "Three Women" Plath achieves a dual misprision. She severs a Western linguistic tradition that, as Margaret Homans has shown, associates entrance into the symbolic order of language with the loss or murder of the mother (*Bearing* 2–6, 41–52); but at the same time she asserts her difference from her mother by rejecting the progenitor's narrowness and control. This complex act of differentiation within assimilation permits the female subject to transcend both the literality of pre-Oedipal language and the particular configurations of the mother's discourse.

Just as Plath seeks to recover her mother's verbal power while transgressing her mother's discursive boundaries, so she revises the texts of her literary mothers, Emily Dickinson and Virginia Woolf. Like many of Dickinson's strongest poems, "Three Women" exposes a drama of physical and psychological pain, but its association of female creativity with childbirth has no precedent in the earlier poet's discourse. Plath defaces Dickinson's image of creative power as a male double named "Tim" (196), as well as her own earlier propensity to figure creativity as a "snakecharmer" or "bull" (*CP* 79, 108). She breaks through the reticence and perfectionism that typify and confine the Dickinson-Moore-Bishop line by substituting a gynocentric aesthetic that announces, "Perfection is terrible, it can't have children" (*CP* 262). Plath misreads Woolf in a related way. As Sandra Gilbert has noted ("House" 216–19), "Three Women" resembles *The Waves*, in which six stylistically uniform voices narrate their diverse experiences. Like *The Bell Jar*, "Three Women" revises the Woolfian text by focusing on the speakers' reproductive experience. Only two of Woolf's characters, Bernard and Susan, have children, and only the latter even briefly represents herself as a parent. Plath's drama of birth, miscarriage, childlessness, and motherhood reconstitutes the Woolfian plot of gain and loss, consciousness and voice, in quite another sense: within a realm that Woolf repressed, and in a genre that she labeled foreign to women's genius. Whereas Woolf evokes the spiritual dimension of men's and women's lives together, Plath suggests meanings specific to women's biological and cultural being. Whereas Woolf aspires to an androgynous style, Plath explores the resources of "womanly" writing (Plath, quoted in Wagner-Martin 218). Whereas Woolf, like Dickinson, figures the artist as a male (Bernard), Plath depicts creators as three ordinary women. Thus "Three Women" simultaneously perpetuates and breaks the precursors' causal chain, moving Woolf's "room of one's own" and Dickinson's "smallest room" out of the "father's house" and into the freehold of women.

In this revolutionary text, then, Plath managed to liberate herself from all sorts of conscious and unconscious restraints. The poem presents an image of a Plath we hardly know, open to others yet not dominated by them, free of both "self-worship and self-loathing" (J 13), not fixated in either anger or despair. "Three Women" achieves its psychological and feminist insight, however, at the expense of insight into issues of class. Although the poem's voices describe themselves as a housewife, a secretary, and a Cambridge student (all roles that Plath herself had played), their discourse deflects economic considerations. If they experienced oppression in housework and office work, or privilege at Cambridge, they choose not to dwell on those conditions. Their monologues share Plath's own ideology, which was relatively class-unconscious, as befits a follower of the Liberal party in Britain and Adlai Stevenson in America. Although Plath received an elite education on sufferance and lived all of her life on the edge of a financial abyss, she did not resolve that contradiction by means of either a conservative identification with the class that trained her or a socialist identification with the class that shared her "insecurity" (J 272). She translated the contradiction into one between the privilege of voice and the oppression of silence. Her first loyalty was to the potential space of the text, which she initially conceived of as "a little colored island of words" (J 321), but which she eventually recognized as being "waist-deep in history" (*CP* 258). Despite her increasing politicization, however, she refused to acknowledge

that the imagination might be an illusion or a luxury properly
subordinated to more basic needs. For her, poetry *was* a basic
need, "like water or bread or something absolutely essential to
me" (Interview 172).

Although the first publication of "Three Women" labeled its
speaking subjects a "wife," a "secretary," and a "young woman,"
thereby adhering to canons of realism, all subsequent editions
identify them simply as "voices," implying a rhetorical basis
for their existence. As voices, they occupy a frontier between
body and text, human intention and the free play of signs.
Their words echo and diverge, neither together nor apart, but
polyphonically suspended in textual space. Although their
words certainly reveal "the individuality of the female response
to their bodies" (Bundtzen 213) and "the threatened and vulnerable identities of women" (Rosenblatt 112), they also encode the
powers, anxieties, aims, and limits of language-production itself. As Roland Barthes said in his last interview, half-jestingly,
"Writing is creation, and to that extent it is also a form of procreation" (*Grain* 365). In the present analysis, I wish to high-
light the degree to which Plath too represents writing as
procreation, as the birthing of language.

The metapoetic code of "Three Women" comes clearest in
the context of women's struggle for literary language in our culture. In *Bearing the Word*, Margaret Homans argues that since
male writers have historically claimed the symbolic order as
their exclusive domain, women writers have characteristically
"literalized" figures as part of an ambivalent turning toward
the only linguistic practices left open to them. She identifies
four vehicles by which they have accomplished this goal: the
transformation of metaphor into actual event; the figure of the
Virgin Mary, giving birth to the male Word; women characters who play the role of a man's amanuensis or translator; and
moments when the female text itself transmits the words of
males. Homans finds that, through these motifs, "the women
writers and their women characters dramatize at once the way
in which the relation of women as women to symbolic language is continually in jeopardy and the hope that the father's
law might cease to be the exclusive language of literary culture"

(33). Homans's analysis is evocative for our reading of Plath, who repeatedly used the figure of the secretary in precisely the way Homans suggests and who also at times associated female language with the unliterary. But in "Three Women" Plath does not move unilaterally from the figurative to the literal ends of the linguistic spectrum; she oscillates between the two. She literalizes the idea of creative making as a childbirth scene, returning literary tropes of pregnancy, labor, and birth to their biological referents; and then, I would suggest, she recomposes that scene as a scene of writing. Swinging between the literal and the figurative, Plath's text escapes the name of the father while avoiding nostalgia for the silence of the mother's body. If the goal of women's writing in the late twentieth century is to discover a capable language free of phallic law, then "Three Women" may prove one of the most significant landmarks in that enterprise.

In a general sense, "Three Women" affirms Erik Erikson's notion that generativity is the "central" human experience (*Childhood* 266–67) and Jean Baker Miller's claim that creativity is an "absolute necessity" for women (44). More narrowly, it examines the role of the author and the work, which Foucault calls the most "fundamental" issue in literary study (*Language* 115). Reflecting on the birth and miscarriage of literary language, the poem evokes what I have called the *creative moment*, in which the writing subject reflects on her own productivity and on her text — the other self to which she feels attached but from which she also feels distanced. Sandra Gilbert has noted that the first woman's infant seems to resemble a poem ("Myth" 255). I wish to go even further in my analysis, positing that each of the poem's three women functions as an alternative guise of the female poet. The first voice produces living but unexceptional texts (like the Plath who feared she was a hack). The third voice gives her creation away (like the youthful Plath who put her husband's career before her own and like the ultimate Plath who yielded her texts to her executor). And the second voice, the most articulate of the three, miscarries her inspiration (like the Plath we most prize today, the one who discovered her power in disaster).

Giving birth may well strike us as an inappropriate metaphor for literary production. Viewed from a social perspective,
the childbirth "metaphor" conspires with patriarchal culture's
regressive desire to valorize women "exclusively as mother," in
Adrienne Rich's words (*Woman* 107). As Nina Auerbach and
Elaine Showalter ("Feminist Criticism") have argued, it essentializes women in terms of a single biological function, and it
blurs the distinction between involuntary and voluntary achievement. Moreover, from a linguistic perspective, the childbirth
metaphor cancels itself, for when the female poet labors to
bear the word, she gives birth not to life but to absence. Plath
herself ultimately recognized the lack of self-referentiality of
the text, alluding at the end of her career to hollows, shreds,
and "dead" children (*CP* 270-72). In making writing a "hollow
and failing substitute for real life" (*J* 312), she placed loss —
"echoes travelling off from the center"— at the heart of her project: loss, the very thing she thought to ward off or defeat.
Thus, to the degree that textual voice functions as a metaphor-
ical replacement for organic being, it proves a dangerous transumption, fostering a habit of mind that allowed Plath, when
textual gratification failed her, to turn to death as her last
metaphor.

If, however, we regard giving birth to texts as a metonym
rather than a metaphor, as a trope of experience rather than of
product, then a quite different critical horizon opens. As Susan
Stanford Friedman has recently shown, women poets ranging
from H.D. to Erica Jong and Lucille Clifton have sought to
resignify "mother-as-poet" in a developing counterpoetic of the
female body (67-75). In "Three Women" above all her other
poems, Plath participates in this refashioning of the female
self. She anticipates Susan Gubar's call for texts that celebrate
"uniquely female powers of creativity without perpetuating
destructive feminine socialization" and that depict creativity as
"act or process" rather than as "artistic object" ("Page" 262-63).
She also prefigures Hélène Cixous's advocacy of female writing
that emanates from "a desire to live self from within, a desire
for a swollen belly, for language, for blood" (261). As I see it,
however, Plath contributes to this counterpoetic neither through

"metaphor" (Friedman 49), which substitutes one competitive term for another, nor through a notion that "women are body" (Cixous 257), which essentializes women, but rather through associative play. Her second and third voices themselves (and the first voice too by the end of the poem) speak and think in metonyms: "Every little word hooked to every little word, and act to act" (*CP* 178). They construct a discursive world of breaking apart and holding on (*CP* 180–81), of severance and adhering (*CP* 182–84). Beyond its evasion of bipolarity and hierarchy, metonymy is a mode of indeterminacy and deferral, for where does the associative chain end? The first voice's child—her living text—will "marry what he wants and where he will" (*CP* 186). Plath is trying to reclaim metonymy for a reconstructed matriarchal community.

In "Three Women," Plath suggests that by giving birth either to child or to trope, the female subject experiences the

Plath with her children, Frieda and Nicholas, in 1962.

Source: Plath Manuscript II. Manuscripts Department, Lilly Library, Indiana University, Bloomington, Indiana.

pain and pleasure of her own generativity and in that sense gives birth to herself. To the degree that textual voice functions as a metonymic link between poetic and empirical experience, between a woman's mental and physical creativity, it unsettles the social codes patriarchal culture employs to define, to delimit, and to "waste" her (*J* 291). Voice as metonym becomes a "magnificent" source of satisfaction (Interview 172).

If Plath frequently complained of the practical incompatibility of motherhood and writing (*LH* 298, 384, 439, 441, 495), she also sought to synthesize "making in all its forms" (*JP* 64). She did not wish to subordinate her career to motherhood (as her mother wanted her to do and had done herself), nor did she wish to forgo motherhood in favor of writing (as her teacher Mary Ellen Chase advocated and as Woolf and Dickinson had done). She tried to finesse her dilemma by viewing childbearing as an impetus to wordbearing (*LH* 450), by regarding each activity as, in Gilbert's word, an "analog" of the other ("Myth" 255). We know that Plath characteristically associated writing with lovemaking, figuration with pregnancy, writer's block with sterility and stillbirth, and words with living beings (*CP* 116, 142, 157, 204; *J* 106, 252, 253, 300, 309; *JP* 65; *LH* 244). It is no accident that she composed "Three Women" midway between two births: that of her second child, Nicholas (in January 1962) and that of her first American book, *The Colossus* (in May of the same year). Yet she also knew that the associations between "children and writing" (*J* 251) were complex, ironic, tenuous, and unstable — capable of being used against as well as for her., Thinking of her texts as deformed or miscarried, she sought to make a strength out of those very weaknesses, just as, thinking herself an inadequate homemaker by Aurelia Plath's standards, she continued to take pleasure in domestic activities.

Thus, in "Three Women" more than in any other text, Plath placed authoring and mothering in metonymic relation to each other, subverting the phallocentric association of pen with penis. The poem's cultural countermyth suggests that if "anatomy is destiny," then women are the natural makers. Foreseeing that female expression would be released only when it became other to the metaphysical oddity or impossibility that patriarchal tradition had made of it, "Three Women" seizes on and elaborates Whitman's tropes of an egg-laying poet and a poetic birth on a "nine-month midnight" (*Leaves* 246).

THE POEM's first voice, that of the wife, progresses in her monologues from narcissistic contentment (*CP* 176–77) through an emotional and physical nadir during heavy labor (*CP* 180) and then back toward recovery (*CP* 185–86). I believe that the feminist critic Bundtzen errs when she accuses the wife's discourse of "sentimental banality" (212), just as the nonfeminist Rosenblatt does when he praises it as "positive" and "normative" (115). From their opposing perspectives, both commentators imply that the wife's utterance reflects the conventional notions of maternity that Plath inherited from her mother and from such books as *The Case for Chastity*, whereas I find that it forcefully revises such notions. The woman's final monologue indicates that her initial smugness has disappeared: she is haunted by dreams of the deformed children she might have had and by fears that her son may not love her (*CP* 185–86). As a result of giving birth, she has grown more complicated and doubtful, exchanging self-satisfaction for a deepened awareness of her vulnerability in a dangerous and unpredictable universe. The experience of childbirth has shifted her ego ideal from being a center of "attention" (*CP* 176) to being "common" (*CP* 186), a change underscored by her position in the text as both the first to speak and the first to stop speaking. Shaken, she has drawn into herself, like one of Dickinson's, H.D.'s, or Moore's armored creatures.

Regarded as a simple mimesis, this voice seems the one furthest from artistic creation, the one who glories in motherhood. But if we regard her metonymically, as a creator in the wide sense, the metapoetic dimension opens. We then see that, having given birth to her "image" (*CP* 183), the first voice expresses a complex of conflicting emotions about authorship: anxiety over the production of "terrible" or ill-formed texts (*CP* 185); satisfaction at having delivered a "normal" text (*CP* 186); desire to live beyond the borders of a single lifetime; fear of artistic greatness, since the "exception" inevitably climbs the "sorrowful hill" (*CP* 186); and finally a resigned awareness that, because signifying power resides in language rather than in the *cogito*, the author's will to power over her text cannot withstand the text's independent "will" (*CP* 186). As Plath wrote in her journal, writing "goes about on its own in the world" (*J* 272). Thus the first voice has relinquished egoistic passivity only to encounter the limits of intention. Nevertheless, the process of giving birth has reaffirmed her femaleness, which she gynocentrically equates with creative "power" (*CP* 180). In delivering her poem-child, she has given birth to a new, more encompassing, language of self-representation, one that includes uncertainty and confusion, fear and desire.

The third voice, that of the Cambridge student, speaks in counterpoint to the first, inverting the predecessor's narrative by emphasizing premature creativity and lost creation. In contrast to the wife, who pronounces herself "ready" (*CP* 177), the student has felt all along that she "wasn't ready" (*CP* 178). Like the youthful Plath, whom Dr. Beuscher characterized as being "afraid of premature choices cutting off other choices" (*J* 273), the student feels dragged apart (*CP* 178), forced to choose between motherhood and the intellectual life. Whereas the wife inhabits a universe of attentive signs, the student's world is "small, mean and black" (*CP* 178). Whereas the wife calls her infant's cry "the hook I hang on" (*CP* 183), the student figures her child's cries as "hooks" that "grate" (*CP* 182). And whereas the wife exclaims, "What did my fingers do before they held him? / . . . / I shall not let go" (*CP* 181), the student says, "I undo her fingers like bandages: I go" (*CP* 184). A walking "wound" (*CP* 184), the student returns alone to Cambridge, where her black gown symbolizes her grief. In a poetic drama centrally concerned with fulfilled and frustrated desire, she alone is left unassuaged, cut off even from the poem's other voices, both of whom find some source of consolation. She concludes:

> What is that bird that cries
> With such sorrow in its voice?
> I am young as ever, it says. What is it I miss?   (*CP* 186)

This conclusion emphasizes the third voice's strong associations with the figure of an apprentice poet. Using imagery that recalls Whitman, Dickinson, Teasdale, and a whole tradition of equating poetry with birdsong, the third voice seems to suggest that utterance arises out of loss. Her discovery resembles that made by the young boy in "Out of the Cradle Endlessly Rocking" and by Plath herself, who published her first poem soon after her father's death and considered herself thereafter to be a professional poet (Butscher 12–13; Interview 167). Conflating Whitman's tropes of a "bird" that is a "solitary singer" and "grass" that is "uttering tongues" (*Leaves* 246–53, 33–35), the third voice calls herself as "solitary as grass" (*CP* 186). The child she relinquishes seems to represent an unsatisfactory text: a "dream" without meaning, an "island" of ugly "cries," a "mouth" that utters "such dark sounds it cannot be good" (*CP* 185, 182). Continuing to "miss" the target, the third voice laments her artistic puerility. Yet the very "sorrow" of her utterance suggests that the necessary precondition for creative success may at last be present. Like the poet-to-be of "Ocean 1212-W," she may stand ready to transform her loss into artistic gain. The infant who seems "carved in wood" (*CP* 182) resembles the compensatory "monkey of wood" that the young girl of the memoir discovers (*JP* 24).

Although in principle all voices in "Three Women" are created equal, the second voice, that of the secretary who miscarries, seems more equal than the others. She speaks the most (twenty-two stanzas, compared with the wife's nineteen and the student's twelve); she speaks last; and of the three she is the most capable of generalization. Whereas the first and third voices faithfully track each other through labor, birth, and post partum reflection, the second voice adheres to a variant pattern. Originating in loss, her discourse expresses anger, self-doubt, self-hatred, and finally self-forgiveness. Employing Holocaustal imagery, she uncovers feelings that remain latent and ideas that remain unthought in the others' discourse. She is the most illuminated consciousness in the poem.

In her initial monologues, the secretary powerfully communicates her skepticism toward men, her anxiety about gender, and her wish to die. Despite having obeyed the patriarchal imperatives "to be blind in love" and "not to think too hard" (*CP* 178), she has not received the promised reward of a child. This bitter failure gives her ironic leverage on masculinist ideology. She accuses men of institutionalizing their power in governments that they control and in a religion that portrays male flatness as "holy" and female roundness as gross (*CP* 179). She associates male culture with "bulldozers, guillotines, white chambers of shrieks" (*CP* 177), a triad that we may translate as destruction, execution, and Nazi torture. Her critique reflects Virginia Woolf's position in *Three Guineas*, and it incidentally prefigures gender analyses by Ruth Bleier, Sherry Ortner, and Michelle Rosaldo and social criticism by Mary Daly, Dorothy Dinnerstein, and Adrienne Rich. But like Plath herself, the secretary internalizes her quarrel with others, lamenting that "I, too, create corpses" (*CP* 182). Having miscarried, she feels disidentified as a woman, reduced in status to a Tiresian "shadow" who functions as neither man nor woman (*CP* 182). Furthermore, her loss reactivates an anterior, unworked-through grief. As a child she had deeply loved a "lichen-bitten name" (*CP* 177), presumably a dead father's, like the "name" carved on stone in "Electra on Azalea Path" (*CP* 117) and *The Bell Jar* (*BJ* 197–98). Fearing that her love has killed both that "dead one" and this "unborn one" (*CP* 178), haunted by Holocaustal images of bodies "mounded" around her (*CP* 181), the second woman feels her old "dead love of death" return (*CP* 177). In her last monologues, however, a process of recovery apparently commences. Her scarring descent into the "inferno" has allowed her to deliver a vital new self, that of an intellectual and an artist (*CP* 184, 186–87).

To pursue our more radical line of interpretation, let us consider the second voice as a figure of the writer whose words have miscarried. From this perspective, the voice resembles that of Sexton, describing words that leak from her pen "like a miscarriage" ("Silence")—or Plath herself, hiding a rejected poem "under a pile of papers like a stillborn illegitimate baby" (*J* 106). The second voice is, after all, a secretary, a position that closely associates her with words. Those words, however, are normally dictated by a male executive. That fact helps to account for her anger at men, and it additionally connects her to women's historical role as transmitters of men's texts (a role played professionally by Aurelia Plath and periodically by Sylvia Plath herself). The second voice explains that when she sits at her desk, the letters proceed metonymically "from three black keys, and these black keys proceed / From my alphabetical fingers" (*CP* 177). She feels simply a "bit" or "cog" in the masculine signifying machine, producing a series of "mechanical" rather than personal "echoes." This situation convinces her that she has lost a "dimension," which I interpret not simply as her baby but as the creative "fulfillment" Plath spoke of so often in letters and interviews (e.g., *LH* 298; Interview 176). Although the second voice has loved a lichen-bitten male name, her failure to give things new names, her own names, leads to a kind of "death" (*CP* 177), akin to what Plath elsewhere terms the "death of the imagination" (*J* 109). Like Plath herself, the second voice feels threatened by maternal as well as paternal presences. While the male "gods" have forced her to remain creatively "flat" (*CP* 179), the female imagoes have collaboratively wished her "barren" and "empty" (*CP* 181–82). As a result, she feels herself "neither a woman . . . nor a man" (*CP* 182)—perhaps evoking Plath's own self-image during her marriage to a husband who insisted that she be neither a "whining poetess" nor a "man-imitator" (*LH* 244, 277) and who moreover encouraged her to perform secretarial chores for him when she was not sewing on his buttons or mending his socks.

If the second voice begins as a silenced artist, a woman forbidden entry into the symbolic order of language except in the role of amanuensis, she ends in revolt:

> I shall not be accused by isolate buttons,
> Holes in the heels of socks, the white mute faces
> Of unanswered letters, coffined in a letter case.   (*CP* 182)

Prodded by her history of defeats, she intends to uncoffin her letters, to unmute her language, to breathe life into her creative corpses, to answer her call. When she states that losing a child resembles losing "an eye, a leg, a tongue" (*CP* 183), her implicit equation reads: child = eye, leg, tongue = vision, standing, voice = poem. Just as the starfish grows back its "arms" (*CP* 184), so she proposes to regenerate the poems that have thus far died aborning. Speaking with "fingers, not a tongue" (*CP* 184), which I interpret as a substitution of textual for phonic voice, she intends to replace her miscarried texts with viable ones: "Nothing has happened / . . . that cannot be erased, ripped up and scrapped, begun again" (*CP* 184). "Like a spirit" or a revitalized imagination (*CP* 184), she concludes her discourse at home in an Eliotesque "lamplight" (*CP* 186), stitching lace onto fabric, an image of nonpatriarchal composition. ("Text," like "textile," derives from *texere*, to weave.) Her last lines allude to three interconnected images that are canonical in our literature: Whitman's "grass," which signifies (among other things) the woven green flag of his disposition, a child, an interpretable hieroglyphic, and uttering tongues (*Leaves* 33–34); Dickinson's "Grass" that is both a sphere of simple green and a sod hiding a volcano (poems 333, 1677); and Stevens's fiction of the "green leaves" covering and curing the barren stone of reality ("The Rock"). Transuming all those complex images of vital poetic art, and Plath's own "flickering grass tongues" as well (*CP* 79), the second voice affirms that for her too, "the little grasses / Crack through stone, and they are green with life" (*CP* 187).

The second voice of "Three Women" inaugurated Plath's period of textual self-realization after years of artistic miscarriage. With this voice, Plath prophesied her own doubling of biographical identity and poetic immanence, bodily woman and textual child. The second voice states, "I recover / From the long fall," though she also braces her hands ominously "as for a fall" (*CP* 187). As always, Plath's powers of prediction were astounding. Yet she may not have understood, however implicit it is in her image of a future fall, that the prophecy would be its own fulfillment—that her dream, which must have seemed so close that she could hardly fail to grasp it, was already behind her.

CHAPTER FOUR

"There Are Two of Me Now"

One face, one voice, one habit, and two persons. . . .
How have you made division of yourself?
—Shakespeare, *Twelfth Night*

God sets us nothing but riddles. Here the boundaries meet and
all contradictions exist side by side.
—Dostoevsky, *The Brothers Karamazov*

PLATH once wrote that her suicide was a knot in
which much was caught (*J* 302). In meditating on the poet, I
have often returned to that knot, and I shall continue to do so.
But there is another knot that also catches much of her creative
drive and poetic vocation. That is the knot she tied with her
husband.

Like Jean Baker Miller's example of "Beatrice," who despite
many accomplishments felt like "no person at all" unless she
was using herself "*with* someone else and *for* someone else" (90),
Plath felt sterile and empty without Ted Hughes. Existing
almost without a skin, she wanted to take her husband into
herself, fusing their egos and confusing their identities. In this
desire she may have sought to reexperience her idealized
pre-Oedipal relationship with her mother—or to repair the
fractures that had actually rent her pre-Oedipal state. On a
conscious level, Plath made her husband into a "model" of her
father rather than her mother (*CP* 224). Nevertheless, as Freud
observed, since the relationship with the mother precedes and
underlies the relationship with the father, "many a woman who
takes her father as the model for her choice of a husband, or as-
signs her father's place to him, yet in her married life repeats
with her husband her bad relations with her mother" ("Female
Sexuality" 258). Mistaking merger for intimacy, Plath attempted

178

to unite with a man who possessed both the controlling imperatives of her mother and the fearsomeness of her father.

If Plath associated her husband with her father and, through
him, with her mother, she similarly associated authorship with
both paternal privilege and maternal creativity, as we have
seen. Fundamentally, her textual activity, like her marriage,
reflected her relationship with her mother. We may speculate
that throughout her life Plath felt the effects of her fissured pre-
Oedipal union with her mother and of their subsequent hypersymbiosis or "osmosis" (*LH* 32). She ambivalently sought to
correct and to reproduce that relationship in her interactions
with both her husband and her texts. Indeed, since her marriage and her career shared a common motive, we cannot fully
distinguish between them. Plath interlaced goals usually kept
separate: affective satisfaction and vocational identity, attachment and autonomy. Understanding her writing and her wedding to Hughes as part of a single package, she exhorted her
textual self to "let flesh be knit, and each step hence go famous"
(*CP* 45). In that dual aim, she masked rather than confronted
the contradictions within her wishes as well as those between
her wishes and the social options available to her. She hoped
that her marriage and her poetic calling would permeate and
reinforce each other, though in the end they proved to be coun-
terweights, opponents in a zero-sum game.

In this final chapter, let us try to fathom the ways Plath's love
life and her creative life merged and divided, and the ways
merger and division governed the internal dynamics of each.
In undertaking this quest, we shall have occasion to study first
her journal, in which she thought she observed her life "unfolding in clear glass" (*J* 161), and then the literary texts of her last
two years, in which her desire for oneness and her contradictory wish for separation played themselves out as a powerful
system of signs. We shall witness her attempt to transform her
husband and herself into duplicates of each other and, when
that attempt failed, her even more complex effort to turn her
texts and herself into self-reflexive doubles.

A MARRIAGE OF POETS

IDENTITY formation can often prove difficult for young women in our society, since they tend to define themselves "in a context of relationship" rather than individually (Gilligan 160–61). Plath's particular way of constructing her identity increased the difficulties she faced. While basing much of her self-concept on competition, she also sought connection and care in a marital union. Moreover, the man she wished to unite with was himself marked by a need for distance and isolation, paradoxically conjoined with elements of dependency. Conflicted within herself and married to a man whose needs were at odds with her own, she lived her emotional life among "uncaged tigers" (*CP* 85). Although she hoped that love could cure her injured self, her affective relationship seemed only to reopen the original wounds. Plath's situation was further complicated by the way she involved her marriage in her drive to become a writer. As we saw in chapter 2, she associated her husband with male poetry. Initially attracted to him as a "colossal" statue of a poet, she introduced herself to him by quoting his verses (*J* III; *JP* 183; Stevenson 74–77; Wagner-Martin 130). Ever after, he remained for her "the Poet of England" (*J* 211), an individual whose essence could be summarized in three words: "He writes poems" (*LH* 234). She wanted to be "married to a poet" (*J* 153) and, implicitly, to poetry itself.

We can gain insight into Plath's attempt to achieve oneness through marriage and at the same time to marry herself to poetry by considering one of the more striking episodes in all of the *Journals*. This paradigmatic episode begins on Plath's last day of teaching at Smith College in May 1958. Professionally and socially, the year had been excruciatingly difficult for her, so much so that she refused to continue teaching a second year despite an invitation to do so. She felt unprepared and inadequate as a teacher, frightened to appear as an authority in classrooms where she had recently sat as a student, and awkward in interactions with colleagues who had once been her teachers. Nevertheless, her notes suggest that she was a more than competent teacher, and her accounts of the applause she received in every class (*LH* 341; *J* 230) indicate that she was successful with her students — and almost pathetically eager for recognition.

Her final day of class was doubly important to her. First, she had completed a task that had initially seemed beyond her. Second, since the day was her last as a teacher, it marked the conclusion of her psychological "moratorium" (Erikson, *Life History* 199–201) and the commencement of her true vocation, writing. So in two senses the day symbolized a rite of passage. Plath wanted to formalize the transition by sharing it with her husband. When the day arrived, she made a "ceremonial stab" at asking Hughes to drive down with her so that she could see him and "rejoice" the very minute she finished teaching (*J* 230). Arranging for him to visit the library and then to wait for her in their car, she stopped alone at the campus coffee shop before class. At the coffee shop, she observed a married colleague, William Van Voris, seeming to flirt with one of his female students. She became absorbed in a vision of male professors taking up with young mistresses, leaving their wives neglected and anguished: "These images piled up. I felt tempted to drop in at the library before class and share with Ted my amusing insight, my ringside seat at Van Voris and the Seductive Smith Girl: or William S. is bad agayne. But I went to class" (*J* 232). Plath's speculations about a colleague's adultery and his wife's death as a consequence — "maybe Jacky will die: she has death, and great pain, written on her stretched mouth" — seems to have represented a working out on a fantasy level of a possibility in her own marriage that she was unwilling to confront directly. But fate was preparing to force her to do so, for the apparent flirtation she had witnessed prefigured the situation in which she almost immediately found herself.

On completing her class, Plath "ran" expectantly to the parking lot, "half-expecting to meet Ted on the way to the car, but more sure of finding him inside" (*J* 232). But the car was empty. She spotted an almost allegorical Van Voris bidding his student good-bye; when he began to approach her, she turned her back on him and got into the car. Resisting an impulse to drive home, perhaps for fear of what she might find there, she drove around campus instead and eventually found her husband returning from Paradise Pond, "where girls take their boys to neck on weekends." She saw that Hughes was looking into the uplifted eyes of a young woman with brownish hair, lipsticked grin, and bare legs: "I saw this in several sharp flashes, like blows. I could not tell the color of the girl's eyes but Ted could, and his smile, though open and engaging as the girl's was, took on an ugliness in context. His stance next to Van Voris clicked into place" (*J* 232-33).

Although the sight disturbed Plath, it did not surprise her, since she "knew" what she would see, and she had known "for a very long time" (*J* 232). Curiously, she identified the young woman with herself: "He thought her name was Sheila; once he thought my name was Shirley" (*J* 233; cf. *J* 137). Plath seems to have foreseen her end in her beginning—when she had observed Hughes with another young woman at a Cambridge party and had stolen him away (*J* 112; *JP* 180-81, 184). Now she correctly guessed that the same destiny awaited her. Her first reaction to Hughes's "infidelity" was to repudiate suicide as a solution, a classic instance of the "negation" that reveals "unconscious and repressed material" (Freud, "Negation" 181-82). "No," she wrote, "I won't jump out of a window or drive Warren's car into a tree, or fill the garage at home with carbon monoxide and save expense, or slit my wrists and lie in the bath" (*J* 233). Instead, she would sublimate her pain and anger in work: "I can teach, and will write and write well. I can get in a year of that, perhaps, before other choices follow." She resorted to just this strategy five years later when Hughes's infidelity became actual.

We can see that Plath's expected day of triumph, her intended private ceremony of maturation and change, turned to ashes as a result of her husband's seemingly casual action. Instead of reaffirming her place in the world, she found herself ontologically insecure—at question and alone. That Hughes should have chosen this day to display his potential for infidelity indicates, at the least, that he was insensitive to her needs. At the most, it suggests that he was actively hostile to her needs, that he unconsciously sought to keep her weak, subor-

dinate, distant, and injured. Plath's psychiatrist hinted at the
latter possibility when she asked Plath (early in their second
set of therapeutic sessions, which began, not coincidentally,
soon after the episode being discussed here): "Would you have
the guts to admit you'd made a wrong choice?" and "Does Ted
want you to get better?" (*J* 270, 272).

Following the incident, according to Plath, Hughes refused
to discuss his motives and feelings openly: "The fake excuses,
vague confusions about name and class. . . . And the complete
refusal to explain" (*J* 233). She responds to the violation of her
attachment with anger directed at herself and at him: "All stu-
pidity and frankness on my side. . . . I made the most amusing, ironic and fatal step in trusting Ted was unlike other vain
and obfuscating and self-indulgent men" (*J* 234). She wonders
why she had made his concerns her own and had wished to see
him at his best, since he clearly "does not care." Then nearly
a month of silence. When her journalistic monologue resumes,
she records physical battles, in which "Ted [bore] bloody claw
marks for a week, and . . . I got hit and saw stars," and an
eventual reconciliation: "Air cleared. We are intact. And nothing . . . is worth jeopardizing what I have, which is so much
the angels might well envy it" (*J* 235).

We might briefly draw several conclusions from this episode.
First, it seems that Plath and Hughes did not have a relationship that allowed them to talk honestly about their feelings, despite Plath's comment about "frankness" on her side. They
substituted charges, counter charges, sulky silences, physical
violence, and "complete refusals to explain" for constructive
conflict. Since they did not share their feelings, they were apt
to misunderstand the role each played for the other. They seem
not to have known each other well, seem almost to have spoken
different languages. Each became, in Hughes's telling phrase,
chapters in the other's mythology ("Notes" 187).

Second, we observe the power of Plath's habit of compart-
mentalizing her psyche into "subdivision after subdivision" (*J*
70). Despite her self-injunctions, in relatively healthy times, to
remain "fluid," she was characteristically rigid in her psychic
structures. She immediately follows her bitter portrait of a mar-

riage to a man who "does not care" with a depiction of a marriage that "the angels might well envy" and seems not to notice
the contradiction. One suspects that, except under her psychiatrist's prodding, she talked no more openly to herself than to
her husband. Despite her luminous intelligence, she often
seemed alienated from herself as well as from him, and in that
sense, as well as in many others, the two were doubles of each
other — pictures of estrangement, of the intellect self-blinded.

We may further posit that Hughes doubled Plath's own ambition and self-doubt back onto herself. It was less a man that
she attempted to marry, less the voice and flesh of the other,
than her own sense of herself as a poet, her own egotism com-
promised by low self-esteem. Locked in a hypersymbiosis with
that image of herself, she found the image resisting her every
effort to change. Dr. Beuscher's questions that Plath tried so
long to evade return to haunt us as they must have haunted
her: "Would you have the guts to admit you'd made a wrong
choice?" and "Does Ted want you to get better?" Married to
Hughes, she was married to her sickness, and just as her anger
reflects the degree to which the marriage did not meet her
needs, her repression of the anger reflects the even greater degree to which she was unwilling and afraid to change.

At such moments as this in *Journals*, as in *Letters Home*, we
may be reasonably certain that the editorial apparatus will do
its best to lead us astray. The editors introduce the episode
thus: "At this time, and for months afterward, Plath began to
feel an upsurge of rage, an emotion she rarely allowed herself.
In the passage that follows it is a rage against her husband in
which a small incident takes on enormous proportions, and is
quickly transferred to some girls in a public park. As Plath
notes eight months later (December 27), the real source is her
father" (*J* 228). According to this theory, Plath's anger at her
father spontaneously combusted at this time, taking the form
of fury at her husband and then, as we shall see, at some young
women in a park. It is an ingenious thesis, though we may wonder why the editors are so eager to jump to a problematic, complex explanation when a simple and obvious one is readily at
hand. They exclude the possibility that when Plath seems to

be, has cause to be, and believes herself to be angry at her husband, she actually *is* angry at her husband. Our skepticism
must increase when we realize that Plath's second episode of
anger, concerning the young women in the park, remains inex-
plicable if we hypothesize that the long-dead father is its "real
source." What has the father to do with three young women
cutting flowers in a park? But it seems possible that a flirta-
tious husband might explain Plath's antipathy toward attrac-
tive young women who break the rules. We might suppose that
Plath unconsciously associated these laughing teenagers with
the grinning teenager she had seen walking with Hughes three
and a half weeks before.

Plath and Hughes first spot the three young women cutting
flowers by a frog pond (*J* 236), just as Plath had spied Hughes
and "Sheila" coming up the road from Paradise Pond. Both
Plath and Hughes express strong moral disapproval of the gig-
gling trio, who want the flowers to decorate for a dance (*J* 237).
It is worth noting that this behavior is abnormal for Plath; nowhere else in the *Journals* does she actively assume the role of
guardian of the public weal. Plath's initial disapproval soon
grows into wild fury and a wish to punish, feelings that appear
to have their "real source" less in thoughts of her father than in
sexual competition. Since she was unable, because of the
dynamics of her marriage, to sustain her anger at her husband
when he failed to provide the care she needed, she has transferred her hostility to his partner in infidelity, here symbolized
by three "brassy" young women (*J* 237). Remonstrating with
one of them, Plath finds herself "wanting strangely to claw off
her raincoat, smack her face, read the emblem of her school on
her jersey and send her to jail." Puzzled by these violent
wishes, she finally concludes: "I can kill myself or — I know it
now — even kill another. I could kill a woman, or wound a man.
I think I could. I gritted to control my hands, but had a flash
of bloody stars in my head as I stared that sassy girl down, and
a blood-longing to [rush] at her and tear her to bloody beating
bits" (*J* 237–38).

Plath was right to be puzzled, for even in her moralistic
inner world, she would not normally have regarded picking

rhododendrons as a capital offense. Her anger at the three young women probably represented a way of gaining imaginary revenge for her husband's unreliability. We note that her imagery of "clawing" and seeing "stars" exactly duplicates her description of her physical fight with Hughes after his flirtation.

A further curious point is that Plath herself had brought scissors to the park that afternoon, intending to cut a flower. She wonders in her journal at her "split morality" (*J* 237), though we might think she does not wonder hard enough. Perhaps the key for us here is that Plath identified her own guilt with that of the young women, just as she had previously identified her initial act of "stealing" Hughes with that of the young woman on the road from Paradise Pond, as indicated by the "Shirley"/ "Sheila" equation (*J* 233). A rigorous moralist and a gifted seer, Plath correctly predicted that her own ultimate punishment would come in the same form as her original transgression. Her justified anger at "Sheila" and her excessive anger at the three young women in the park may reflect a need to deny her own crime of man stealing and her consequent sense of marital illegitimacy (analogous both to her habitual theft of writing paper and her feelings of textual illegitimacy and to Esther Greenwood's theft of flowers at her father's grave and her feelings of biological illegitimacy [*BJ* 198, 39]). At the same time, Plath's anger reflects her desire to punish criminal behavior like her own. Her fury at the three young women starkly exposes her hidden guilt, her self-hatred. She may have chosen to continue in a marriage that caused her considerable pain in order both to justify her past actions (her "wrong choice," as Dr. Beuscher put it) and to punish herself for those actions.

The episodes of Hughes's flirtation and Plath's rage reveal her difficulty in sharing complex or painful feelings with her husband. For example, Plath and Hughes seem to have conspired to deflect her anger at him onto scapegoats: to three young women in a park, to her father, to the world in general. This is not to deny that Plath experienced anger at others, but to suggest that Hughes frequently functioned in her aversions as a hidden object. We glimpse this phenomenon in "The Other" and "Words heard by accident over the phone," which project the speaker's marital resentment onto her rival, and in "Daddy" and "Lady Lazarus," which project it onto a father figure. Although Plath believed that her husband was a "substitute" for her father (*J* 280), she failed to recognize the extent to which the reverse was also true. Hughes was the most immediate "daddy" in her life, the nearest "jealous god" in that pantheon that gave her life much of its meaning and more of its anguish. Hughes was also, and this would have been even harder for Plath to grasp, the nearest "medusa," whose threat of a poisoning, paralyzing interdependence was exceeded only by his threat of withdrawal. We see in these flirtation and revenge episodes the anger, indirection, and suppression that marked Plath's affective life, as well as the dangerous attempt to construct her reality through a process of doubling.

RATHER THAN being isolated incidents, the flirtation and revenge episodes bring to the fore conflicts inherent in Plath's marriage, divisions that undermined her conscious wish to declare "that 'I' and 'you' are one" (Freud, *Civilization* 66). Despite her compulsive attempts to idealize the relationship, it seems to have been a compound of hurt, argument, and loneliness. Toward the end, Plath's poetic speaker would plaintively ask herself, "Does nobody love me?" (*CP* 211), but such doubts appeared as early as the honeymoon in Spain. Although the marriage impressed Plath as a canny career move—"Living with him is like being told a perpetual story. . . . I . . . feel a new direct pouring of energy into my own work" (*J* 145)—it was also an emotional disappointment, as a long journal entry a month after the wedding suggests: "Wrongness grows in the skin and makes it hard to touch. Up, angry, in the darkness, for a sweater. No sleep, smothering. Sitting in nightgown and sweater in the dining room staring into the full moon, talking to the full moon, with wrongness growing and filling the house like a man-eating plant" (*J* 146). The quarreling newlyweds go for a sullen walk together, avoiding "killing words" only by becoming "silent strangers" to each other (*J* 146–47). The entry concludes on a note of frank disillusionment: "The wrongness is growing, creeping, choking the house, twining the tables and chairs and poisoning the knives and forks, clouding the drinking water with that lethal taint. Sun falls off-key on eyes asquint, and the world has grown crooked and sour as a lemon overnight" (*J* 147).

This passage forecasts the tenor of the entire marriage, which Plath habitually describes in medusan metaphors of poison, suffocation, and paralysis. Her only alternative vocabulary is the idealized one of a perfect union—a repression regularly vanquished by emotional reality, only to resurrect itself just as regularly. Skipping the idealized passages, in which Plath insists, despite massive evidence to the contrary, that she and her husband are "amazingly compatible" (*J* 246), we witness a succession of scenes involving "killing words" or "silent strangers."

Marital blues, in fact, become the journal's mournful leitmotif. Plath tells of "anger" jolting "like heartburn in the throat" (this on their first stay with Hughes's family in Yorkshire) (*J* 154). She contemplates writing a story about a woman "with a poet husband who writes about love, passion—she, after glow of vanity and joy, finds out he isn't writing about her (as friends think) but about Dream Woman Muse" (*J* 174). She wonders "if I am alive, or have been ever" after hearing Hughes tell her, "I want to get clear of this life: trapped" (*J* 202). She runs to watch a neighborhood fire, "hoping for houses in a holocaust, parents jumping out of the window with babies" (*J* 210). She praises the plays of Strindberg for reflecting her own personal life (*J* 204). She has "absurd" quarrels with Hughes (*J* 219), a "fanatic" who unnerves her with his "continuous 'What are you thinking? What are you going to do now?'" (*J* 246). She contemplates writing a story entitled "The Button Quarrel" but then adds, "Not really fight about that. Fight about his deep-rooted conventional ideas of womanhood, like all the rest of the men, wants them pregnant and in the kitchen. Wants to shame her in public" (*J* 277; cf. *J* 43, in which she expressed her youthful anxiety that her marital partner would reject sexual equality). She records tirades, gripes, irritations, "acrid fights" (*J* 278), a dream of "running after Ted through a huge hospital, knowing he was with another woman"

(*J* 279), "a miserable dowie dowie fight over nothing, our usual gloom" (*J* 297), "hostile silences" (*J* 304). A recurrent theme of her journal entries is "anger at Ted" (*J* 346). Although Plath sees that it is "dangerous to be so close to Ted day in day out" (*J* 328), she cannot forge an independent existence. She feels alienated from him, yet needs to feel attached.

If Plath ultimately converted her experience of the conflict between self and other into a textual issue—the tension between subject and language—she also portrayed it, especially in her early stories, almost transparently as domestic crisis. In "Stone Boy with Dolphin," for example, a young woman feels rejected by a handsome, statuesque poet and bites him viciously on the cheek (*JP* 173–95). In "That Widow Mangada," a newlywed couple allow their honeymoon to be ruined by friction with their landlady (*JP* 226–45). In "The Wishing Box," a wife who dreams less vividly than her husband commits suicide (*JP* 204–10). In "The Snowman on the Moor," "The Fifty-ninth Bear," and "Mothers," a married couple argue incessantly, their quarrels terminating in either the wife's obedience or the husband's violent death (*CP* 58–59; *JP* 105–14, 10–19). In "Sweetie Pie and the Gutter Men," a wife feels estranged from her sculptor-husband (*JP* 131–42), while in "Day of Success," a housewife with a playwright-husband muses: "*It won't happen right away. Breakups seldom do. It will unfold slowly, one little telltale symptom after another like some awful, hellish flower*" (*JP* 83). "The Rabbit Catcher" and "Event" describe a man and a woman who are wired together yet "dismembered" (*CP* 193–95). And Plath's lost novel had marital unhappiness and divorce as its theme (Kroll 66; Wagner-Martin 236).

In her psychoanalytic sessions with Dr. Beuscher in 1958–59, Plath was encouraged to think seriously about her motives and desires. She came to a somewhat deepened understanding of her complex feelings about her husband. Ceasing to idealize him, she began to dispense with her unworkable myth of her marriage. She acknowledged the dissatisfying lack of warmth in the relationship: "Hugging. I have never found anybody who could stand to accept the daily demonstrative love I feel in me, and give back as good as I gave" (*J* 286). But in December

1959 the two of them moved to England, where Hughes could "be his best" (*J* 293). From that moment on, Plath's attitudes reverted to their primitive state: bitter discontent alongside an idolatry that caused her to imagine her husband as her "salvation" (*J* 322). She resurrected her myth of a perfect marriage, despite apparently daily dissatisfactions. But her fear of critically examining the myth evidently exceeded her pain in living it. We might hypothesize that her reason for acquiescing in Hughes's desire to return to England was not that he would be "his best" there but that she could escape her analysis there, could escape those resonant questions, "Would you have the guts to admit you'd made a wrong choice?" and "Does Ted want you to get better?"

Stunned at her lack of compatibility with her husband—his complaints, orders, and silences, his attempts to control her, his displays of indifference, his refusal to share his inner life, and her own complaints, self-blamings, and jealousies, her wishes for control and privacy—Plath eventually sealed herself off from him. This self-imposed isolation paradoxically complemented her dependence on him. She hounded him with her attention, as he hounded her; yet at the same time she could not communicate openly with him. Like John Crowe Ransom's "Equilibrists," the two remained "close, but untouching in each other's sight." Plath's tendency to keep herself secret from her husband became an increasingly important strategy after the flirtation episode and her subsequent period of psychoanalysis. During that analysis, we find journal notations like the following: "How to develop my independence? Not tell him everything. Hard, seeing him all the time" (*J* 278); "Telling Ted nothing. DOING" (*J* 288); "Don't share sorrow with Ted of rejection" (*J* 291); "Must try poems. DO NOT SHOW ANY TO TED" (*J* 295); "Tell T. nothing" (*J* 304); "Keep my sorrows and despairs to myself" (*J* 322). Just as she sought to keep her mother both near her and away, so she wished both to speak and not to speak to her husband. Before gaining insight into these complicated feelings, however, she broke off the analysis and moved to England. Although the ersatz "journal" that survives from England contains no injunctions to "tell Ted nothing," it contains few references to Hughes at all. Plath seems entirely alone, of "interest" to "nobody" (*J* 333), wearing a dead mask similar to the one she had worn in her depression of nearly a decade before (*J* 67).

THE NATURE of Plath's marriage affected her creative life in fundamental ways. First, her deferring to her husband and her frequent unhappiness with him inhibited her writing. Her marriage became one long writer's block, a prolonged period of artistic frustration in which she could not give herself credit even for the poems and stories that she did write. It is hardly coincidental that the creative drive that produced *Ariel, The Bell Jar,* and the lost manuscripts arose simultaneously with her final separation.

Second, Plath's relationship with her husband, though founded on the structure of her mother relation, confirmed a model for her relation to men generally, and therefore to the institution of literature, which has historically been a male preserve. Her rebellion against poetic forms and conventions reflected on a symbolic level her suppressed wish to rebel against her husband's power. In Plath's eyes, Hughes was not merely an individual man. He was "this poet" (*LH* 234), an archetype of the artist—and therefore, in a curious twist, an avatar of her own artistic desires as well. He was poetry considered as an external body of works, and he was her own innate poetic capacity, separated and reified, endowed with a force and a will of its own. Thus Hughes stood at once for the living tradition that inspired and subjugated her and for her own latent gift, her own central self.

Plath was strongly attracted to Hughes as a sort of dominator—one who could overmatch her in wildness and thereby domesticate her. Although he was not remarkably prepossessing, she rarely described him without indicating his "hugeness" (*LH* 234). On their first meeting he was "that big, dark, hunky boy" (*J* 111)—and he always remained for her "big" (*J* 133, 145, 151, 241), "colossal" (*J* 111), "large, hulking" (*LH* 233), "creative in a giant way" (*J* 240), a man who "can break walls" (*J* 142), a "Goliath" (*LH* 244), a "god" (*J* 165), a "patriarch" (*J* 312).

Surely this exaggeration of Hughes's size and power attests to Plath's desire for him to play a fatherly role toward her. Equally, it suggests phallic admiration, just the sort that Plath came to critique so tellingly in "Three Women." Hughes was her "male totem" (*J* 273), for Plath had been trained by a patriarchal social structure to associate phallicism with literary creation. As we have seen, this general cultural bias was reinforced by her family myth, in which the father had been a writer while the mother was a mere transcriber (though in reality the mother wrote at least some of the father's words). For most of Plath's career up through 1961 and periodically even after that date, she fancied that men possessed writing and kept it to themselves: "Ideas of maleness: conservation of creative power (sex and writing)" (*J* 273). It is no accident that one of the givens of their marriage was that she would type and mail his poems. If Ophelia represents Hamlet's phallic signifier (O phallus) or his affective capacity (O feeling), Hughes seems to have represented Plath's own creative drive phallicized.

Plath integrated her husband into fantasies of rape that predated him. One adolescent journal passage indicates the "Leda and the Swan" pattern of her imaginings: "Stretching out on the rock, body taut, then relaxed, on the altar, I felt that I was being raped deliciously by the sun, filled full of heat from the impersonal and colossal god of nature" (*J* 27). She later transformed this motif into a desire to be raped by the god of poetry. We might speculate that because she felt unworthy (of love or poetry), she wished punishment; or that because the dominant ideology glorified female passivity, she felt compelled to "sacrifice" herself (*CP* 23); or that because poetry seemed to be aggressively male, she preferred being assaulted by it to being left alone. Perhaps she fantasized being overpowered in order to displace awareness of the violence in herself, the violence of a female who wishes to seize the male role of poetry. Whatever the motivation, she frequently depicted Hughes not simply as big but as dangerous as well. During their courtship she called him a "black marauder" and a "panther" (*CP* 22–23; *J* 131–33); she declared herself "hungry" for his "big smashing creative" love (*J* 131); she felt that his words "ripped" her to bits (*J* 142).

Judith Kroll is right to observe that part of Plath's presentation of Hughes "is as a reformed or reformable destroyer" (249). After the marriage, Plath continued to entertain violent fantasies concerning him, but with growing ambivalence. On one occasion she ran out of the house following a nighttime quarrel, sat in a park, and then spotted him striding down the street: "He paused, stared, and if he weren't my husband I would have run from him as a killer" (*J* 219). Characteristically, the two reconciled without discussing or altering their feelings, apparently preferring to keep their fantasy lives intact. Later Hughes gassed an injured bird to death — ostensibly an act of mercy but possibly an oblique threat to Plath as well, since she identified herself with the "panic bird" (*J* 247–48, 263, 268). Her description of the dead bird — "composed, perfect and beautiful in death" (*J* 248) — strangely foreshadows her last self-representation as a being who has been "perfected" (*CP* 272).

Plath's need to marry a genius, colossus, or god (*J* 259, III, 165) conflicted with her desire to be a genius, colossus, and god herself (*LH* 468; *J* 56, 131). She wanted it both ways, to be married to genius and to be a genius, and her conception of the two roles made them mutually exclusive. She married Hughes believing that he was "a better poet" than she (*J* 172) and that his vocation was "so much stronger" than her own (*J* 329). "I am so glad Ted is first," she wrote. "All my pat theories against marrying a writer dissolve with Ted: his rejections more than double my sorrow & his acceptances rejoice me more than mine" (*J* 154). But at the same time, she wanted to be a writer with her own rejections and acceptances, and her notion of literary talent was based on competition. Hughes's success, she admitted in her franker moods, was an obstacle to her own — "something I must cope with" (*J* 172). To be a god herself she needed to be married not to a bigger god, a rival who could and would overpower her, but to a supporter and inspirer, a male muse. At one point in her journal she tried to unite the disparate images, referring to the "buried male muse and god-creator risen to be my mate in Ted" (*J* 223). But the images of muse and god-creator repelled each other: the one nurtured, the other dominated and inhibited.

Hughes himself refused to play anything like the role of
Plath's muse. As a result, Plath retreated from her hope of living with a muse to the gloom of living with a rival. Instead of
her mate pouring energy into her work as she had expected
him to do (J 145), he humbled her with his successes, like the
husband in "The Wishing Box." She increasingly turned away
from him, as we have seen, blaming herself for her dependence, vowing to show him none of her work. The journals for
the years 1958–59 constitute a monotonous, continuous com-
plaint, in which she describes herself as paralyzed, choking,
suffocating, and stifled. She had thought she wished to "try my
force against his" (J 112), but it turned out that she did not. Unwilling to compete directly against the "biggest, most imaginative" mind she knew (J 145), she risked creative frustration and
silence.

If Plath could not defeat her image of Hughes as a dominating god with her wistful hope that he would play her muse, she
did invent an alternative myth that promised to meet her needs
(and those of her husband) more successfully. This was the
myth of the double. Through this invention Plath (and
Hughes) could have it both ways. As her double, he needed
neither to subjugate nor to inspire her. The idea of doubling
could eliminate the rivalry between them, just as it lessened
the need for intimacy in their marriage. As doubles, they felt
no threat to their selfhood, for they were not confronted with
an alien presence, nor did they have to communicate since
they were not really other. Thus the myth of the double worked
to reduce anxiety both in their creative lives and their affective
relationship. They were neither supportive of nor antagonistic
toward each other's work. They were two halves of a single
child, romping in Elysian fields of the imaginary.

Plath's attempt to make Hughes into her double had a substantial history and prehistory. As a teenager, she had written
to her pen pal Eddie Cohen, "I love you because you are me"
(J 16). Later she had regarded her lover, Richard Sassoon, as
an alter ego, imitating his odd Harry Crosbyesque prose style
in her letters to him. When she met Hughes, she immediately
noted his equivalence to her, calling him "the only one there

huge enough for me" (*J* III). As their relationship progressed, the similarities increased. In such poems as "Pursuit," "Ode for Ted," "Faun," "Song for a Summer's Day," and "The Glutton," she wrote in a Hughesian style on Hughesian themes, as Margaret Dickie Uroff has shown (70-84). During the early years of their marriage, Plath adopted Hughes's favorite writers as her own (Blake, Hopkins, Lawrence, Thomas); fasted when he fasted; wrote productively when he wrote productively; and became interested in subjects he was interested in (ouija, tarot, horoscopes, fertility myths, exotic plants and animals, the white goddess, arcana). Conceiving of her husband as her "male counterpart," she thought that they had "mystically become one," with "no barriers" and a single skin between them (*LH* 264, 276; *J* 246).

Seeing her husband as her double reduced the tension between them, regressively reinstated the pleasure associated with infantile existence, and above all relieved the pressure on Plath to write her own texts. If he was an emanation of her, his accomplishment would count as hers. Once she thought of writing an autobiographical novel about "big, blasting dangerous love" and the "double theme" (*J* 151). Although she may have been thinking of the heroine as being divided in herself, her juxtaposition of "love" and "double" suggests that she thought of love as a form of doubling. In truth, doubling was Plath's fundamental way of ordering all aspects of her world. It was a dangerous way, as she herself occasionally realized, because it turned people, events, or concepts with points of similarity into identities, and dynamic or ambiguous entities into static, monolithic ones. When Plath wrote in her journal that she felt she had made her husband up (*J* 240), or when she wrote in her poetry that he sprang out of her head (*CP* 38), she was not far wrong. Plath and Hughes seem to have been married to what Eliot in *The Family Reunion* called "that other person, if person, / You thought I was" — an image of their own idea of themselves. Plath thought her husband to be "so perfectly the male being complement to me" (*J* 156), her "black complement power" (*J* 165). Implicitly she and Hughes, Hughes and his work, she and her work, and Hughes's work and her own work comprised a series of specular images: "I live for my own work, without which I am nothing. My writing. Nothing matters but Ted, Ted's writing and my writing" (*J* 204).

Nevertheless, two incompatible notions contended behind Plath's harmonized image of her husband as her double: the notion that they were each other's match, bringing out each other's best effort through competition; and the notion that he was her superior, writing poetry better than her own. She could engage in a healthy competition with a peer, or she could vicariously share in the accomplishments of a superior. Those two notions refused to blend, and they never accorded with the reality of her situation. As a result, Plath's assertions of doubleness with Hughes are usually followed by expressions of anger at him. For she found that her contest with Hughes did not bring out her best work but rather paralyzed her. In actuality, Hughes did not welcome her competition, and she, in her weakness, feared the consequences of her competition, feared that she might lose or, perhaps even worse, might win. Nor did she long enjoy the vicarious pleasure of his successes—partly because his successes were not sufficiently great, but more centrally because her own ambition did not allow her to take full satisfaction in merely being a poet's wife. She wanted to be the "Poetess of America" (*J* 211) in her own right and could not really accept his achievements as her own.

Plath sought to see herself and Hughes as doubles in order to create grounds for marriage and then in order to save their marriage (and to evade it). The effort ultimately shipwrecked on the rocks of a vain reality. As she and her husband told each other less and less, as they ceased reading each other's work, as they closed off from each other, the myth of the double disappeared from her representations of the marriage, to be replaced by silence. As the myth vanished from Plath's life, however, it began to take new form in her poetry and fiction, where it found a more habitable environment. She had initially discovered the double in her literary studies—in her aborted senior thesis on twins in Joyce and in her completed thesis on doubles in Dostoevsky—and it was in literature that the motif could best flourish. Unlike the human psyche, the text was two-dimensional and exposed. Plath's binary structuring of feelings and ideas having brought grief to her personal life, she instinctively turned to a realm where such structuring would have a greater chance of success. Writing was a world without people, without the "voice" that "is always that of someone else" (Stevens), without "*ces voix d'enfants, chantant dans la coupole*" (Verlaine, Eliot). It was a domain of mute and controllable signs, themselves structured by a binary code of sameness and difference.

As Plath lost comfort in regarding her husband as a double, she found relief by writing poems and stories that imaged her pain. She increasingly used the figure of the double to evoke her sense of inner division, especially the conflict she experienced between creative and uncreative feelings. The double evoked as well the text's own uncanny ability to echo the authorial subject, to become a second self. Thus the line dividing her inscribed texts from her psychic one became increasingly uncertain, mirrorlike, shadowy. By investing so heavily in her artistic activity, by displacing libido from her object relations to words as self-objects, Plath may have hoped to recapture the lost pre-Oedipal oneness. She may have been relieving the anxiety of separation by filling in the "potential space" between self and other "with creative playing, with the use of symbols, and with all that adds up to a cultural life" (Winnicott 109). Or she may have wished to explore a distinctively female "web of connection" (Gilligan 62) between social and linguistic worlds, to reexamine boundaries and hierarchies, to discover a postmodern poetics of one's own. Whatever our exact interpretation, we now need to refocus our attention on the texts Plath wrote in her last two years, for in them we see how she transformed doubling from a crumbling foundation of her personal life to a solid cornerstone of her art.

MIRROR

Although as a young girl Plath thought of herself as a potential double of Alice (*J* 21, 181; *CP* 324; Aurelia Plath, Letter), she did not go through the looking glass herself. Instead of entering the "abstract, Platonic realm out of time and flesh on the other side of all those mirrors" (*J* 117), she continued to look at the glass, observing how she and her world were reflected in it. That she saw through the glass darkly hardly needs to be emphasized, though later I shall point up her tragic final effort to dispense with her glass, to see existence face to face. For now, let us consider what it meant for Plath to construct a landscape of textual doubles.

Although Plath sometimes spoke of accepting "conflict, uncertainty, and pain as the soil for true knowledge" (*LH* 311), she more characteristically channeled ambiguity and contradiction into sets of bipolar oppositions. For example, she would habitually envision herself as a doubled being, composed of an outer false self in combat with a hidden true self, or a "murderous" self in combat with a "good" self (*J* 176). Those sets of selves did not consistently correlate with each other: at times she equated her murderous self with her false self and at other times with her true self. In the early stages of her marriage, as we have seen, she tried to view her husband as a projection of her inner true self. He was the "god" within her, her "black complement power" (*J* 165), her hypostatized soul, or at least he was a mirror that "reflected" her innermost feelings back to her (*J* 179). But as her marital relationship soured, she came to regard her texts as her essential double: "And so to the mirror — twin, Muse" (*J* 194). As her effort to merge with another failed, she refocused her attention on the other within her, while attempting to merge with the other self of her texts. In her writing she could live a second freer, deeper life. She could create an identity more satisfying than the one that emerged from her day-to-day existence.

Writing, the home of the specular "I" rather than the social "I," could well express her sense of doubleness because so much of her hidden self centered on the issue of creativity. Plath saw herself as a material husk encasing a creative or spiritual seed. The seed was sometimes agonizingly diminished or concealed, sometimes vigorous and ready to germinate. At unimaginative times she would feel "sterile, empty" (*LH* 130), but at times of imaginative accomplishment (for example, when

composing the *Ariel* poems) she could claim, "I am a genius of
a writer; I have it in me" (*LH* 468). At those moments when the
seed seemed to have vanished and she was faced with only
material existence, she would feel despair: "I must get back
into the world of creative mind: otherwise, in the world of pies
and shin beef, I die. The great vampire cook extracts the
nourishment and I grow fat on the corruption of matter, mere
mindless matter" (*J* 157). She would confront "the deadness of
a being to whom nothing can happen, who no longer creates"
(*J* 164). But at moments of inner "fulfillment," she would experience an "intense sense of living . . . richly and deeply" (*LH*
298, 235). She would hear her "deep self" speaking (*J* 165).

From a very early date, Plath sensed that the artistic mirror
could reflect her divided being. She entitled her Smith College
honors thesis "The Magic Mirror," and she proposed calling a
projected autobiographical novel "The Girl in the Mirror" (*J*
168). She conceived of the mirror itself as a doubled figure. On
the other side of it lay the "Platonic realm" (*J* 117) inhabited by
a Stevensian fantastic consciousness, while on this side lay "the
surface texture of life" which "can be dead, was dead for me"
(*J* 181). The mirror therefore mediated between the ideal world
of dream and the actual world of matter. Separated, each was
moribund, but brought into contact, each came to life. Yet if
Plath sought an Emersonian unity, she still saw two. Although
she hoped the process of composition could integrate her vision, she found that her imaginative mirror, like Hawthorne's
in "The Custom House," was tarnished, exposing only its own
limitations and opacities, reflecting merely an abyss that divided the axis of vision from the axis of things. At the best of
times, Plath's mirror revealed two selves struggling to merge,
but it never quite depicted the achievement of wholeness. Perhaps the specular image itself, as an emblem of Lacan's *stade du
miroir*, inherently signified unrejoinable separation. Whatever
the explanation, intimations of unity warded off the mirror image and reduced Plath to silence. And with the termination of
the composing process came the relapse into personal doubleness, the disconnection of body and spirit, and the need to attempt creative operations once more. Plath's Sisyphean labor,

therefore, was to inscribe an unfinishable poem of the self. She was condemned always to begin and never to complete.

Frightened by her psychic mobility and her sense of indistinct boundaries, Plath generally sought to fix her experience on a bivalent scale (x———x rather than xxxxxxxx). As Pamela J. Annas has noted, Plath saw herself "trapped between sets of mutually exclusive alternatives" (*Disturbance* 161). Balancing each idea or force with its obverse negation, she postulated God and devil, Jew and Nazi, good and bad, joy and despair, friend and enemy, matter and creative spirit. This way of seeing led her inevitably to the figure of the double. Like Baudelaire, who stabilized his fluid sense of reality by dualizing "l'idéale" and "la gouffre," and like Dickinson and Frost, who countered an impulse to merge with cosmic paranoia, Plath structured her world as a Manichean battle of opposites. The structure exposes the limits of her lifelong wish for oneness. For however much she yearned to recover the "vast similitude" that Whitman said "interlocks all" (*Leaves* 261), she even more deeply needed to keep envisioning divided selves in worlds of contradiction.

Rather than suggesting a gradual self-education or a process of change responsive to objective reality and subjective needs, Plath's late poetry typically depicts the self as undergoing a clash of opposites. In "Face Lift," for example, two individualities compete for possession of a single body: an aging, false face and a new one constructed by a surgeon (*CP* 155–56). When the young face triumphs, the hated old one is relegated to a "jar" (reversing the imagery of "Medusa," "Daddy," and *The Bell Jar*, in which the true self is trapped in a "bottle," "shoe," or "jar"). But the true self achieves only a pyrrhic victory in "Face Lift," for as it ages it too will inevitably be imprisoned in what R. D. Laing called a "false-self system" (100–112). In Plath's construction, when the creative dimension disappears, selfhood devolves into a futile proliferation of objects: "suitcases" out of which "the same self unfolds like a suit" (*CP* 264–65). The outer world similarly devolves; reflections, shadows, and echoes duplicate or invert it, revealing a hidden presence or, more frequently, an absence. Beneath Plath's "double vision" (*J* 177) lurks a nihilistic fear that being is nothingness. Only the creative act may prove something, but even that something ceases with the conclusion of each new poem. Writing is a self that also requires a perpetual face-lift.

A catastrophic sense of loss and a need for recovery seem to underlie Plath's interest in the double. At least she obsessively attributed such losses and attempted restitutions to her protagonists. She sought to reconstitute her own identity as a textual immanence, and though that immanence inevitably remained a fiction, a function of linguistic convention, the recurrent patterns that tie the texts together do evoke a compelling image of authorial psyche in the process of constructing reality. As a result, Plath seems to have found her "true" self enacted more revealingly and satisfyingly in her poems than in her social existence. We may speculate that she eventually became enmeshed in what John Irwin has called "the suicidal, incestuous struggle between the writer and the other self of his book" (20). Encountering a double more meaningful than her empirical self, she at first felt comforted and relieved, but then haunted and possessed. When that double, which had virtually become her real existence, reached its limit and began to deliquesce, she may have attempted to become *its* double in turn. She may have undergone her suicide ritual at least partly to recapture her identity from her poems.

Several of Plath's critics have analyzed the dialectical systems at work in her texts, noting that Plath's "I" frequently experiences a "tension between false and true selves" (Kroll 10) or seeks a "rebirth of the self" (Rosenblatt 31). Judith Kroll and Jon Rosenblatt discuss this motif in terms of initiatory ritual, Lynda Bundtzen in terms of female identity in *The Bell Jar*, Pamela Annas in terms of socialization, and Susan Van Dyne in terms of the struggle for authorship in the bee poems. Outside of Plath studies, C. F. Keppler, Robert Rogers, and John Irwin have provided further clues to the way Plath must have understood the double. Irwin, for example, traces an American genealogy of the double from Poe through James to Faulkner and Hart Crane. Although Plath was influenced by Poe and James, her relation to Crane is most interesting of all. She read Crane but never mentioned him in her essays, letters, or journals. This repression may have occurred because her own work restages his central agon, in which (as Irwin says with remarkable insight) an oscillation between the speaker's story and the author's own story "evokes the oscillating relationship between a writer and his book, evoking it as a kind of incestuous doubling in which the writer, through an oblique repetition, seeks revenge against time" (1). In the pages that follow, I wish to take these analyses and hints in some new directions, suggesting the sources, the strengths, and the limitations of Plath's figure of the double and finally the manner in which the figure shaped her career.

ALTHOUGH Plath's tendency to structure in doubles was evidently characterological, perhaps dating from the "awful birthday of otherness" (*JP* 23), it acquired literary dimension from her study at Smith. There she wrote papers on Thomas Mann's dualisms and Nietzsche's epigram that "pain is also a joy, curse is also a blessing, night is also a sun" (Indiana mss.). In her senior year, after recovering from her first suicide attempt, she wrote a highly personal term paper for Professor George Gibian entitled "The Devil's Advocate," in which she confessed that the conflicts and dichotomies in Dostoevsky's novels were echoed in her own mind (Indiana ms.). She added that while she accepted the Russian novelist's idea of regeneration through suffering, she did not share his religious faith; it was precisely her conviction of oblivion after death that had reassured her when, after months of despair, she had tried to take her life.

The next semester, she expanded this paper into her honors thesis, a more methodical study called "The Magic Mirror: A Study of the Double in Two of Dostoevski's Novels" (Smith ms.). Here she described the double as an attempt to solve the enigma of identity, and more specifically as an emblem of "the fundamental duality of man." In the individual's attempt to read the riddle of his soul, she wrote, he comes "face to face with his own mysterious mirror image, an image which he confronts with mingled curiosity and fear." Plath preferred the treatment of the double in *The Brothers Karamazov* to that in *The Double* because the former text distinguishes psychical from physical doubling, making the metaphysical dimension of the phenomenon clear both to the character of Ivan and to us. The important aspect of the thesis from our perspective, however, is not its thoughtful commentary but the impact the study had on Plath's own developing tropology. She claimed that the double did not merely illuminate the psyche of Dostoevsky's characters but formed the core of Dostoevsky's "polemical philosophy," his way of seeing, which she herself found so congenial.

Plath's propensity to portray through polarities must have been strengthened by the texts she read in preparing her thesis — not only the two Russian novels but also Hawthorne's "Monsieur du Miroir," Poe's "William Wilson," Stevenson's *Dr. Jekyll and Mr. Hyde*, and Wilde's *The Picture of Dorian Gray*. Although early studies of the double in German romanticism by Wilhelmine Krauss and Ralph Tymms were available to her, she seems not to have read them. She did read Ernest Simmons's *Dostoevski: The Making of a Novelist*, but she dismissed its brief comments on the double as simplistic. Dostoevsky, Hawthorne, Poe, Stevenson, Wilde — and, I might add, Shakespeare, Hoffmann, the Brontës, Melville, Dickens, Twain, James, Conrad, Kafka, Faulkner, Woolf, and Jean Stafford — these were the writers she contested, the rivals she sought to beat. Her most obvious swerve from them was to put a motif associated with narrative and drama to sustained, intense use in lyric poetry.

In addition to literary texts, Plath read medical, psychological, and religious studies as background for "The Magic Mirror." One, by Edward Lazell, asserts that the schizophrenic's "disharmony of thought and disorganization of personality" (589) develop from "the pressure of the reality principle," a burden that society itself has placed on him (627). Another, by Stanley Coleman, claims that whereas Guy de Maupassant was haunted by a hallucination that projected his libido "as enemy and destroyer" (257-62), Fyodor Dostoevsky expressed his "intrapsychic conflict" by composing narratives about doubles (255, 262-68). Plath read Freud's "A Neurosis of

Demoniacal Possession in the Seventeenth Century" and also "Dostoevski and Parricide," which posits an "intimate connection" or doubling between Dostoevsky's characters and his personal experience (224). Most important, however, she studied James Frazer's chapter "The Perils of the Soul" in *The Golden Bough*, Otto Rank's chapter "The Double as Immortal Self" in *Beyond Psychology*, and Freud's commentary on doubling in "The Uncanny." It seems that Frazer supplied Plath with instances of doubling, while Rank and Freud provided a conceptual framework in which to place the instances. Her own later texts evoke these three earlier texts in innumerable ways.

Anthropologists today (for example, Gaster and Littleton) reject the theory and methodology of *The Golden Bough*, but that rejection need not concern us, as it would not have concerned Plath. John Vickery has shown that such writers as Yeats, Eliot, Lawrence, and Joyce "perused the book casually or piecemeal" rather than systematically (38), since they were more attracted to its style, structure, narratives, and images than to its argument. Plath, too, was more interested in the book as a rich work of the imagination than as science, which she abhorred. The underlinings and notations in her copy of the 1922 abridgment (given to her by her mother in 1953 and now at Smith) suggest that she read it with an eye for stories or customs that illustrated the themes most interesting to her: identity and doubling. Her markings appear most frequently in the chapter "The Perils of the Soul," especially in sections called "The Soul as a Manniken" and "The Soul as a Shadow and a Reflection." Receiving fewer markings are chapters titled "The King of the Wood," "Sympathetic Magic," "The Magical Control of the Weather," "The Sacred Marriage," "The Worship of the Oak," "Tabooed Acts," "The Propitiation of Wild Animals by Hunters," "The Transference of Evil," and "Public Scapegoats." The remaining chapters show no annotation. Although Vickery does not mention Plath, her career supports his thesis that *The Golden Bough* "has been and continues to be of seminal importance in the forging of twentieth century literature" (135).

In "The Perils of the Soul," Frazer explains that in preindustrialized cultures the "animal inside the animal, the man inside the man, is the soul" and that death is "the permanent absence of the soul" (178). All living creatures, then, possess two distinct selves, an outward body and an inward soul. The inward soul, however, is all too apt to become outward itself; it may escape through body apertures, it may be abducted by ghosts or demons, or it may become threateningly manifest in dreams, hallucinations, reflections, shadows, or pictures (189). Plath was to express precisely this anxiety in her poetry:

> I do not trust the spirit. It escapes like steam
> In dreams, through mouth-hole or eye-hole. I can't stop it.
> One day it won't come back.   (*CP* 172)

Frazer observes that "often the soul is conceived as a bird ready to take flight" (181), an image Plath transumed in her journal references to her "Panic-Bird." Plath underscored Frazer's comment that the tribe members of "the Baganda believe that every person is born with a double" (40). She believed such a thing herself, though for her that alter ego was an authentic or creative self rather than a traditional soul. As I have suggested, she variously posited both spatial and temporal doubles: inner seed/outer husk and old self/new self, the latter duality possibly being a modern variant of Frazer's "god who annually died and rose again from the dead" (325). Frazer's stories must have confirmed Plath in her notion that to be alive was to be and to see double and that death was simply the loss of doubleness. She must have recognized in herself regressive elements of Frazer's "savage," who is beset by spiritual danger because he believes that if his double "is detached from him entirely (as he believes that it may be) he will die" (181).

If Frazer's fund of myths strengthened Plath's sense of the double from the inside, Rank provided her with a sophisticated schema that allowed her to know it intellectually, from the outside. *Beyond Psychology* (1941) is the primary basis for Plath's analysis in her honors thesis. Virtually all the footnotes concerning doubling refer to it, and her very contrast between Dostoevsky's two novels derives from it. Plath's bibliography also includes a second Rank work, "The Double" (1919), which is a ten-page abstract in English of his early essay "Der Doppelgänger" (1914; revised 1925). But Plath's text itself refers only to *Beyond Psychology*. The distinction between the two works is important, since Rank's perspective shifted significantly in the time between their writing. In "The Double," Rank, still a loyal follower of Freud, attributed doubling to the hero's and the author's guilt concerning autoeroticism. In *Beyond Psychology*, however, he dropped the notions of repressed sexual desire and guilt evasion, instead placing the topic in the context of spiritual and creative needs. He suggested that the artist's unique capacity to reveal the hidden immortal self and to combine it with the viable, socialized self performed a heroic function for society.

In *Beyond Psychology*, Rank traces the evolution of the double from its origins in preindustrialized societies (like the ones whose stories and customs Frazer recounted) to its manifestations in modern literature. Rank asserts that although the double began in primitive religion as a symbol of the individual's "immortal soul," it has increasingly become the opposite in our overcivilized culture, "a reminder of the individual's mortality, indeed, the announcer of death itself" (74, 76; quoted in "Magic Mirror" 1). For the "modern personality type," the double often indicates the "almost pathological loss of one's real self through a superimposed one," or it may represent the evil or repressed characteristics of its master, thereby presaging his ultimate destruction (*Beyond* 66, 70; quoted in "Magic Mirror" 2). Plath described her thesis to her mother by alluding to the two types of double, putting Rank's modern conception before Frazer's ancient one: "All fascinating stuff about the ego as symbolized in reflections (mirror and water), shadows, twins — dividing off and becoming an enemy, or omen of death, or a warning conscience, or a means by which one denies the power of death (e.g., by creating the idea of the soul as the deathless double of the mortal body)" (*LH* 146). Although Plath herself warned against reducing the rich variety of uses to which the double motif might be put, we may identify both of these historical possibilities — the double as immortal spirit or as harbinger of death — in the deep structure of her various uses of the trope. In addition, we may glimpse Rank's admiration for the "true artist type" as a modern hero (97) in Plath's emphasis on the redemptive power of her own creative self.

Plath's sense of Rank's work may have been mediated by her knowledge of Freud's "The Uncanny" (1919), which comments on the earliest version of "Der Doppelgänger" (1914). Freud treats Rank's essay with surface respect, accurately summarizing its finding that "from having been an assurance of immortality, [the double] becomes the ghastly harbinger of death" ("Uncanny" 387). But curiously, Freud almost exempts the double from his category of the uncanny. For Freud, "the uncanny is nothing else than a hidden, familiar thing that has undergone repression and then emerged from it" (399). In the uncanny experience, some infantile fear or desire, or primitive belief, returns to consciousness in symbolic form. Yet Freud thought that the double does not really manifest this process, deriving instead from our propensity toward "self-observation" (388). The "new meaning" in the "old idea of a 'double'" is the division "between the critical faculty and the rest of the ego, and not . . . the antithesis discovered by psycho-analysis between the ego and what is unconscious and repressed" (388). Freud here takes pains to devise a nonpsychoanalytical explanation for the phenomenon, possibly as a result of anxiety about his follower's precursory work in the area.

Whatever the reason for his departure from Rank, Freud concludes his discussion with a frank confession of confusion: "But, after having thus considered the manifest motivation of the figure of a 'double,' we have to admit that none of it helps us to understand the extraordinarily strong feeling of something uncanny that pervades the conception," which he finally attributes to the figure's primitive origins (388–89). Thus Freud places the double in an uncomfortable borderland between the uncanny and the self-critical and hastens on to discuss more clear-cut "forms of disturbance in the ego." His next example of the uncanny, however, is even more problematic: a personal anecdote telling of his inability, one summer day, to escape from a street thronged with prostitutes in a provincial

Italian town. Although he repeatedly sought to leave, he help-
lessly found himself back on the same narrow street each time
and soon began "to excite attention" (389–90). Freud wishes
the incident to illustrate repetition-compulsion, but it also suggests sexual fear, obsessiveness, and shame. The anecdote may
relate to the anxious discussion of Rank that precedes it, the
connecting link being Freud's concern for his manhood.

There is no telling the degree to which Freud's uncertainty
about the meaning of the double affected Plath's own understanding. Except in the bibliography of her thesis, she does not
mention the essay. We may suppose that Freud helped to com-
plicate Rank's analysis for her, even more than Rank complicated it himself in *Beyond Psychology*. Freud raised the possibility
that the double could serve as a metaphor for a rational exam-
ination of the self. The double, then, was not limited to appearing as immortal soul or harbinger of death; it could also
function as the evaluator of the ego in its status quo state, as an
instrument of self-criticism and change. I believe that we see
elements of all three roles in Plath's various ways of employing
the figure.

IN TURNING to Plath's use of mirror images in her poetry, we
find that "Face Lift" again provides a useful point of departure
(*CP* 155–56). Jenijoy La Belle remarks in her study of mirror literature, *Herself Beheld*, that "looking-glass scenes" typically reveal "an intimate and significant relationship between the
mirror and a woman's conception of what she is" (2). In just
that spirit, the narrating character of "Face Lift" confronts several competing ego images, each of which seems to fix her identity in a different configuration. First she asserts that "the
dewlapped lady / I watched settle, line by line, in my mirror"
is "done for"; then, when her "mummy-clothes" are removed
after the operation, she observes a new self, "swaddled in
gauze, / Pink and smooth as a baby." The mirror thus confirms
the death of an aged, meretricious identity and the birth of a
new one. But the woman implicitly seeks spiritual renewal
rather than cosmetic change alone, and the exclusively material terms in which the mirror "frames" her sabotage that very

possibility. Therefore the poem's ostensibly positive paradigm of death and rebirth takes on a sinister coloration. The phrase "she's done for" anticipates "somebody's done for" in the later "Death and Co.," while the image of a "baby" self prefigures the death symbol of "Getting There." The "face lift" seen in the mirror becomes simply a premonitory metaphor in Plath's final drama of rebirth into death.

Although Frazer explained that "some people believe a man's soul . . . to be in his reflection" (192), Plath generally uses the mirror reflection in the more modern fashion, as a fatal omen. The reflection is not the soul exposed to danger, it is the danger itself. For what Plath's mirror cannot reflect is precisely the soul; it reveals "nothing but blood" (*CP* 259). Although Plath did not really believe in the soul at all, she did make a crucial substitution for it. Stevens's "Interior Paramour," who resembles Plath's "creative mind," says that "God and the imagination are one," and Rank too speaks of the process whereby spiritual and artistic values may absorb each other. Plath simply translated Frazer's and Rank's traditional imagery of the "immortal soul" into her own secularized vocabulary of creativity. But she projected her skepticism about her artistic prowess — skepticism on display throughout her writing, perhaps most overtly in "The Wishing Box" — by depicting a mirror that fails to make the creative dimension manifest. Her mirror reflects the empirical identity she knew existed but not the textual immanence that alone could be real for her. There is a discontinuity, therefore, between the figure of lack and the texts that contain the figure. Torn between Plath's need to realize a self in the act of writing and her deep-seated uncertainty about her ability to do so, the poems implicitly fissure. Their inner contradiction becomes Plath's characteristic mode of eloquence and thought, her distinctive poetics of self-doubt.

We witness another self-subverted denial of figurative power in "Mirror" (*CP* 173–74). This poem, a dark revision of Hawthorne's "Monsieur du Miroir," rescues the specular double from silence while rendering the double's origin mute. The mirror represents itself as incapable of figuration:

> I am silver and exact. I have no preconceptions.
> Whatever I see I swallow immediately
> Just as it is, unmisted by love or dislike.

This claim to passive veridicality, however, does not accord with the mirror's actual role of dominating and interpreting its world. Its eye is like that of an imperious "little god," its heart is hard as the opposite wall it reflects. The poor voiceless woman who bends over it, searching for "what she really is," recoils in horror at what she sees. "In me," the mirror boasts, "she has drowned a young girl, and in me an old woman / Rises toward her day after day, like a terrible fish." Although the mirror may function as a Jungian lake of the unconscious (as Timmerman and La Belle have suggested), it even more clearly functions as a Rankian double, "threatening" rather than "consoling" (*Beyond* 76). A devil who triumphs in mortal decay, like the cloaked intruder in Poe's "Masque of the Red Death," it engages in temporal as well as spatial doubling, replacing the drowned girl first with a middle-aged woman of tears and agitation, then with an old woman resembling one of Robert Lowell's cars, and finally with the blankness of a wall. The mirror simultaneously abjures the Christian promise of immortality, the humanist notion of a continuous, valuable self, and Plath's hope of creativity. Rank asserts that in modern times the double has moved from a being that promises "personal survival" to "an opposing self, appearing in the form of evil which represents the perishable and mortal part of the personality" (*Beyond* 81–82). Exactly so in "Face Lift" and "Mirror."

Plath's mirror poems originate in her doubts about her creativity and then reinforce those doubts. They almost all reveal a person who feels "sterile, empty" (*LH* 130). Because she increasingly believed that "I am what I am, and have written" (*J* 176–77), Plath's sense of selfhood depended on her feeling of imaginative fulfillment. Her interaction with systems of written language was not subsequent to her self but creative of self. When her mirrors show an individual lacking in creativity, therefore, they expose a self already disintegrating. Whereas the women writers studied by La Belle generally use specular imagery to suggest either internalized social norms or female self-fashioning, Plath uses it to figure the death of the imagination. Whitman's disturbing "A Hand-Mirror" provides perhaps the closest analogue: "Hold it up sternly—see this it sends back, (who is it? is it you?) / Outside fair costume, within ashes and filth." In Plath's "Totem," for example, the barren self comes equipped with "folding mirrors" and "short circuits" (*CP* 265). In "Last Words," the dying speaker says, "My mirror is clouding over— / A few more breaths, and it will reflect nothing at all" (*CP* 172). In "Morning Song," the cloud "distills a mirror to reflect its own slow / Effacement" (*CP* 157). In "Insomniac," an anguished man's head "is a little interior of gray mirrors," an "alley of diminishing perspectives" through which significance drains like water (*CP* 163). In "The Courage of Shutting Up," eyes resemble mirrors "in which a torture goes on" (*CP* 209–10). In "Leaving Early," the mirror transforms a vase of chrysanthemums into an enemy host (*CP* 146), while in "Purdah" and "The Couriers" it reveals a world of withering male abuse (*CP* 242, 247).

In Plath's last week of writing, however, a significant change occurred. The contradiction between figure and poem began to evaporate. The first intimation of this shift appears in "Child," which laments that the young girl resembles a non-reflective ceiling rather than a "pool in which images / Should be grand and classical" (*CP* 265). For the first time, a mirror positively combines associations of mortal life and art. As we saw in chapter 2, "Words" similarly ties mirror imagery to creativity (*CP* 270). The sap (or poetic process) can establish a "mirror" capable of covering over the white skull of mortality, even though the words themselves (the texts) come to seem dry. "Kindness" at first reminds us of Plath's established mode of mirror symbolism, as the mirrors fill with a friend's uncomprehending smiles, another reflection of appearance devoid of reality (*CP* 269–70). Nevertheless, the poem also insists on the unempirical fact that for the speaker "the blood jet is poetry, / There is no stopping it." This poem contains more than the mirror can reflect, more than the material husk. We find another departure as well, in the equation of poetry with blood. Spirit and body permeate rather than oppose each other.

"Contusion," written on the penultimate day that Plath composed poetry, includes the most significant change of all (*CP*
271). When the poem concludes, "the mirrors are sheeted," we
wonder why they need to be sheeted, why they do not simply
cloud up and go blank as in earlier poems of cessation. Frazer
can help us here. He asserts that when a death occurs in a
house, there is a "widespread custom of covering up mirrors"
to prevent the ghost of the departed from carrying away a
mourner's soul, projected outward in the shape of his mirror
reflection (192). Furthermore, "the reason why sick people
should not see themselves in a mirror, and why the mirror in
a sick-room is therefore covered up, is also plain; in time of
sickness, when the soul might take flight so easily, it is particularly dangerous to project it out of the body by means of the
reflection in a mirror." The mirrors of "Contusion" are sheeted
to prevent the loss of the soul. Whereas in earlier poems mirrors represent physical vision alone, here they include spiritual
vision as well, which Plath understood as poetic vision.

In different ways, then, "Words," "Kindness," and "Contusion" all imply a connection between body and poetry. Plath's
last poems may tell us that she believed she had finally fulfilled
an infantile wish, had discovered an enduring double. For that
reason, her "I" could claim to feel "perfected" (*CP* 272). Although Plath seemed uncertain where mirrors fit into this new
world she inhabited, she did appear to recognize that a real
transformation had occurred in her sense of self. She had
located her double not in her mother or husband, not in an
other at all, but in her creativity, which was marked by her
texts. Her way of observing momentous change was through
the Frazerian metaphor of death and resurrection. Perhaps to
celebrate the alteration that had taken place in her writing, or
perhaps to mourn its passing, she enacted the metaphor in her
life — a confusion of realms that proved fatal.

SHADOW

SHADOW IMAGERY complements Plath's imagery of
mirror reflections. Rank, generalizing from Frazer's anecdotes,

traces the presentation of the second self "by one's own shadow or reflection" back to the human race's earliest conceptions of the soul (*Beyond* 71–74; Frazer 189–91). Of the two images, shadow is the more archaic and unalterable. Shadow returns perpetually with the sun, like a returning soul. Since it is not as lifelike as reflection, it resists being made into a figure for mortal or moral decay. It tends to remain just what it has been in many different cultures through time, a symbol of the individual's spiritual essence.

As a writer, Plath liked to repeat old themes and to recapture popular traditions, employing ancient beliefs as an antidote to an oversocialized, superrationalized civilization. More to the point, she used these images as an antidote to her personal oversocialization and superrationalism, as an outlet for her frustrated emotions. But as we have seen before, she insisted on revising such images, no matter how venerable and hardy, to make them apply to her own situation. Thus she made the shadow evoke what was for her the equivalent of spiritual essence — imaginative identity. In Plath's shadow poems, this "most vital part" of the self is prevented from coming into being not only by the corporeal, factitious mask we see revealed in the mirror poems, but also by external authoritarian figures. If the mirror poems dramatize a struggle that takes place wholly within the self, the shadow poems usually imply a conflict between the self and others. But again the poems vibrate with an inner contradiction: they figure the death of figuration. Plath's shadow adumbrates what cannot appear in her mirror, the ghost of creativity. Shadow betokens the imaginative self that might have been but was forbidden to be, the self that has been defeated and destroyed.

In "The Colossus," the textual "I" states that her "hours are married to shadow" — that is, to the soul of the inanimate and oppressive father-husband who lives only in her anamnesis (*CP* 129–30). As a result, she herself becomes increasingly shadow-like. Indeed, she is the only shadowbeing in the scene, since the "colossus" stands in the sun, making the shade that she lives in. Plath often equated "sun" with the "saying of poems" (*LH* 244) and darkness with creative dearth. We remember that she complained of living in the "shadow" of the powerful males to whom she was attached yet by whom she felt frustrated and intimidated. So often in the journals and letters, as in her poems, the "I" fails to make a shadow of her own: "Apathetic about my work—distant, bemused, feeling, as I said, a ghost of the world I am working in, casting no shadow" (*J* 221). Existence in and as a shadow in "The Colossus" thus represents the creative half-life that is, rather than the full life that might have been. The "I" does not possess her own shadow, her own creative identity, but is possessed by that of another. Frazer tells us that "injury done to the shadow is felt by the person or animal as if it were done to his body," and conversely, "it may under certain circumstances be as hazardous to be touched" by the shadow of another (190).

In two later poems, Plath's speaker defiantly attempts to avoid being touched by her oppressor's shadow. In "Gulliver" she identifies herself with the Lilliputians who, more like the villagers in "Daddy" than Swift's originals, actively "hate" their colossal visitor (*CP* 251). She demands that the giant "step off seven leagues" so that the "shadow" of his lip might become a remote abyss. She thus hopes to depersonalize and distance the giant, perhaps only to submerge him in the superego but at least to be free of his externalized control. In "Medusa" (*CP* 224–26), the creative threat appears as a woman, indeed as the mythic figure Freud identified with "the terrifying genitals of the Mother" ("Medusa's Head" 106). The "I" has a keel, perhaps her poetic gift, that enables her to flee the mother-deity's "mouth-plugs" and ability to strangle. Rather than being caught in Medusa's shadow, the "I" herself casts a momentary shadow on Medusa's minions (st. 2).

If Plath's protagonist at times struggles mightily against shadows, she is more likely to capitulate to them. In "The Jailer," for example, her defeat is absolute (*CP* 226–27). She describes herself as but a "lever" of her jailer's "wet dreams," as being "drugged and raped," "hung, starved, burned, hooked." As much as we sympathize with her in her suffering, her submission at the end recalls Freud's disparaging comment about Dostoevsky, that rather than becoming a liberator of humanity

he "made himself one with their gaolers" ("Dostoevski" 223); or
it may recall Orwell's Winston Smith, learning to love Big
Brother. It certainly evokes the Deutschian myth of feminine
masochism. But the speaker's self-subordination to an abuser
should also suggest to us her perceived lack of alternatives. Her
dilemma parallels that described by the poet herself in her journals. Plath portrays herself there as a woman deprived by her
poet-husband of her "own inner life," hounded by his "fanati-
cism," plagued by his "continuous 'What are you thinking?
What are you going to do now?'" (J 246–47). In the poem, this
destructive male figure becomes a demon of possession and dependency. His female victim, threatened with psychological
extinction, images her anguish in metonyms and metaphors of
shadow: a night in a "black sack," a day full of "holes," a black
woman enslaved to a white man's sadistic desires, a marriage
to "distant thunder, / In whose shadow I have eaten my ghost
ration." Unlike Eliot's thunder over Himavant, this cloud
steals rather than gives life. Shadow existence in Plath's poetry
implies the political failure to extricate oneself from illegitimate and destructive authority, and more specifically the inability to function freely as a woman artist. Like an Orwellian
party member being vaporized for thought-crime, like Celan's
ash-haired Shulamith being granted "a grave in the air" by the
Nazis, like the person in "Belsen — physical or psychological"
(LH 560), the "I" becomes but a "ghost" of herself.

Plath's shadow imagery emphasizes an abiding sense of in-
substantiality. As in William James's evocation of melancholy,
"persons move like shadows, and sounds seem to come from a
distant world" (Varieties 129). In "Tulips," for example, a faceless, hospitalized woman sees herself as "a cut-paper shadow,"
wishing to "efface" herself entirely (CP 160–62). In "Crossing
the Water," other "cut paper" individuals traverse a landscape
of "shadows" (CP 190). To be a shadow in shadowland is to be
unreal: not a body without a soul, as depicted in the mirror
poems, but a spirit detached from actuality, a condition that
Frazer says must bring death. Plath's shadow almost always
suggests feelings of affective or artistic loss. In "Elm," love is
but a "shadow" that has gone off (CP 192). In "Three Women"

the second voice, the one who has miscarried her creativity, sees herself as but "a shadow" who enters "abyss after abyss" (*CP* 182). In "A Life," an Eliotesque woman drags "her shadow in a circle," the shadow resembling "a sheet of blank paper" (*CP* 149–50). As we might expect, such shadows bring anguish. The woman of "Tulips," for example, feels that she is silently suffocating—a powerful misprision of Dickinson's "shadows" that "hold their breath" (poem 258). We remember that when Benito Cereno is asked at the end of his ordeal, "What has cast such a shadow upon you?" he responds, "the Negro." Like Melville's Babo and James's "black stranger" in "The Jolly Corner," the "Negro . . . shadow" in "Thalidomide," the shadow-imprisoned "negress" in "The Jailer," and the shadow-casting blackberries in "Ariel" all represent the uncanny return of the repressed. For Plath, this return means a reencounter with feelings of marginality and bereavement.

Shadows, then, evoke the painful half-life one lives on the edge of annihilation. But to *have* a shadow, not of a cut-paper figure but of a human being, implies wholeness. Such moments occur rarely in *Ariel*, and they all involve children, which, as we have seen, Plath associated with poetry. In "Candles," for example, the candlelight provides the speaker and her daughter with protective shadows that "stoop over like guests at a christening" (*CP* 148–49). Similarly, in "By Candlelight," a shadowy light flickering on the protagonist and her infant son wards off the threatening "sack of black" (*CP* 236–37). Although these two poems suggest that affective connection and creative fulfillment can defy the black sack that is "everywhere, tight, tight!" Plath more typically represents the self as but a shadow of a dominating authority figure, or as a phantom of the creative self she might and should have been. In this characteristic guise, the shadow poem becomes the sickly, thin double of the unwritten poem. An image of absence, it substitutes for and points toward its opposite, the textual immanence that otherwise does not exist.

Why was Plath unable or unwilling to break free from her cell without a number? Why did she consign her "I" over and over again to a prison of shadows? Perceiving herself to be not

a "whole person" but a "knot of nerves, without identity," a
"reflection," a "wild dispersal," and a "fragmentary welter" (*J*
17, 108, 257, 307), she may have felt free to represent herself only
as the appendage or image of another. In her depression and
uncertainty, perhaps she feared that the alternative to her
shadow existence was an inability to represent herself at all. As
a shadow she had at least a "ghost ration" of creative identity,
but as herself she had none. Her mirror reaffirmed that lack
constantly, as did her recurrent artistic frustrations, her failed
quests for "plot," her extended writer's blocks — and beneath
those problems the messages she received about herself from
her affective relationships. Such was her artistic dilemma. Although she could hope to write herself out of the "hole" or
"abyss" in which she was trapped (*LH* 466; *CP* 182, 251), she
could write only by representing the tenuousness of her existence. Between the desire and the act lay the shadow.

Moreover, as a female latecomer burdened by male precursors whom she considered "the really good boys" (*J* 108), Plath
almost unavoidably represented herself in terms of their tropes.
In composing a textual immanence that was a shadow, for example, she created a double of Eliot's striding and rising "shadow"
that yields to fear in a handful of dust, of Roethke's "shadow
pinned against a sweating wall," and of Yeats's "image, man or
shade" called death-in-life or life-in-death; a double of Peter
Schlemihl's cast-off shadow, of the Faulknerian shadow that ac-
companies Quentin Compson on his last day of life, and of Conrad Kurtz, whom Marlow calls a shade or shadow; a double
even of Hans Christian Andersen's "The Shadow" and Stevenson's "little shadow that goes in and out with me." (Plath's
mother read Andersen's fairy tales and Stevenson's verses to her
as a young girl.) Certainly Plath attempted to make imaginative
space for herself by "misreading" her precursors, but she doubted
her success. Despite her career-long search for her own "voice,"
she found that she would often merely "mouth other poets,"
"shovel the hole full of other people and their words," "copy" (*J*
33, 86, 199). She feared doubling in the weak sense, with an attenuated sameness instead of an amplified difference. She feared
that her work was but a shadow of its predecessors.

Related to this intertextual viewpoint is the even more unsettling one that Plath partially repressed: the linguistic. From this perspective we see that words are inherently creatures of the labyrinth and the wind, "substanceless . . . shadows" (*CP* 239). They slip through anyone's fingers. Plath generally attributed her difficulties in achieving self-representation to her own ineptitude or to a male-dominated, hierarchical, and belated culture, but her textualizing project was also sabotaged by language itself, which contains its own treacherous holes. The shadow imaged the gap separating word from intention — the limits an errant medium imposed on her attempted "dialogue" between "Writing" and "Life" (*J* 108). She pursued two mutually exclusive goals: to represent accurately and to free words from any referential aspect whatever. The shadow expressed the impossibility of the former wish, just as the "suicidal" drive into the sun in "Ariel" expressed the impossibility of the latter. Only at extreme moments, such as we find exhibited in her last poems and in passages of her journal, did Plath explicitly recognize that "the words dissolve and the letters crawl away" (*J* 298). But the figure of the shadow implicitly testifies to this fearful insight throughout her canon. Shadow in this sense signifies not a failure to misread strongly enough but the inevitability of miswriting.

If the mirrors in Plath's last poems attest to a new, positive association of creativity with the self, the shadow of "Edge" suggests a counterpoint of linguistic alienation (*CP* 272–73). The reification of creativity into text has estranged it as an object, while the words themselves remain forever distinct from meaning, which depends on the contextual factors situating the words. In the last lines Plath is known to have written, the shadow of textual indeterminacy darkens and subverts the quest for self-representation. What Roland Barthes was to call the mobile, blank "edge" of discourse, "the place where the death of language is glimpsed" (*Pleasure* 6), arises to challenge the continuous, cultured edge that Plath's poetry also possesses. If we attend to what might be called its underthought, "Edge" resembles a poetic epitaph. The "illusion" of a "necessity" flows through the woman's "scrolls" (of writing); her coiled children (her pages of poetry) are "folded" back into her emptied-out self; her (metrical) "feet" "seem to be saying: / We have come so far, it is over." But in what sense can the woman be "perfected" when her texts merely contain, in Barbara Johnson's phase, endlessly "warring forces of signification" (5)? The words "illusion" and "seem" imply the possibility that the unfortunate woman has fatally misread her own texts, just as the poet has miswritten her poem to the degree that it evades her intentions. The texts may actually be telling the woman to *live*, though she interprets them contrarily. On an edge between metaphysics and indeterminacy as well as between life and death, Plath's last poem gapes at the space separating words from their referents and meanings, while the moon's shadows "crackle and drag" to commemorate the dissolution.

DEATH

IN ADDITION to projecting the double as reflection or shadow, Plath portrayed it in a variety of alternative forms. She had learned from Rank that the double came into vogue in German romanticism as a mode of questioning identity (*Beyond* 67–68). The figure, Rank argued, developed from a split between the intellect and the irrational forces unleashed by the French Revolution. In the nineteenth and twentieth centuries, writers have employed the figure to represent a wide range of divisions within the self — as, for example, between conventional morality and criminal impulses (Dostoevsky's novels), materialism and spirit (James's "The Jolly Corner"), submission and rebellion (Gilman's "The Yellow Wallpaper"), survival and suicide (Woolf's *Mrs. Dalloway*), conscience and vice (Poe's "William Wilson"), repression and desire (Brontë's *Wuthering Heights*), or repression and violence (Stevenson's *Dr. Jekyll and Mr. Hyde*). Plath, whose habit of seeing in polarities was brought to consciousness by Rank, used the double figure almost compulsively as she proceeded in her own inquisition of the self. It appears in poem after poem and story after story. Although the referential aspect of the figure may shift, the epistemology it manifests — the effort to structure self-knowledge dialectically — remains constant.

Doubles such as Johnny Panic, the speaking tree of "Elm,"
and the salesmen of "Death and Co." all resemble Rank's "modern" type: a secularized projection of Christian doom, an
omen of death (*Beyond* 76). Rather than the spiritual or immortal self, this double represents the profane self, capable of per-
secuting and punishing its alter ego, as do Golyadkin Junior,
Smerdyakov, and the devil in the Dostoevsky novels Plath
wrote about so perceptively. In her own Dostoevskian texts,
Plath used the double to evoke the psychic death that occurs in
moments of creative and affective sterility. These texts suggest
that when the potential space of imaginative and emotive free
play contracts, aspects of the self break down and break off, become grotesque in Sherwood Anderson's sense of partialness
passing for wholeness, and prey on one another like monsters
of the deep.

In "Johnny Panic and the Bible of Dreams" (*JP* 152–66), for
example, the "I" explains at the outset: "Maybe a mouse gets
to thinking pretty early on how the whole world is run by these
enormous feet. Well, from where I sit, I figure the world is run
by one thing and this one thing only. Panic with a dog-face,
devil-face, hag-face, whore-face, panic in capital letters with
no face at all — it's the same Johnny Panic, awake or asleep" (*JP*
152). Like the cognate "Panic-Bird" of the *Journals*, Johnny
Panic incarnates the narrator's fear — her fear, for instance, of
"those great originals" at the bottom of a semitransparent lake
(*JP* 154–55). This image, like so many others in Plath's canon,
implies an anxiety about precursors, about the mermen, snake
charmers, and colossi who haunted her psyche and utterance.
Johnny Panic, whose single "Word" obliterates the narrator's
own verbal play (*JP* 166), is a herald and a cause of her extinction (*JP* 166).

Similarly in "Elm" (*CP* 192–93), the taunting tree is the
double of the weak and dissatisfied "you." Although the "you"
(the ego) fears "the bottom" (the repressed material of the id),
the elm does not fear it, for it has "been there." Thus the poem
projects the psyche's forbidden impulses onto the tree, in a
kind of antithetical completion of Frost's "Tree at My Window." But as we saw in chapter 3, the two selves soon battle for

position. As the "you" reclaims its aggressive instincts from the elm, the tree becomes the passive and "terrified" one. It fears the "dark thing" inhabiting it — a panic bird projecting the destructive power newly unleashed in the "you." The tree has been demonized by the "face" in its "branches," an image of the transformed "you" superimposed on the tree by the windowpane's reflection. The selves of the poem, divided by "faults," reunify only in a violence that can "kill."

"Death and Co." (CP 254–55) concerns two uncanny figures, one condorlike and the other masturbatory, who correspond to the bifurcated deathwish of the desperate woman who encounters them. In one of her BBC broadcasts, Plath said that the poem suggests "the double or schizophrenic nature of death — the marmoreal coldness of Blake's death mask, say, hand in glove with the fearful softness of worms, water and other katabolists" (CP 294). Beyond the schizophrenic nature of death, the salesmen evoke the double nature of the immobilized speaker herself, aggressive and passive, or overtly aggressive and passively aggressive. Plath's doubles — like the maiden aunt of "The Tour," the malicious neighbor of "Eavesdropper," and Doreen of The Bell Jar — frequently stand for the hidden or "dirty" side of a disintegrating "I." Although the double of "Death and Co." is itself divided into opposing halves, both announce that "somebody's done for."

The double of "In Plaster" (CP 158–60), though similar in deathly purport to the ones I have been discussing, is distinct in what it represents. The hospitalized narrator exclaims that "there are two of me now," a new "white person" encasing the "old yellow one" (st. 1). Part spirit ("one of the real saints") and part matter ("like a dead body"), the narrator's white plaster cast initially exhibits a "slave mentality" but soon becomes a "superior" and "resentful" agent of death (st. 1, 3, 6), like Moby Dick in Ahab's diseased imagination or Smerdyakov in Ivan's. Although the speaker once thought of "making a go of it together," she now plots revenge: "I'm collecting my strength; one day I shall manage without her, / And she'll perish with emptiness then, and begin to miss me" (st. 8). Whereas Lynda Bundtzen plausibly interprets the plaster double as Plath's

confining "good-little-girl" persona (85), I would alternatively
suggest that this "white person" projects the external other
brought into intimate association with the self. For Plath, the
other who unites with the self as an indispensable sustainer
threatens to become an intolerable weight. Hence the patient's
ambivalent dependency and revolt: she rebels so that the
double will "miss" her.

This threat of punishing through leaving, as a way of regaining control over a situation, played a recurrent role in Plath's
emotional life. Her father seemed to have gained permanent
power over her by dying, making her "miss" him ever after,
making her "perish with emptiness." Rebelliously, she repeated the tactic herself on the two other individuals who mattered most to her, and who also seemed prone to withdraw
their love as a token of disapproval. Plath's first attempt to kill
herself, reflected obliquely in the final plotting of "In Plaster,"
may be interpreted as an effort to punish her mother for guid-
ing her along paths that she found inimical. Plath may have
been trying to "manage without her," and in the aftermath she
did indeed gain some of the adult authority she had been seeking. Plath's second and successful suicide attempt, prefigured
by "In Plaster" and accomplished less than two years after its
composition, may be seen as an effort to punish her husband —
again for manipulating her but more importantly for abandoning her, much as her father had seemed to do. Hughes's rejection was fully deliberate, unlike her father's, and it encompassed
her not simply as an affectional being but as a sexual partner
and a creative artist. The devastation must have been complete,
and the need for revenge and for recovery of authority overwhelming. Although "In Plaster" does not prophesy Hughes's
humiliation of Plath, it does reflect the manifest strains in their
relationship, which we have previously seen expressed in her
journals. Change the pronoun, and the poem's final lines may
well correlate with Plath's motivation in her last desperate
months: she would "manage" without him, so that he would
"perish with emptiness" and begin to "miss" her. It hardly
needs saying that the wish for the other to "miss" her undermines the very possibility of her "managing" on her own.

"In Plaster," then, deals less with the tortured self alone than with the self's tortured relations with the other. As we have seen, Plath both approached and avoided those she loved, in a sense internalizing her parents' troubled marriage, in which her mother ambivalently yearned for union while her father ambivalently fled from contact. Plath's wish for fusion was a way for her to reconstitute the pre-Oedipal oneness, to diminish the risks of intimacy, and to avoid the pain of loss and loneliness. She did indeed live her life "in plaster," cementing her emotions or allowing them to be cemented by others, and then seeking to free herself from those casts, only to realize her dependence on them. The way she and her culture constructed her human relations meant that the other was both necessary to her health and a sinister force that prevented her from achieving independence. No wonder she felt suffocated and paralyzed, imprisoned and poisoned. Those most precious to her all became doubles who threatened to inhabit, to inhibit, and to destroy her.

Plath's double frequently takes this form of an oppressive other—in early stories like "Sunday at the Mintons' " and "The Wishing Box," and more indelibly in the late poetic tetralogy of "Daddy," "Medusa," "The Jailer," and "Lady Lazarus." Although the doubles in these texts all have a connective or syntagmatic relation to the protagonist—all are either husbands or blood relations—they are also related to her through paradigmatic contrast, as Hyde is to Jekyll. The character of Daddy, for example, is to the "I" as a Nazi is to a Jew (*CP* 222–24). He splits into two relatively interchangeable avatars, the "black man" who is Daddy proper and the "man in black" who is his successor, the husband. At the end this two-faced oppressor seems to merge back into the injured "I" herself, since she ultimately assumes his signification of murderousness: "Daddy, I have had to kill you," "If I've killed one man I've killed two—." The other has ceased to be contrastive or even "other" as the "I" takes Daddyesque pleasure in the act of violence.

We must now supplement, and to some degree qualify, our earlier view of "Daddy" as an act of rebellion by reconsidering it in terms of diabolical possession. For embedded in Plath's strike for freedom was her characterological ambivalence, expressed as a skepticism about her control even over the rhetoric of control. Plath came to write "Daddy" after years of active interest in the phenomenon of possession. In preparing her honors thesis of 1955, she read "A Neurosis of Demoniacal Possession in the Seventeenth Century," in which Freud analyzes the case of Christoph Haitzmann, a painter who gave his bond to the devil and who was exorcised by priests. In Freud's analysis, Haitzmann was motivated by grief over the death of his father, intensified by anxieties concerning his livelihood as an artist. Freud suggests that Haitzmann's train of thought was as follows: "Owing to my father's death I am despondent and can no longer work; if I can but get a father-substitute I shall be able to regain all that I have lost" (446). An "eternal suckling," Haitzmann followed a path leading "from his own father" to "the devil as a father-substitute" and finally "to the pious Fathers" (470–71). The psychological themes that Freud finds interwoven into this story — grief, doubts about working capacity, desires for substitution and for exorcism — certainly had continuing applicability to Plath's own psychological situation.

In 1958, in the midst of her "fury" at her husband's flirtation, Plath returned to the theme of possession, immersing herself in T. K. Oesterreich's *Possession: Demoniacal and Other*, which gives examples of the phenomenon "from the most ancient times down to the present day" (ix). Although Oesterreich ascribes possession to "auto-suggestion," the strength of his book lies not in its analysis but in its wealth of memorable illustrations. Plath seems to have been fascinated by the sheer power of the narratives — story after story of individuals being taken over by the soul of a dead person, an animal, or a diabolical force. The book contains numerous instances of possession by the "devil," of the inner divisions entailed by such possession, and of exorcism. Oesterreich quotes one investigator's assertion that possession often originates in the victim's unsorted feelings toward a deceased loved one (116; quoted in *J* 258). The possessed person, usually female, typically loses her individuality, becoming changed in appearance and prone to violence. Crucially, she is always deprived of her voice. The male demon speaks for her, in a "strange voice" that may betray "a coarse and filthy attitude, fundamentally opposed to all accepted ethical and religious ideas" (21). For example, Oesterreich tells of a young Polish-Jewish woman who was possessed by a "dibbuck"—the spirit of a German-speaking Christian man who had drowned himself in despair (207-10). He also tells of the maid of Orlach, attacked by a "black spirit" who came to her "in human form" (but with a face she could never clearly describe) and who made himself master of "her whole interior" (21, 94, 108-9; mentioned in *J* 257).

Under the stress of Hughes's desertion, Plath seems to have turned again to these "diverting—but also inspiring—*metaphors*" (*J* 257) as a structure for her poetry. One can discern them, put to her own purposes, in "Daddy" and in the other poems of the tetralogy. As in Freud's and Oesterreich's stories, Plath's Daddy is a "devil," a spirit "so black no sky could squeak through" (st. 10-11). He is also a "bag full of God," recalling Freud's notion that God and the devil are doubles, projecting opposite aspects of the father. As in Oesterreich, the possessor speaks a "strange" and "filthy" language (21), an obscene "gobbledygoo" that renders his victim unable to "speak" (st. 5-6, 9). While possessed by this demon, however, Plath's "I" becomes possessed by a second individuality, which may contain the seeds of an authentic, creative identity: she begins "to talk like a Jew" (st. 7). Oesterreich mentions cases "in which possession by an evil spirit alternates with possession by a good one" (27). For Plath's speaker, the good spirit entails not merely moral virtue but the ability "to talk," a topic I shall return to in a moment. Like the tree and the woman in "Elm," and like the yellow and white selves of "In Plaster," the diabolical and Jewish spirits of "Daddy" contend for mastery. Despite appearances, the "man in black" may ultimately win. For though the poem's conclusion resembles an exorcism ritual, the "I" seems not to expel her "devil" but to give him full expression for the first time. Her vicarious brutality, her endorsement of "the killing of the father by the brothers banded together" (Freud, *Civilization* 131), signals the defeat of her hopes for autonomy, creativity, and an "ethic of care" (Gilligan 164). Furthermore, her guilt over this transformation appears to doom her. Her last words imply that she herself will now complete Daddy's task for him: "Daddy, daddy, you bastard, I'm through" (st. 16).

The remaining poems of the tetralogy—"Medusa," "The Jailer," and "Lady Lazarus"—similarly concern destructive and unconquerable possessors. In the Gothic universe of these poems, the other enters the female subject, takes charge of her, and steals her life. John Irwin has attributed the "annihilating union" of self and other to regressive narcissism:

> The ego loves the double as a copy of itself, but it simultaneously hates and fears the double because it is a copy with a difference — the double is the ego shadowed by the unconscious, the ego tinged with its own death. Thus in doubling, the ego takes the embodiment of its own death as its object of sexual desire, and the murder of the double becomes . . . the suicidal return to the womb, the sexual reentry into Mother Death. (90–91)

Although this interpretation certainly has relevance to Plath, we should remain aware that the situation is complicated by her desire for authority. Plath structured her confrontation with the double around her creative self-doubt. When we consider "Daddy" from this perspective, we see even more clearly than before that the poem ends in defeat for the speaker. As Margaret Homans (*Women Writers* 220–21), Margaret Dickie Uroff (160–61), and Guinevara Nance and Judith Jones (129) have suggested, the "I" never achieves an adequate self-representation. Thus the poem reveals not simply her hidden death-wish but also her discursive failure, her experience of the limits of both rebellion as an imaginative act and doubling as a means of self-observation. Although Plath claimed that her protagonist "has to act out the awful little allegory before she is free of it" (*CP* 293), her protagonist in fact has no language of self beyond the allegory and therefore can never be free of it.

As we know, the poem opens with the "I" rejecting any representation of herself that relies on Daddy's definition of her, in which she has "lived like a foot" for thirty years. She has "had to kill" him in order to discover a more acceptable self-representation. She then proceeds to describe herself not as a daddy's girl but as a Jewish or Gypsy victim of the Fascist's crimes, and finally as a violent rebel. Daddy descends the ladder from "God" to "swastika" and "devil." Although the tropes have undergone a chiasmic reversal, however, little has actually changed, since the "I" still represents herself in stereotypes dependent solely on her relation to Daddy. By relabeling the godlike father a devil and her submissive self an insurrectionist, she has simply inverted the values while keeping the terms of the equation constant. Indeed, as the poem proceeds, the original paradigm of daughterly devotion returns and interferes with the revised one of daughterly hatred: "At twenty I tried to die / And get back, back, back to you." (st. 12). The daughter's initial submissiveness, never truly given up, resurfaces in the form of adult masochism and incest fantasy. Once afraid of her father's "black shoe," she now "adores" his "boot in the face." When the effort to "get back" fails, she revives the devotion myth in terms of a substitute, the vampire-husband "who said he was you."

In the last stanza, the "I" finally severs herself from both of these daddy figures. But by vicariously placing her boot in Daddy's face, by terminating his doubling presence in herself, she has also killed the only speaking voice of the poem. Without Daddy, the "I," who has defined herself only in terms of him, has no further means of self-reference. In other words, the poem moves not from oppression to self-mastery but from limited self-mastery to a void. The "I" initiates language by simultaneously posing and deposing the self that is a passive instrument of her father's desire; she then experiments with a new self-representation as a rebel, which proves spectacular but transitory; and she concludes by relinquishing her claims to any self-representation at all. If the figure of Daddy personifies male poetic tradition, the poem signifies Plath's difficulty in textualizing a self free of masculine conventions, her unwillingness to move confidently in the direction suggested by "Three Women." If Daddy personifies hierarchical and abusive uses of power, then the poem signifies her difficulty in inventing a textual being independent of such structures. In either case, despite its surface note of triumph,

"Daddy" forecasts the silence Plath plunged into during her final days. And considering that her life had narrowed to an obsessional quest for vocational and textual identity to compensate for her lost affectional and social identity, we understand that that final "I'm through" does prefigure not merely the cessation of utterance but attempted suicide as well.

Plath's sequence of father hatred, symbolic parricide, and the resultant impulse both to celebrate and to mourn accords with Freud's speculations about Dostoevsky's psychic history in "Dostoevski and Parricide." "Daddy" remains quite faithful to Freud's pessimism about the outcome of such a history: "One wished another person dead, and now one *is* this other person and is dead oneself" (229). Plath's poem, a "self-punishment for a death-wish against a hated father" (229), demonstrates the limited life span of her October poetic voice by enacting its extinction.

In "Daddy" and the other poems of the tetralogy, the double proves less a means to self-knowledge than an emblem of the irony of the enterprise. Plath's "I" turns others into images or counterimages of the self, and the self into images or counterimages of others. Each new poem, each new attempt to represent a being, in effect represented what the being was not. Calling such poems "light verse" (Alvarez, *Beyond* 56) or, alternatively, "gruesome" (*LH* 472) could not disguise their alienation from her original need in composing them.

WE ARE NOW prepared to consider Plath's most significant use of the double motif, her trope of an authentic, creative "deep self" trapped in an inauthentic, material self (*J* 165). This trope suggests the ubiquitous romantic and postromantic duality between one's empirical identity and a more essential "imaginative power" (Wordsworth), "real Me" (Whitman), "man below the man" (Stevens), "self aetherial" (Pound), or "mind which creates" (Eliot). It also suggests the contrast common in women's poetry between the conforming self and a disruptive "concealed" self (Dickinson), "woman, wild" (Mary Coleridge), "innermost me" (Teasdale), or "daemon" (Isabella Gardner). More disquietingly, however, Plath's dichotomy resembles

R. D. Laing's imagery of schizophrenia, as both David Holbrook (13-14, 35-37, 152-53, 174-77, 252-54) and Alan Williamson (31-32) have observed. We recall that the bibliography of Plath's honors thesis included an article on schizophrenia by Edward Lazell and that she again associated doubling with schizophrenia in her BBC broadcast of fall 1962 (*CP* 294). Although it is not clear that Plath actually had a copy of Laing's *The Divided Self* in her hands, she would unquestionably have known about the book. It was published in London in 1960, and its ideas were in the air. Plath's texts of 1962-63 almost certainly reflect Laing's eloquent evocation of mental illness, employing his metaphors to suggest the dimensions of her own creative crisis.

Of course we cannot tell precisely where Laing's influence leaves off and Plath's own life experience begins. Although she was not a schizophrenic, she did suffer from "depressive illness" (Andreasen, "Ariel's Flight" 3, 8-9), and its symptoms can mimic those of schizophrenia. In her month of greatest poetic productivity, October 1962, she exhibited manic hyperactivity and flight of ideas together with depression. By February 1963 she had entered into a fully depressive phase, and the pain caused her to stop writing. We might postulate that Plath's depressive sequence was triggered by the departure of her husband; by the birth of her second child; by her artistic frustration; by her economic difficulties; by her knowledge that Dickinson, Woolf, Lowell, and Roethke had experienced similar sequences; or by some combination of these, in conjunction with endogenous factors (see Andreasen; Bowlby; Goodwin and Guze; Winokur, Clayton, and Reich).

Whatever the precipitating events and feelings, it is clear that between October 1962 and February 1963 Plath textualized a condition of psychic disturbance within the imagistic framework Laing established. In her last bursts of writing, we glimpse something analogous to schizophrenia's core traits (cognitive slippage, anhedonia, interpersonal aversiveness) and fundamental symptoms (tone at odds with content, autism, loosening of associations, extreme ambivalence). By placing *The Divided Self* and Plath's texts on the same plane, we glimpse the unsettling interplay that may occur between mental and creative crisis (as James, Freud, Andreasen, Hatterer, and Storr have shown). We also sense the disparities in adaptiveness, purpose, and power that separate psychological extremity per se from the kind of imaginative passion Plath experienced.

In Plath's late writing, as in the discourse of Laing's patients, the world is empty and dead, and the somatic self also feels dead. Within that somatic self, however, "something of great worth" has been "deeply lost or buried" (Laing 223). Laing posits that the breach between the body and this "true" self is both painful — something the sufferer wants mended — and desired as a basic means of defense (173). The self progressively withdraws from the body, seals itself in an interior castle, and becomes charged with hatred for all that is "there" (174). Then it loses its sense of its own reality, no longer viewing its inward chamber as a safe haven but seeing it as a prison, a hell. The true self feels "persecuted within [its] chamber by split concretized parts of itself or by its own phantoms which have become uncontrollable" (174). The sufferer sinks into an endless time of "barren, arid desolation," a "death in life" (222), from which the only plausible escape is suicide: "If I'm dead I can't be killed" (174).

Up to a point, this pattern corresponds to the one we observe in Plath's art. Nevertheless, neither her actual nor her represented psyche deteriorated into "chaotic nonentity" (Laing 175). Nor did her discourse become incoherent, though it loosened its tie to conventional sequencing and exhibited something akin to Hart Crane's "logic of metaphor" (*Poems* 221). Plath's depression simply intensified her normal way of structuring things, which was to split them into opposed categories — into a war between what was real or creatively meaningful and what was material, factitious, malevolent, oppressive, or alien. Moreover, instead of inexorably withdrawing ever deeper into its cocoon, Plath's depicted self typically struggles to reemerge into the light, though that struggle never completely succeeds. Plath dramatized the desire of the "deep self" to transform its false-self system, to become free and whole.

The Bell Jar prefigures the doubling imagery of Plath's late poetry. As Esther Greenwood moves through her suicidal crisis, she experiences the same series of feelings Laing observed in his patients: "arid desolation," the separation of bodily self from another "deeply lost or buried" self, and the wish to die (Laing 222–23, 174). Wherever she goes, Esther seems to be under a "glass bell jar," stewing in her own "sour air" (*BJ* 222), just like the patient who says, "I felt as though I were in a bottle. . . . The air is so very stale" (Laing 182–83). Living an existential death, Esther attempts to slash her wrists but cannot do it: "It was as if what I wanted to kill wasn't in that skin or the thin blue pulse that jumped under my thumb, but somewhere else, deeper, more secret, a whole lot harder to get at" (*BJ* 176). Like the patient who "wants to be dead and hidden in a place where nothing can touch him and drag him back" (Laing 191), Esther finally swallows pills in a basement, "crouching at the mouth of the darkness, like a troll" (*BJ* 200). She hopes to terminate not only her somatic self but the troll-like "deeper" self sequestered within (*BJ* 176). Nevertheless, by the novel's end Esther recovers. Her false-self system dead and "buried," she now feels "free," though still faced with a confusing world of "question marks" (*BJ* 288, 290). Perhaps Plath wrote *The Bell Jar* in order to reexperience her suffering and to retrieve her cure. Perhaps it was a way of foreseeing or warding off a recurrence of that pain and loneliness in her present life. For certainly the bell jar did "descend again" (*BJ* 286), and she did try again to dislodge it and escape.

The conflict between false and true selves reached its apex in Plath's poems of October 1962. In the very first poem of that month, "The Detective," a prevaricating man murders a woman's deep self, while her physical being survives (*CP* 208–9). Within days, however, a different paradigm appeared, in which the inner seed strives to defeat the outer husk and to live an independent existence. As Susan Van Dyne has shown, Plath's worksheets for the bee poems represent a "search for an authentic and autonomous self" (3). In "Stings," for example, the "I" acquires a beehive, which she regards as a metaphor for human identity (*CP* 214–15). Envisioning a "queen" that is either absent from the hive or "unqueenly and even shameful," she compares that failed queen to the drudgelike women at the bee meeting and then to herself. But the sight of a brooding male figure on the sidelines, with "lips like lies," rekindles her faith in her deep self. Realizing that she too has "a self to recover," a Dickinsonian "queen," she imagines a revived queen bee flying

> More terrible than she ever was, red
> Scar in the sky, red comet
> Over the engine that killed her —
> The mausoleum, the wax house.

Thus the wax house, or false-self system, contains a powerful inner being with "lion-red body" and "wings of glass," a poetic self capable of both flight and violence.

In "Ariel" (*CP* 239–40) and "Purdah" (*CP* 242–44), similarly, the speaking subject removes an outer "doll" composed of "dead hands, dead stringencies" to reveal a "White Godiva" or "lioness," a spirit of unveiled female rebelliousness. Like the red queen of "Stings," sailing ambiguously through the sky as either a "scar" or a "comet," the White Godiva and the lioness are at once emblems of injury and prophecies of artistic greatness. In "Lady Lazarus," too, a powerful deep self eventually emerges from its encasing system (*CP* 244–46). Although the protagonist initially attempts suicide to free herself from a body that her "enemy" defines as his "opus," she fails, remaining fixed in an existence that is material without being real (as Fitzgerald says of the world that killed Gatsby). She herself learns to speak the dead language of that dead world, exacting a "charge" for her word or touch. She becomes but a collection of fraudulent relics, since the god within is hidden, even from herself. Ultimately, however, the god escapes, leaving only more relics behind — a wedding ring, a gold filling. Since the social world, like the Third Reich, apprehends its victims as things rather than as precious human beings, her deep self can evade its grasp — but only at a cost. Instead of a being "full of wings, otherworldliness" (*CP* 258), she emerges as a homicidal maniac, eating men "like air."

Poems like "Stings," "Ariel," "Purdah," and "Lady Lazarus"

share a vision of the destructiveness of the livid, reddened, scarred, or leonine true self. This self resembles the schizoid individual as described by Laing: "If there is anything [he] is likely to believe in, it is his own destructiveness. He is unable to believe that he can fill his own emptiness without reducing what is there to nothing" (99). But we can find another, more compelling explanation for the destructiveness of the being Plath termed in her journal "this murderous self" and "the fearful beast in myself" (*J* 176-77). In Plath's drama, the inner being has been denied so painfully and for so long that when it rises out of the ash it has virtually no being to be, has nothing to take account of but its own anger, its long frustration, its desperate effort to rise. It becomes a figure of revenge or, conversely, of self-annihilation.

In the poems of Plath's last creative burst, written between January 28 and February 5, 1963, the speaker acknowledges her inability to realize herself positively. Her hidden self personifies the wish to cast off the false-self system, and since it is only a wish, its repeated appearances have the effect of immobilizing her imagination. It leads to no further wishes, and certainly not to a vision of an individuality apart from the Manichean war of opposites. Prolonged suffering has swept aside the image of autonomous yet caring female selves contained in "Three Women." Instead of growth and transformation, Plath's final poems reverberate with a sense of futility and fate, with allusions to fixed stars, doom marks, and Greek necessities. In "Words," when the buried self escapes into the words of a text, its significance dries up (*CP* 270). In "Contusion," after an inner pit pivots the outer "sea," it immediately disappears (*CP* 271). In "Balloons," the delightful "soul animals" also vanish (*CP* 271-72). And in "Edge," the deep self has petrified into a "dead body" with two dead children (*CP* 272-73). In this last poem, the struggle of the inner self to emerge has ended. The "woman"—no longer the poem's voice but a voiceless object of the poem's gaze—is inorganic through and through. The true self, which was revealed as no more than the battle against its outer double, has died, and with that death comes the death of representation.

To guess the final significance of Plath's use of the double, we must backtrack to her poetics. As we have observed, Plath's true self was essentially her "creative mind" (*J* 157), her interior "genius" that allowed her to feel an "intense sense of living richly and deeply" (*LH* 468, 235). Her false-self system was everything that hid, blocked, stifled, or defeated her creativity. This division corresponds not only to the distinction a poet like Whitman makes between the "Me myself" and the self defined by "trippers and askers" ("Song of Myself"), but also to the distinction Harold Bloom makes between the "poet-in-a-poet" and the "person-in-a-poet" (*Map* 19). The "person-in-a-poet" lives a life, ordinary or unordinary, while the "poet-in-a-poet" voices poems. Although Plath spent her career constructing a "dialogue" between those two identities, by the end she had given up on the "person-in-the-poet." Her true self was the one that waxed in the composition process and waned when the process concluded.

In her loneliness and suffering, Plath seized the poetic act itself as her most desired double. In one sense it was her opposite: in literary creation she felt alive, whereas at all other times she felt dead. But in another sense the poetic act replicated her. One might argue that she merely used her life experience as a pretext for her word making, as her mentor Lowell claimed to do ("In Conversation" 19). Yet even if the analogies between life experience and art were only pretext, the autobiographical matter finally loomed large, laden with power. And the analogies were undoubtedly more than just pretext. They helped Plath to libidinize language; to fulfill her need for osmosis with someone or something outside herself; and to construct a regulated self-image in a realm of freedom. Frazer wrote, in a sentence Plath underlined, that "primitive man regards his name as a vital portion of himself" (244). Plath similarly hoped that her texts would magically name her, would become organic extensions of her, transforming her identity. In every character, every situation, every image, every word choice, she saw reflections or shadows of her own character, of the individuals closest to her, of her own ways of knowing and feeling.

We might speculate that Plath became oppressed by the notion that, as Bloom suggests, every poem contains an "image
or lie of voice" (*Breaking* 4). She must have found her personal
voice being drowned out by the one that arose from her texts.
The image of her true self in her writing must eventually have
begun to plague her. As we have seen, the true self had
difficulty developing once it had emerged, but there was a problem beyond that. It demanded that all other selves be sacrificed
to it. Yet Plath had more than one need. She needed to live as
a person as well as a poet; she needed to touch and to be
touched. Her textual self demanded constant attention, like a
monster. It threatened to die every day and every moment that
she was not creating, for it had no other means to sustain itself.
It lived on air, on her. It could not represent itself as being,
only as becoming — and it required that she sacrifice her existence to it. Plath's true self had become yet another tyrant, a
"devil," a "jailer," a "vampire." Her desire had been to release
the trapped being, the poet locked within her, and she had become a slave to that desire. She did not know how to give it up.

But then the monster began to expire. As Plath ran out of
pretext or out of language, as her verbal constitution of self
reached its limit and then withdrew, the potential space of her
texts attenuated, like the guttering candles or emaciated people she wrote about so memorably. Her relationship to words
was failing, just as her affective relationships had failed, and
perhaps now she felt the full brunt of her losses. In her anguish, she may have even come to think that her "true self"
had in fact been estranged from her all along, had not truly
been her. Whatever the causes, one can feel the will to create
melt away in those last spare, almost affectless poems. One
thinks of Bartleby's response to his employer:

"Why, how now? what next? do no more writing?"
"No more."
"And what is the reason?"
"Do you not see the reason for yourself?" (Melville, "Bartleby" 38)

Then again, perhaps Plath was not simply a victim. When
she saw herself trapped in a true self grown increasingly alien,

she may have decided to "thrust through the wall" of her prison, as Ahab says (Melville, *Moby-Dick* 144). She may have intended to strike "through the mask" by giving meaning and validity to her empirical self. And as she transferred her attention to this empirical being, her *pneuma* began to lose energy and power, to weaken and to die like so many of her defeated doubles, to whisper, like the voice of "Daddy," "I'm through." According to this line of reasoning, Plath tried to reinvest her empirical self with desire by making it double the same myth she had evoked in her poetry: that of death and rebirth. As intertextual act and trope, Plath's transformative myth engendered, orchestrated, and relieved some profound human emotions; but made actual, it turned malign. In attempting to continue her art through other means, Plath brought her struggle with her textual echo to an abrupt conclusion, terminating her pain at the cost of her words. In a sense her poetic voice had not weakened and died at all, but had captured her person. The double as immortal soul had quite literally turned harbinger of death, for if Plath's poetry initially seemed to be saving her life, it ended by consuming her. The shadow jumped off the wall, the image leapt out of the mirror, annihilating their origin.

WORKS CITED

Parenthetical page references in my text to Plath's major works have been abbreviated as follows: *The Bell Jar: BJ*; *The Collected Poems: CP*; *Johnny Panic and the Bible of Dreams: JP*; *The Journals: J*; and *Letters Home: LH*. References are to clothbound editions, as indicated below. Clothbound and paperback editions of *Collected Poems* have the same pagination, as do cloth and paper editions of *Johnny Panic*. Readers wishing to locate quotations in paperback editions of the other three volumes may find the following information helpful: the Bantam paperback edition of *The Bell Jar* runs ninety pages shorter than the Harper & Row clothbound edition; the Ballantine paperback edition of *The Journals* varies at any point from the Dial clothbound edition by no more than two pages plus or minus; and the Bantam paperback edition of *Letters Home* runs eighty-eight pages longer than the Harper & Row clothbound edition.

PRIMARY TEXTS

Beckett, Samuel. *The Unnamable.* New York: Grove, 1958.

Bishop, Elizabeth. *Complete Poems: 1927–1979.* New York: Farrar, Straus & Giroux, 1980.

Crane, Hart. *Complete Poems and Selected Letters and Prose.* Ed. Brom Weber. Garden City, N.Y.: Doubleday-Anchor, 1966.

Dickinson, Emily. *Letters of Emily Dickinson.* Ed. Thomas H. Johnson. Cambridge: Harvard UP, 1958.

——. *Poems of Emily Dickinson.* Ed. Thomas H. Johnson. Cambridge: Harvard UP, 1955.

Dostoevsky, Fyodor. *The Brothers Karamazov.* 1880. Trans. Constance Garnett. New York: Random House/Modern Library, 1950.

Eliot, T. S. *Complete Poems and Plays, 1909–1950.* New York: Harcourt, Brace & World, 1971.

Fitzgerald, F. Scott. *Letters.* Ed. Andrew Turnbull. New York: Scribner's, 1963.

Hughes, Ted. Foreword. *Journals.* By Sylvia Plath. New York: Dial, 1982. xi–xiii.

————. Introduction. *Collected Poems*. By Sylvia Plath. New York: Harper & Row, 1981. 13–17.

————. Introduction. *Johnny Panic and the Bible of Dreams*. By Sylvia Plath. New York: Harper & Row, 1979: 1–9.

————. *New Selected Poems*. New York: Harper & Row, 1982.

————. "Notes on the Chronological Order of Sylvia Plath's Poer: s." 1966. *The Art of Sylvia Plath*. Ed. Charles Newman. Bloomington: Indiana UP, 1970. 187–95.

————. "Sylvia Plath and Her Journals." 1983. *Ariel Ascending: Writings about Sylvia Plath*. Ed. Paul Alexander. New York: Harper & Row, 1985. 152–64.

Lowell, Robert. "After Enjoying Six or Seven Essays on Me." *Salmagundi* 37 (Spring 1977): 112–15.

————. *Collected Prose*. Ed. Robert Giroux. New York: Farrar, Straus & Giroux, 1987.

————. *Day by Day*. New York: Farrar, Straus & Giroux, 1977.

————. Foreword. *Ariel*. By Sylvia Plath. New York: Harper & Row, 1966. ix–xi.

————. *For the Union Dead*. New York: Farrar, Straus & Giroux, 1964.

————. *History*. New York: Farrar, Straus & Giroux, 1973.

————. *Life Studies*. New York: Farrar, Straus & Cudahy, 1959.

————. *Lord Weary's Castle and the Mills of the Kavanaughs*. 1946, 1951. Cleveland: World/Meridian, 1961.

————. "Robert Lowell in Conversation." Interviewer A. Alvarez. *London Observer*, July 21, 1963. 19.

————. "Talk with Robert Lowell." Interviewer A. Alvarez. *Encounter*, Feb. 1965. 39–43.

Melville, Herman. "Bartleby." *Piazza Tales*. 1856. New York: Henricks House, Farrar, Straus, 1948. 16–54.

————. *Letters*. Ed. Merrell R. Davis and William H. Gilman. New Haven: Yale UP, 1960.

————. *Moby-Dick*. 1851. New York: Norton, 1967.

Millay, Edna St. Vincent. *Collected Poems*. New York: Harper & Row, 1956.

Milton, John. *Paradise Lost*. 1667, 1674. Ed. Merritt Y. Hughes. New York: Odyssey, 1935.

Moore, Marianne. *Complete Poems*. New York: Macmillan, 1967.

Plath, Aurelia Schober. Introduction. *Letters Home: Correspondence, 1950–1963*. By Sylvia Plath. Ed. Aurelia Schober Plath. New York: Harper & Row, 1975. 3–41.

————. Letter to Steven Gould Axelrod, August 14, 1983.

————. "Letter Written in the Actuality of Spring." *Ariel Ascend-*

ing: Writings about Sylvia Plath. Ed. Paul Alexander. New York: Harper & Row, 1985. 214-17.

——— . Talk, Wellesley College Club, March 16, 1976. Unpublished ms. at Smith College.

Plath, Otto. *Bumblebees and Their Ways*. New York: Macmillan, 1934.

Plath, Sylvia, ed. *American Poetry Now: A Selection of the Best Poems by Modern American Writers. Critical Quarterly Poetry Supplement* 2, 1961.

——— . *The Bell Jar*. 1963. New York: Harper & Row, 1971.

——— . *Collected Poems*. Ed. Ted Hughes. New York: Harper & Row, 1981.

——— . Interview. *The Poet Speaks*. By Peter Orr. New York: Barnes & Noble, 1966. 167-72.

——— . *Johnny Panic and the Bible of Dreams: Short Stories, Prose, and Diary Excerpts*. New York: Harper & Row, 1979.

——— . *Journals of Sylvia Plath*. Ed. Frances McCullough and Ted Hughes. New York: Dial, 1982.

——— . *Letters Home: Correspondence, 1950-1963*. Ed. Aurelia Schober Plath. New York: Harper & Row, 1975.

——— . "The Magic Mirror: A Study of the Double in Two of Dostoevski's Novels." Unpublished ms. at Smith College.

Rich, Adrienne. *The Fact of a Doorframe: Poems Selected and New, 1950-1984*. New York: Norton, 1984.

——— . *Of Woman Born: Motherhood as Experience and Institution*. 1976. Toronto: Bantam, 1977.

——— . *On Lies, Secrets, and Silence: Selected Prose, 1966-1978*. New York: Norton, 1979.

Roethke, Theodore. *Collected Poems*. Garden City, N.Y.: Doubleday, 1966.

——— . *On the Poet and His Craft: Selected Prose*. Seattle: U of Washington P, 1965.

Sexton, Anne. "The Barfly Ought to Sing." *The Art of Sylvia Plath*. Ed. Charles Newman. Bloomington: Indiana UP, 1970. 174-81.

——— . *Complete Poems*. Boston: Houghton Mifflin, 1981.

Shakespeare, William. *Complete Works*. Ed. Hardin Craig. Chicago: Scott, Foresman, 1961.

Stevens, Wallace. *Collected Poems*. New York: Knopf, 1954.

Teasdale, Sara, ed. *The Answering Voice: One Hundred Love Lyrics by Women*. Boston: Houghton Mifflin, 1917.

——— . *Collected Poems*. New York: Macmillan, 1937.

Thomas, Dylan. *Collected Poems*. New York: New Directions, 1957.

Whitman, Walt. *Leaves of Grass*. 1891-92. Ed. Harold W. Blodgett and Sculley Bradley. New York: Norton, 1968.

Woolf, Virginia. *The Common Reader*, First Series. 1925. New York: Harcourt Brace Jovanovich/Harvest, n.d.

——. *Moments of Being: Unpublished Autobiographical Writings*. Ed. Jeanne Schulkind. New York: Harcourt Brace Jovanovich, 1976.

——. *Mrs. Dalloway*. 1925. New York: Harcourt Brace Jovanovich/Harvest, n.d.

——. *A Room of One's Own*. 1929. New York: Harcourt, Brace & World/Harbinger, n.d.

——. *Three Guineas*. New York: Harcourt, Brace & World, 1938.

——. *To the Lighthouse*. New York: Harcourt, Brace & World, 1927.

——. *The Waves*. New York: Harcourt, Brace & World, 1931.

——. *A Writer's Diary*. Ed. Leonard Woolf. 1954. New York: Harcourt Brace Jovanovich/Harvest, n.d.

SECONDARY TEXTS

Aird, Eileen. *Sylvia Plath: Her Life and Work*. New York: Harper & Row, 1973.

Alvarez, A. *Beyond All This Fiddle*. London: Allen Lane-Penguin, 1968.

——. *The Savage God: A Study of Suicide*. 1971. New York: Bantam, 1973.

——. "Sylvia Plath." 1963. *The Art of Sylvia Plath*. Ed. Charles Newman. Bloomington: Indiana UP, 1970. 56–68.

Ames, Lois. "Sylvia Plath: A Biographical Note." *The Bell Jar*. By Sylvia Plath. 1963. New York: Harper & Row, 1971. 291–311.

Anderson, Charles R. *Emily Dickinson's Poetry: Stairway of Surprise*. New York: Holt, Rinehart & Winston, 1960.

Andreasen, Nancy. "Ariel's Flight: The Death of Sylvia Plath." *Saturday Evening Post*, March 1975. Typescript at Smith College, dated 1973. 1–15.

——. "Creativity and Psychiatric Illness." *Psychiatric Annals* 8.3 (Mar. 1978): 23–45.

Annas, Pamela J. *A Disturbance in Mirrors: The Poetry of Sylvia Plath*. New York: Greenwood, 1988.

Auerbach, Nina. "Artists and Mothers: A False Alliance." 1978. *Romantic Imprisonment: Women and Other Glorified Outcasts*. New York: Columbia UP, 1986. 171–83.

Axelrod, Steven Gould. "Plath's Literary Relations: An Essay and an Index to the *Journals* and *Letters Home*." *Resources for American Literary Study* 14.2–3 (Spring and Autumn 1984): 59–84.

————. *Robert Lowell: Life and Art.* Princeton: Princeton UP, 1978.

Balint, Alice. *The Early Years of Life.* New York: Basic, 1954.

Banning, Margaret. *The Case for Chastity.* New York: Harper, 1937.

Barthes, Roland. *Criticism and Truth.* 1966. Trans. Katrine Pilcher Keuneman. Minneapolis: U of Minnesota P, 1978.

————. *The Grain of the Voice: Interviews 1962–1980.* 1981. Trans. Linda Coverdale. New York: Hill and Wang, 1985.

————. *The Pleasure of the Text.* 1973. Trans. Richard Miller. New York: Hill and Wang, 1975.

————. *The Rustle of Language.* 1964–78. Trans. Richard Howard. New York: Hill and Wang, 1986.

Bate, W. Jackson. *The Burden of the Past and the English Poet.* New York: Norton, 1972.

Bedient, Calvin. "Sylvia Plath, Romantic." *Sylvia Plath: New Views on the Poetry.* Ed. Gary Lane. Baltimore: Johns Hopkins UP, 1979. 3–18.

Bell, Quentin. *Virginia Woolf: A Biography.* New York: Harcourt Brace Jovanovich, 1972.

Bleier, Ruth. *Science and Gender.* New York: Pergamon, 1984.

Blessing, Richard Allen. "The Shape of the Psyche: Vision and Technique in the Late Poems of Sylvia Plath." *Sylvia Plath: New Views on the Poetry.* Ed. Gary Lane. Baltimore: Johns Hopkins UP, 1979. 57–73.

Bloom, Harold. *Agon.* New York: Oxford UP, 1982.

————. *The Anxiety of Influence.* New York: Oxford UP, 1973.

————. *The Breaking of the Vessels.* Chicago: U of Chicago P, 1982.

————. *A Map of Misreading.* Oxford: Oxford UP, 1975.

————. *Poetry and Repression.* New Haven: Yale UP, 1976.

————. *Wallace Stevens: The Poems of Our Climate.* Ithaca: Cornell UP, 1977.

Boose, Lynda E. "The Father and the Bride in Shakespeare." *PMLA* 97.3 (May 1982): 325–47.

Borroff, Marie. *Language and the Poet: Verbal Artistry in Frost, Stevens, and Moore.* Chicago: U of Chicago P, 1979.

Bowlby, John. *Attachment and Loss.* Vol. 3. *Loss: Sadness and Depression.* London: Hogarth, 1980.

Broe, Mary Lynn. *Protean Poetic: The Poetry of Sylvia Plath.* Columbia: U of Missouri P, 1980.

————. "A Subtle Psychic Bond: The Mother Figure in Sylvia Plath's Poetry." *The Lost Tradition: Mothers and Daughters in Literature.* Ed. Cathy N. Davidson and E. M. Broner. New York: Ungar, 1980. 217–30.

Bundtzen, Lynda K. *Plath's Incarnations: Woman and the Creative Process.* Ann Arbor: U of Michigan P, 1983.

Butscher, Edward. *Sylvia Plath: Method and Madness.* 1976. New York: Pocket, 1977.

Cam, Heather. "'Daddy': Sylvia Plath's Debt to Anne Sexton." *American Literature* 59.3 (Oct.1987): 429–32.

Cameron, Sharon. *Lyric Time: Dickinson and the Limits of Genre.* Baltimore: Johns Hopkins UP, 1979.

Chodorow, Nancy. *The Reproduction of Mothering.* Berkeley: U of California P, 1978.

Cixous, Hélène. "The Laugh of the Medusa." 1975. Trans. Keith Cohen and Paula Cohen. *New French Feminisms: An Anthology.* Ed. Elaine Marks and Isabelle de Courtivron. 1980. New York: Schocken, 1981. 245–64.

Coleman, Stanley. "The Phantom Double: Its Psychological Significance." *British Journal of Medical Psychology* 14.3 (1934): 254–73.

Daiches, David. *The Novel and the Modern World.* Chicago: U of Chicago P, 1939.

———. *Virginia Woolf.* Norfolk, Conn.: New Directions, 1942.

Daly, Mary. *Beyond God the Father: Toward a Philosophy of Women's Liberation.* 1973. Boston: Beacon, 1985.

De Lauretis, Teresa. "Rebirth in *The Bell Jar.*" *Women's Studies* 3 (1975): 173–83.

Derrida, Jacques. *Of Grammatology.* 1967. Trans. Gayatri Chakravorty Spivak. Baltimore: Johns Hopkins UP, 1976.

———. *Writing and Difference.* 1967. Trans. Alan Bass. Chicago: U of Chicago P, 1978.

Deutsch, Helene. *The Psychology of Women,* Vol. 1. *Girlhood.* 1944. New York: Bantam, 1973.

Diehl, Joanne Feit. *Dickinson and the Romantic Imagination.* Princeton: Princeton UP, 1981.

Dinnerstein, Dorothy. *The Mermaid and the Minotaur.* New York: Harper & Row, 1976.

Drew, Elizabeth. *The Modern Novel: Some Aspects of Contemporary Fiction.* New York: Harcourt Brace, 1926.

Erikson, Erik. *Childhood and Society.* 2nd ed. New York: Norton, 1963.

———. *Life History and the Historical Moment.* New York: Norton, 1975.

Fabricant, Carole. *Swift's Landscape.* Baltimore: Johns Hopkins UP, 1982.

Fleiss, Robert. *Ego and Body Ego.* 1961. New York: International UP, 1970.

Foucault, Michel. *Language, Counter-memory, Practice: Selected Essays and Interviews.* 1962–72. Trans. Donald Bouchard and Sherry Simon. Ithaca: Cornell UP, 1977.

——. *Madness and Civilization.* 1961. Trans. Richard Howard. New York: Vintage, 1971.

——. *The Order of Things: An Archaeology of the Human Sciences.* 1966. New York: Vintage, 1973.

Frazer, James G. *The Golden Bough: A Study in Magic and Religion.* Abridged ed. 1922. New York: Macmillan, 1943.

Freud, Sigmund. *Beyond the Pleasure Principle.* 1920. Trans. James Strachey. *Standard Edition.* Vol. 18. London: Hogarth, 1955. 7–64.

——. *Civilization and Its Discontents.* 1930. Trans. Joan Riviere and James Strachey. *Standard Edition.* Vol. 21. London: Hogarth, 1961. 64–145.

——. "Dostoevski and Parricide." 1928. Trans. D. F. Tait. *Collected Papers* Vol. 5. London: Hogarth, 1950. 222–42.

——. "Female Sexuality." 1931. Trans. James Strachey. *Collected Papers.* Vol. 5. London: Hogarth, 1950. 252–72.

——. *Inhibitions, Symptoms and Anxiety.* 1936. Trans. Alix Strachey. New York: Norton, 1959.

——. *The Interpretation of Dreams.* 1900. Trans. A. A. Brill. *Basic Writings.* New York: Random House/Modern Library, 1938. 181–549.

——. "Leonardo da Vinci." 1910. *Collected Papers* Vol. 11. London: Hogarth, 1957. 63–137.

——. "Medusa's Head." 1922. Trans. James Strachey. *Collected Papers* Vol. 5. London: Hogarth, 1953. 105–6.

——. "Mourning and Melancholia." 1917. Trans. James Strachey. *Standard Edition* Vol. 14. London: Hogarth, 1957. 243–58.

——. "Negation." 1925. Trans. Joan Riviere. *Collected Papers* Vol. 5. London: Hogarth, 1953. 181–85.

——. "A Neurosis of Demoniacal Possession in the Seventeenth Century." 1923. Trans. Edward Glover. *Collected Papers* Vol. 4. London: Hogarth, 1925. 436–72.

——. *New Introductory Lectures on Psychoanalysis.* 1933. Trans. James Strachey. *Standard Edition* Vol. 22. London: Hogarth, 1962. 3–182.

——. "Some Psychic Consequences of the Anatomical Distinction between the Sexes." 1925. Trans. James Strachey. *Collected Papers* Vol. 5. London: Hogarth, 1953. 186–97.

——. "The Theme of the Three Caskets." 1913. Trans. C. J. M. Hubback. *Collected Papers* Vol. 4. London: Hogarth, 1925. 244–56.

——. *Three Case Histories.* 1909, 1911, 1918. Trans. New York: Macmillan, 1963.

———. *Totem and Taboo.* 1912. Trans. A. A. Brill. *Basic Writings.* New York: Random House/Modern Library, 1938. 807–930.

———. "The Uncanny." 1919. Trans. Alix Strachey. *Collected Papers* Vol. 4. London: Hogarth, 1925. 368–407.

Friedan, Betty. *The Feminine Mystique.* 1963. New York: Norton, 1974.

Friedman, Susan Stanford. "Creativity and the Childbirth Metaphor: Gender Difference in Literary Discourse." *Feminist Studies* 13.1 (Spring 1987): 49–82.

Frye, Northrop. *Fables of Identity: Studies in Poetic Mythology.* New York: Harcourt Brace & World, 1963.

Gaster, Theodor H. Editor's Foreword. *The New Golden Bough: A New Abridgement.* By James G. Frazer. 1959. New York: New American Library, 1964. xv–xxiv.

Gelpi, Albert. *The Tenth Muse: The Psyche of the American Poet.* Cambridge: Harvard UP, 1975.

Giannotti, Thomas. "A Language of Silence: Writing the Self in Yeats and Synge, Joyce and Beckett." Diss. U of California, Riverside, 1985.

Gilbert, Sandra M. "A Fine, White Flying Myth: The Life/Work of Sylvia Plath." 1978. *Shakespeare's Sisters: Feminist Essays on Women Poets.* Ed. Sandra M. Gilbert and Susan Gubar. Bloomington: Indiana UP, 1979. 245–60.

———. "In Yeats's House: The Death and Resurrection of Sylvia Plath." *Critical Essays on Sylvia Plath.* Ed. Linda W. Wagner. Boston: G. K. Hall, 1984. 204–22.

Gilbert, Sandra M., and Susan Gubar. *The Madwoman in the Attic: The Woman Writer and the Nineteenth-Century Literary Imagination.* New Haven: Yale UP, 1979.

———. *No Man's Land: The Place of the Woman Writer in the Twentieth Century,* Vol. 1: *The War of the Words.* New Haven: Yale UP, 1988.

Gilligan, Carol. *In a Different Voice: Psychological Theory and Women's Development.* Cambridge: Harvard UP, 1982.

Goodwin, Donald W., and Samuel B. Guze. *Psychiatric Diagnosis.* 2nd ed. New York: Oxford UP, 1979.

Gubar, Susan. "'The Blank Page' and the Issues of Female Creativity." *Critical Inquiry* 8.2 (Winter 1981): 243–64.

Guillory, John. *Poetic Authority: Spenser, Milton, and Literary History.* New York: Columbia UP, 1983.

Hamilton, Ian. *Robert Lowell: A Biography.* New York: Random House, 1982.

Hatterer, Lawrence J. *The Artist in Society.* New York: Grove, 1965.

Hoffman, Steven. "Impersonal Personalism: The Making of a Confessional Poetic." *ELH* 45 (Winter 1978): 687–709.

Holbrook, David. *Sylvia Plath: Poetry and Existence*. London: Athlone, 1976.

Homans, Margaret. *Bearing the Word: Language and Female Experience in Nineteenth-Century Women's Writing*. Chicago: U of Chicago P, 1986.

———. *Women Writers and Poetic Identity: Dorothy Wordsworth, Emily Brontë, and Emily Dickinson*. Princeton: Princeton UP, 1980.

Horney, Karen. *Feminine Psychology*. New York: Norton, 1967.

Irwin, John T. *Doubling and Incest/Repetition and Revenge: A Speculative Reading of Faulkner*. Baltimore: Johns Hopkins UP, 1975.

Jacobus, Mary. "The Difference of View." *Women Writing and Writing about Women*. Ed. Mary Jacobus. London: Croom Helm, 1979. 10–21.

James, William. "Genius." 1896. *William James on Exceptional Mental States*. Ed. Eugene Taylor. New York: Scribner's, 1983. 149–65.

———. *The Varieties of Religious Experience*. 1902. New York: New American Library, 1958.

Johnson, Barbara. *The Critical Difference: Essays in the Contemporary Rhetoric of Reading*. Baltimore: Johns Hopkins UP, 1980.

Juhasz, Suzanne. *Naked and Fiery Forms: Modern American Poetry by Women, a New Tradition*. New York: Harper & Row, 1976.

———. *The Undiscovered Continent: Emily Dickinson and the Space of Mind*. Bloomington: Indiana UP, 1983.

Kelley, Alice Van Buren. *The Novels of Virginia Woolf: Fact and Vision*. Chicago: U of Chicago P, 1973.

Keppler, C. F. *The Literature of the Second Self*. Tucson: U of Arizona P, 1972.

Kramer, Lawrence. "Freud and the Skunks: Genre and Language in *Life Studies*." *Robert Lowell: Essays on the Poetry*. Ed. Steven Gould Axelrod and Helen Deese. New York: Cambridge UP, 1986. 80–98.

Krauss, Wilhelmine. *Das Doppelgänger in der Romantik*. Berlin: Emil Ebering, 1930.

Kristeva, Julia. *Desire in Language: A Semiotic Approach to Literature and Art*. 1969, 1977. Ed. Leon Roudiez. Trans. Thomas Gora, Alice Jardine, and Leon Roudiez. New York: Columbia UP, 1980.

Kroll, Judith. *Chapters in a Mythology: The Poetry of Sylvia Plath*. New York: Harper & Row, 1976.

Krook, Dorothea. "Recollections of Sylvia Plath." *Sylvia Plath: The Woman and the Work*. Ed. Edward Butscher. New York: Dodd, Mead, 1977. 49–60.

La Belle, Jenijoy. *Herself Beheld: The Literature of the Looking Glass*. Ithaca: Cornell UP, 1988.

Lacan, Jacques. "Desire and the Interpretation of Desire in *Hamlet.*" 1959. Ed. by J.-A. Miller. Trans. James Hulbert. *Literature and Psychoanalysis.* Ed. Shoshana Felman. Baltimore: Johns Hopkins UP, 1982. 11–52.

———. *Ecrits: A Selection.* 1966. Trans. Alan Sheridan. New York: Norton, 1977.

———. *The Four Fundamental Concepts of Psycho-analysis.* 1973. Ed. J.-A. Miller. Trans. Alan Sheridan. New York: Norton, 1981.

———. *The Language of the Self: The Function of Language in Psychoanalysis.* 1956. Trans. Anthony Wilden. New York: Delta, 1968.

Laing, R. D. *The Divided Self.* 1960. New York: Pantheon, 1969.

Lane, Gary. "Influence and Originality in Plath's Poems." *Sylvia Plath: New Views on the Poetry.* Ed. Gary Lane. Baltimore: Johns Hopkins UP, 1979. 116–37.

Lazell, Edward W. "Schizophrenia." *Modern Abnormal Psychology: A Symposium.* Ed. W. H. Mikesell. New York: Philosophical Library, 1950. 585–628.

Littleton, C. Scott. *The New Comparative Mythology.* 3rd ed. Berkeley: U of California P, 1982.

Lucas, Dolores Dyer. *Emily Dickinson and Riddle.* DeKalb: Northern Illinois UP, 1969.

Lukacher, Ned. *Primal Scenes: Literature, Philosophy, Psychoanalysis.* Ithaca: Cornell UP, 1986.

Marcus, Jane. "Art and Anger." *Feminist Studies* 4 (1977): 69–98.

Martin, Jay. *Who Am I This Time? Uncovering the Fictive Personality.* New York: Norton, 1988.

McClatchy, J. D. "Short Circuits and Folding Mirrors." *Sylvia Plath: New Views on the Poetry.* Ed. Gary Lane. Baltimore: John Hopkins UP, 1979. 19–32.

McCullough, Francis. "Editor's Note." *Journals.* By Sylvia Plath. New York: Dial, 1982. ix–x.

———. Letter. *New York Review of Books,* Jan. 18, 1990. 53.

Miller, Alice. *For Your Own Good: Hidden Cruelty in Child-Rearing and the Roots of Violence.* 1980 Trans. Hildegarde Hannum and Hunter Hannum. New York: Farrar, Straus & Giroux, 1983.

Miller, J. Hillis. *The Linguistic Moment: From Wordsworth to Stevens.* Princeton: Princeton UP, 1985.

Miller, Jean Baker. *Toward a New Psychology of Women.* 2nd edition. Boston: Beacon, 1986.

Mossberg, Barbara Clarke. *Emily Dickinson: When a Writer Is a Daughter.* Bloomington: Indiana UP, 1982.

Nance, Guinevara A., and Judith P. Jones. "Doing Away with Daddy: Exorcism and Sympathetic Magic in Plath's Poetry."

1978. *Critical Essays on Sylvia Plath*. Ed. Linda W. Wagner. Boston: G. K. Hall, 1984. 124–30.

Newman, Charles. "Candor Is the Only Wile—The Art of Sylvia Plath." *The Art of Sylvia Plath*. Ed. Charles Newman. Bloomington: Indiana UP, 1970. 21–55.

North, Michael. *The Final Sculpture: Public Monuments and Modern Poetry*. Ithaca: Cornell UP, 1985.

Oates, Joyce Carol. "Soul at the White Heat: The Romance of Emily Dickinson's Poetry." *Critical Inquiry* 13.4 (Summer 1987): 806–24.

Oesterreich, T. K. *Possession: Demoniacal and Other*. London: Kegan Paul, 1930.

Olsen, Tillie. *Silences*. 1978. New York: Delta, 1979.

Ong, Walter J. *Fighting for Life: Contest, Sexuality, and Consciousness*. Ithaca: Cornell UP, 1981.

———. *Interfaces of the Word: Studies in the Evolution of Consciousness and Culture*. Ithaca: Cornell UP, 1977.

Ortner, Sherry. "Is Female to Male as Nature Is to Culture?" *Feminist Studies* 1 (1972): 5–31.

Ostriker, Alicia. *Stealing the Language: The Emergence of Women's Poetry in America*. Boston: Beacon, 1986.

———. *Writing Like a Woman*. Ann Arbor: U of Michigan P, 1983.

Perloff, Marjorie. "Extremist Poetry: Some Versions of the Sylvia Plath Myth." *Journal of Modern Literature* 2 (Nov. 1972): 581–88.

———. "Sylvia Plath's 'Sivvy' Poems: A Portrait of the Poet as Daughter." *Sylvia Plath: New Views on the Poetry*. Ed. Gary Lane. Baltimore: Johns Hopkins UP, 1979. 155–78.

———. "The Two *Ariels*: The (Re)making of the Sylvia Plath Canon." *American Poetry Review* 13 (Nov.–Dec. 1984): 10–18.

Piaget, Jean. *The Child's Conception of the World*. Trans. Joan Tomlinson and Andrew Tomlinson. London: Routledge & Kegan Paul, 1929.

Pollak, Vivian R. *Dickinson: The Anxiety of Gender*. Ithaca: Cornell UP, 1984.

Quinn, Bernetta. "Medusan Imagery in Sylvia Plath." *Sylvia Plath: New Views on the Poetry*. Ed. Gary Lane. Baltimore: Johns Hopkins UP, 1979. 97–115.

Rank, Otto. *Beyond Psychology*. 1941. New York: Dover, 1958.

———. *Der Doppelgänger: Eine Psychoanalytische Studie*. 1925. Trans. and ed. Harry Tucker, Jr. *The Double: A Psychoanalytic Study*. Chapel Hill: U of North Carolina P, 1971.

———. "Der Doppelgänger." *Imago: Zeitschrift für Anwendung der Psy-

choanalyse auf die Geisteswissenschaften Vol. 3. Ed. Sigmund Freud. Leipzig: Internaionaler Psychoanalytischer Verlag, 1914. 97–164.
———. "The Double." Abstracted from "Der Doppelgänger." *Imago* Vol. 3. 1914. Trans. Louise Brink. *Psychoanaltyic Review* 6 (Jan. 1919): 450–60.

Reichert, John. "Do Poets Ever Mean What They Say?" *New Literary History* 13 (Autumn 1981): 53–68.

Roche, Clarissa. "Sylvia Plath: Vignettes from England." *Sylvia Plath: The Woman and the Work*. Ed. Edward Butscher. New York: Dodd, Mead, 1977. 81–96.

Rogers, Robert. *The Double in Literature*. Detroit: Wayne State UP, 1970.

Rosenblatt, Jon. *Sylvia Plath: The Poetry of Initiation*. Chapel Hill: U of North Carolina P, 1979.

Rosenman, Ellen Bayuk. *The Invisible Presence: Virginia Woolf and the Mother-Daughter Relationship*. Baton Rouge: Louisiana State UP, 1986.

Rosenthal, M. L. *The New Poets: American and British Poetry since World War II*. London: Oxford UP, 1967.

Rosenthal, Melinda. "Obtaining Her Own Extent: The Singular Quest of Emily Dickinson." Diss., U of California, Riverside, 1989.

Rourke, Constance. *American Humor*. New York: Harcourt Brace, 1931.

Russ, Joanna. *How to Suppress Women's Writing*. Austin: U of Texas P, 1983.

Schwartz, Murray M., and Christopher Bollas. "The Absence of the Center: Sylvia Plath and Suicide." *Sylvia Plath: New Views on the Poetry*. Ed. Gary Lane. Baltimore: Johns Hopkins UP, 1979.

Seager, Allan. *The Glass House: The Life of Theodore Roethke*. New York: McGraw-Hill, 1968.

Showalter, Elaine. "Feminist Criticism in the Wilderness." *Critical Inquiry* 8.2 (Winter 1981): 179–206.

———. *A Literature of Their Own: British Women Novelists from Brontë to Lessing*. Princeton: Princeton UP, 1977.

Silver, Brenda R. "*Three Guineas* Before and After: Further Answers to Correspondents." *Virginia Woolf: A Feminist Slant*. Ed. Jane Marcus. Lincoln: U of Nebraska P, 1983.

Simmons, Ernest J. *Dostoevski: The Making of a Novelist*. 1940. New York: Vintage, 1962.

Squier, Susan M. *Virginia Woolf and London*. Chapel Hill: U of North Carolina P, 1985.

Starobinski, Jean. *Words upon Words*. 1971. Trans. Olivia Emmet. New Haven: Yale UP, 1979.

Steiner, George. *Language and Silence: Essays on Language, Literature and the Inhuman*. 1967. New York: Atheneum, 1970.

Stevenson, Anne. *Bitter Fame: A Life of Sylvia Plath*. Boston: Houghton Mifflin, 1989.

Storr, Anthony. *The Dynamics of Creation*. New York: Atheneum, 1972.

Tabor, Stephen. *Sylvia Plath: An Analytical Bibliography*. London: Mansell, 1987.

Timmerman, John H. "Plath's 'Mirror.'" *Explicator* 45 (1987): 63–64.

Transue, Pamela. *Virginia Woolf and the Politics of Style*. Albany: SUNY Press, 1986.

Tymms, Ralph. *Doubles in Literary Psychology*. Cambridge: Bowes & Bowes, 1949.

Uroff, Margaret Dickie. *Sylvia Plath and Ted Hughes*. Urbana: U of Illinois P, 1979.

Van Deusen, Marshall. "Dickinson's 'Further in Summer than the Birds.'" *Explicator* 13.5 (March 1955): item 33.

Van Dyne, Susan R. "'More Terrible Than She Ever Was': The Manuscripts of Sylvia Plath's Bee Poems." *Stings: Original Drafts of the Poem in Facsimile Reproduced from the Sylvia Plath Collection at Smith College*. By Sylvia Plath. Northampton: Smith College Library Rare Book Room, 1982. 3–12.

Vickery, John B. *The Literary Impact of* The Golden Bough. Princeton: Princeton UP, 1973.

Wagner-Martin, Linda W. *Sylvia Plath: A Biography*. New York: Simon and Schuster, 1987.

Walker, Cheryl. *The Nightingale's Burden: Women Poets and American Culture before 1900*. Bloomington: Indiana UP, 1982.

Watts, Emily. *The Poetry of American Women from 1632 to 1945*. Austin: U of Texas P, 1977.

Wesling, Donald. "Difficulties of the Bardic: Literature and the Human Voice." *Critical Inquiry* 8 (Autumn 1981): 69–81.

Williamson, Alan. *Introspection and Contemporary Poetry*. Cambridge: Harvard UP, 1984.

Winnicott, D. W. *Playing and Reality*. London: Tavistock, 1971.

Winokur, George, Paula J. Clayton, and Theodore Reich. *Manic Depressive Illness*. St. Louis: C. V. Mosby, 1969.

Winters, Yvor. *In Defense of Reason*. New York: Swallow, 1947.

Wolff, Cynthia Griffin. *Emily Dickinson*. New York: Knopf, 1987.

Zwerdling, Alex. *Virginia Woolf and the Real World*. Berkeley: U of California P, 1986.

INDEX

Designed by Susan Bishop

Composed by A. W. Bennett, Inc., in Baskerville text and display
Printed by the Maple Press Company on 50-lb. Glatfelter Eggshell Cream